The FORGOTTEN Cup

The FORGOTTEN Cup

History of the Mitropa Cup, Mother of the Champions League (1927-1940)

Jo Araf

First published by Pitch Publishing, 2023

Pitch Publishing
9 Donnington Park,
85 Birdham Road,
Chichester,
West Sussex,
PO20 7AJ
www.pitchpublishing.co.uk
info@pitchpublishing.co.uk

© 2023, Jo Araf

A CIP catalogue record is available for this book
from the British Library.

ISBN 978 1 80150 437 9

Typesetting and origination by Pitch Publishing
Printed and bound in India by Replika Press Pvt. Ltd.

CONTENTS

Introduction 9

From Amateurs to Professionals: Genesis
  and Evolution of European Football 14

1927 – Steel Sparta 29

1928 – Fradi and the First Treble in History 46

1929 – Champions in Europe, Bit-Part Players
  in Hungary 57

1930 – The Rapidgeist 70

1931 – The Year of the First Times 85

1932 – Bologna, a Walkover Victory 98

1933 – Matthias Sindelar and the Coffee House Team 115

1934 – Bologna, Italy's Most Danubian Team 130

1935 – Raymond Braine: Outcast in Antwerp,
  King in Prague 144

1936 – Austria Vienna, Europe in the DNA 156

1937 – Dr Sárosi's Star Shines 166

1938 – Josef Bican and the Other Face of Prague . . .184

1939 – Béla Guttmann: All Roads Lead to Budapest 204

1940 – The Old Continent Under Iron and Fire . . .219

What Happened to the Mitropa? 232

Mitropa Cup Final Statistics, 1927 to 1939 238

Thanks 246

Bibliography 248

Index of Names .252

To my parents

INTRODUCTION

CONTEMPORARY FOOTBALL fans may be surprised to learn that the Mitropa Cup, an ante litteram version of the Champions League, was in fact an affair reserved for clubs from nations, with the exception of Italy, which have now disappeared from the map of football that counts. Countries such as Austria, Hungary and Czechoslovakia evoke, in the most scattered exploits, outstanding performances that can be traced back to a few editions of World Cups or European Championships that took place over the decades. In the same way, modern fans might be surprised that European football was dominated almost 100 years ago by teams that have now fallen into oblivion. A quick glance at the list of Mitropa winners, for example, reveals the absence of the German, Spanish, Dutch and English[1] teams that would dominate the scene after the Second World War. In addition, when fans think of the Mitropa their minds tend to go to the most recent editions, those played between 1979 and 1992 which were reserved for the winners of the nations' respective second divisions.

---

1 British football was a case in point: having come into being some three decades before European football and considering itself to be of a higher calibre at the time, England would not have contemplated participating in the international competitions of the day.

The event, which in each European nation took on one or more different names[2] – in Italian newspapers, for example, it was renamed the Coppa Europa, not to be confused with the Coppa Europea, which was the International Cup (played by nations, not clubs) – took its name from the German company Mitropa AG, founded in 1916, which managed the sleeping and dining cars of the trains that travelled through Central Europe.[3] Starting in the 1920s, Mitropa AG began to sponsor sporting events, albeit indirectly and by granting discounts, and thanks to the founding of the Mitropa competition it acquired a hitherto unheard-of customer: the fan who travelled across the continent to attend their team's away matches.

However, some clarifications are necessary: although the tournament was in fact a progenitor of the Champions Cup, the latter would later enjoy a much greater resonance by virtue of a decidedly amplified media exposure. A key role in slowing down the metamorphosis of football into a fully fledged international product was played by the sports publications of the 1920s: soaked in propaganda and strongly influenced by the unstable political and diplomatic relations of those years, they dispensed rivers of ink to praise their own clubs, often concealing the successes of teams from rival countries. This happened for two reasons: on the one hand it was the local sport that had to be celebrated and on the other hand the fans' interest in foreign championships and competitions was at the time a marginal phenomenon, something that would take hold only a few years later. A

---

2 The official name of the competition was La Coupe de l'Europe Centrale and it was stamped on the trophy by the jewellers who made it. However, in none of the participating countries was the tournament called this. In Austria it was Mitropapokal, in Hungary Mitropa Kupa or Középeurópa Kupa (KK) and in Czechoslovakia Středoevropský pohár.

3 For convenience we will refer to the Mitropa Cup from here on.

good example of this is the chronicle of the first World Cup in history, played in Uruguay, in which Italy, like the other main European football powers, did not participate. On 31 July 1930, the day after the final between Uruguay and Argentina, *La Gazzetta dello Sport* dedicated to the match a paragraph about ten lines long on the last page and nothing more, while a different article appeared on the cover about Italian footballers and rowers about to start the World University Championships. Similarly, on the day of the final, in the edition of the then weekly *Guerin Sportivo*, an article entitled *Argentineide* was published. The piece mentioned two players who would take part in the match, Juan Evaristo and Guillermo Stabile, but not because they were involved in the event of the day, but rather because of market rumours that the two would move to Roma and Genova at the end of the competition.[4] More generally, the World Cup in Uruguay was the subject of scanty articles with few details.

The same trend concerned, at least during the early years, the matches of the Mitropa: with the exception of *La Gazzetta dello Sport*, no Italian newspaper dedicated itself to the first two editions of the event, those of 1927 and 1928, due to the absence of Italian teams. And the *Gazzetta* itself would in many cases not print match reports the following day. This attitude would change considerably from 1929,[5] the year that marked the beginning of Italian participation.

Due to the political vicissitudes of the time, the tension, as well as in the newspapers, was often palpable on the playing field: when the Italian teams faced Austrian,

---

4 Two clarifications: 1. The negotiation for Juan Evaristo never went through. 2. I refer to Genoa as Genova because from 1928 to 1945 the fascist government in Italy forced the club to take the name Genova.

5 The 1929 edition was the first in which Italian teams participated following the introduction of the single-round championship.

Hungarian or Czechoslovakian teams, the matches often pitted youngsters who had been orphaned during the Great War against each other. This was the case for, among others, two of the most representative champions of the period: Ambrosiana's star player Giuseppe Meazza and his Austrian alter ego Matthias Sindelar. In spite of these circumstances, when the competition began, Italy's newspapers did not hide their feelings: the football of Central Europe, that which was played along the Danube in particular in Austria, Hungary and Czechoslovakia and which the Italians called 'Danubian football' was the model to follow. Rapid Vienna, for example, were described as the team to beat and any defeat suffered by an Italian team would not be seen as a disgrace. But there is another phenomenon that would testify to the high opinion in which Italian football held Central European football: the large number of coaches born under the Austro-Hungarian Empire who coached in Italy during the 1920s and '30s. In every single season between 1927 and 1939, more Danubian coaches sat on the benches of Italian clubs than Italian ones. This led to an interpenetration between the Italian style of play, of a purely defensive nature and inspired by the English school carried out by Vittorio Pozzo, and the Central European style of play, which favoured an offensive game of short passes borrowed from Scottish coaches – and in some cases from English coaches but supporters of the Scottish model – who had settled on the continent in previous years.

The tendency to prefer Magyar and Austrian coaches waned slightly – without disappearing – in the first years after World War II, partly because of the relationship between Italy and Austria and partly because of the successes that Pozzo had achieved with the Italian national team. The fact of having won two World Cups, two

International Cups and the Olympic Games in Berlin[6] led several clubs to turn towards the Italian style of play.

Compared to today's Champions League, there were also differences in the rules: if the two teams scored the same number of goals in the first leg and the second leg, a play-off was played. And if at the end of the play-off the result was still tied, a second one would be played, as penalties were not yet allowed. The format, however, despite some variations in the number of participating teams and the number of federations involved, would maintain its consistency over time. It never featured rounds and only in some editions would a preliminary round be introduced.

Over the years, there were other organisational and political changes that influenced the tournament, including the opening to seven federations in 1937 – the year in which Mitropa took on more or less the features of today's Champions League – or the Anschluss of 1938, which coincided with the exclusion of the Austrian teams and, for reasons of political expediency, of the Swiss ones. Then, in 1940, due to the winds of war that were blowing ever more threateningly over Europe, the event was interrupted.

But to better explain the scenario of European football at the time, a brief historical excursus is necessary, which begins with the arrival of the ball – *foot-ball* – in Europe, continues with the advent of professional football and culminates, if one can say so, with the birth of the first international tournaments.

---

6 The Berlin Olympic Games were a case in point: they pitted players against each other who did not enjoy professional status and therefore were not the same as those who competed in the World Cup and other competitions.

FROM AMATEURS TO PROFESSIONALS: GENESIS AND EVOLUTION OF EUROPEAN FOOTBALL

IN FACT, cross-border football took root in Europe almost at the same time as local football. The first attempt to create a competition between clubs from different nations dates back to 1897, just a few years after the first football teams appeared in continental Europe. The Challenge Cup, or Challenge Kupa as it was known in Budapest, was founded in Vienna by John Gramlick, a prominent member of the Vienna Cricket and Football Club. The tournament adopted the knockout format from the very first edition and began as a sort of progenitor event of the Vienna Cup, only to become a competition open to the best teams gathered under the Habsburg crown a few years later.

Despite the noble intentions of the founders, fair play did not always prevail on the field: due to the growing anti-Austrian sentiment in the various provinces of the Empire, the matches often ended in brawls. The organisers had decided that the cup would be awarded once and for all as soon as a team had won it for the third time, but then went back and decided to continue after 1904, the year that coincided with the third success of WAC (Wiener

Athletiksport Club). It was also agreed that the defending champions could keep the cup until 1 April the following year and that at the end of the tournament the winners would each receive a gold medal. While the teams from Budapest and Prague participated free of charge as guests, the teams from Vienna were required to pay an entry fee of 20 crowns.

The key year in the Challenge Cup's progress towards becoming an international competition was 1901, when two Bohemian teams, Ceski AFC and Slavia Prague, battled it out in Prague to decide which team would face the Austrian champions in Vienna. Slavia won and six months later the red-and-whites played the final against WAC. It was the first time that two European teams played each other in an official trophy match. The match ended 1-0 to the Austrians thanks to a goal scored by Josef Taurer, a player now forgotten, who collected some respectable records: only 13 days before, Taurer had scored the first goal in the history of the Austrian national team against Switzerland and the following year he would repeat the feat in an officially recognised match against Hungary.

The 1902 edition was the first to which teams from Budapest were invited and a few years later a representative from Moravia, DFC Brno, and a team from outside the Empire, the Germans of VfB Leipzig, would appear, two clubs now defunct but at the time among the continent's best. The Challenge Cup was also the showcase for the first stars of the Danube firmament to make a name for themselves and be worshipped by their fans: among those idolised in Budapest, for example, were Imre Schlosser, who would later become one of the most prolific strikers in the history of football, and Gáspar 'Gazsi' Borbás, to whom FTC and national team goalkeeper Alajos Fritz dedicated a poem in which he depicted him as the soul of his team and the best Hungarian player. For their part, Austrian fans had cultivated an adoration for Jan Studnicka, WAC's star player, known for his irresistible dribbling and deformed legs often depicted by the cartoonists of the time; Ludwig Hussak, star of the Vienna Cricket and Football Club and captain of the Austrian national team; and Willy Schmieger. In the years between the wars, Schmieger would become the country's best-known sports broadcaster, and was a forward in the Wiener Sport-Club team, with whom he won the Cup in 1911.[7]

The Challenge Cup was played until 1911, despite a temporary suspension between 1906 and 1908. The matches, which at the time were not very well attended, were mostly played on uneven and unmaintained ground. From time to time there were curious episodes that would become customary over the years. For example, when a ball was kicked outside the playing area, fans would sometimes try to take it away as a souvenir, unleashing the wrath of the players eager to resume the game.

The competition was always won by teams from Vienna, except in one case, in 1909, the year of the only Hungarian success by FTC, later known as Ferencváros. The local press reported:

'FTC managed to bring the cup to Hungary after an extremely intense struggle. The team had to face three very strong opponents in one week and played without Rumbold. In addition, the main problem of the attack was that Seitler was sick. Because of this, the player worked hard to follow the ball but could not do much more. The defence was excellent, especially Fritz!'

---

7 An employee of RAVAG, Schmieger was one of the European pioneers in the field of sports radio commentary and a controversial figure. However, in this work I will only mention his contribution to the game of football.

The referee of that match was Hugo Meisl, a former footballer and the major driving force and visionary within football at the time, the man who more than anyone else worked to make football become a business and a mass product as we know it today. A character without whom, probably, this book would never have seen the light. In order for football to become as popular in continental Europe as it was in England, Meisl and some of his colleagues used to invite British teams to play friendly matches on the Old Continent. British football was 30 years ahead of its time and was well known in Vienna and the surrounding area, so much so that every time an English or Scottish team faced a Central European outfit the crowds were drawn to the playing fields. The first time an English team travelled to Vienna was on Easter Sunday 1899, when Oxford University defeated a local selection 15-0. The game was repeated the following day, but the outcome was almost identical: 13-0 to the visitors.

These were years in which the gap between the English masters and their European pupils was evident, both from a collective and individual point of view. Defeats by visiting British teams were formative for Austrian football: Robinson, for example, goalkeeper of Southampton, would be remembered in Vienna for his unprecedented interpretation of the role and would be long imitated by his local colleagues. Thanks to his innate agility, the extraordinary defender was able to dive from one side of the goal to the other and neutralise his adversaries' low shots. This type of save would set the standard in Vienna and be renamed *Robinsonade*.

As the years went by, the difference between Austrian and British clubs became smaller and smaller. Some good individual performances did not go unnoticed and on one occasion Glasgow Rangers decided to offer First Vienna goalkeeper Karl Pekarna a contract after a friendly match in the Austrian capital. He was the first European player to go to the United Kingdom, although that spell was cut short after just one match: Pekarna, deemed unfit for the task, was sent back.

Thanks to the efforts of Hugo Meisl, who as his brother Willy recalled in his work *Soccer Revolution* squandered a small fortune in organising friendly matches between Viennese and foreign teams, tours of English teams to continental Europe became more frequent and in 1905 a mixed mini-tournament would end in an all-British final. Tottenham and Everton faced off in front of a record crowd of 10,000 spectators! In all likelihood it was then that Meisl realised he was on the right track. He would do everything in his power to encourage the development of football and in 1912, when Austria took part in the Stockholm Olympics, the first event in which football became a truly respected discipline, Austria went to Sweden with an English coach. His name was James 'Jimmy' Hogan and in the years to follow he would shape European football like few others.[8]

Despite being English, Hogan decided to import the philosophy of Scottish football, known in the UK as 'the passing game' or 'combination football'.[9] Danubian football, in contrast to the English style of 'kick and rush', provided a strong cohesion between departments, the emphasis on short passes and a module, the 2-3-5, known as 'the Method', which would take root without distinction in the various countries of Central Europe. It included two full-backs, which today would be the central defenders, a

---

8 Jimmy Hogan and his impact on European football is a matter of debate. However, the coach is cited by most as one of the fathers of continental football.

9 In Austria it would soon be renamed *Donaufußball*.

three-man midfield line composed of the so-called 'halves' or 'supports', as the Italian newspapers called them, two wings, usually exempt from defensive duties, and the forwards. The characteristics of the centre-forward were different from those of the English centre-forwards: he was something between a false nine and a *trequartista* – also defined as a centre-forward – capable of receiving the ball to feet and sending his team-mates, the 'inside forwards', who acted as real strikers, towards the goal, to positions from which they could shoot easily.

Hogan came from the Dutch team of Dordrecht and arrived in Vienna at the behest of Meisl who, after a disappointing friendly match between Austria and Hungary that ended in a draw, had asked Howcroft, the referee, if he knew of a coach who could lead his national team. Howcroft's advice fell on his compatriot Hogan, 28 years old at the time. At the Olympics in Sweden, the Austrian players, Hogan and Meisl (present as referee) got a taste of how football would evolve in the following years. Meisl had also made the acquaintance of his Italian alter ego, Vittorio Pozzo, a figure with whom he would share the European stage in later years.

But the giant steps that the new-born football movement was taking were frustrated only two years later by the outbreak of the Great War. The conflict pitted nations against each other that had only a few years earlier begun to forge their first sporting relationships. Not only that, but on 28 July 1914, the day on which the Austro-Hungarian Empire declared war on Serbia, many of the English pioneers and those who had given an important impulse to the game of football over the years became 'persona non grata', 'enemies on foreign soil', and consequently were taken prisoner. Among them was Hogan: only two days before the start of the conflict the coach had gone to the British Consulate in Vienna to ask if he and his family should return to England in a hurry. He said he was reassured that there was no real danger, but two days later war was declared, he was taken from his home in the middle of the night and put in a cell 'along with thieves and murderers'.

A similar fate had befallen other British footballers who had contributed to the development of European football in previous years. Among them were John Cameron, then coach of Dresdner, Steve Bloomer, coach of Britannia Berlin 92 and John Pentland, who had just arrived in Germany to lead the German national team that was due to take part in the 1916 Olympic Games. The three were sent to the Ruhleben labour camp, not far from Berlin. Here, together with other inmates from the world of football, they created a very popular championship. Fortunately, none of these personal events ended in tragedy: Bloomer, for example, told how life in Ruhleben was not so terrible and that he had often had the feeling that it was worse for the guards than for the prisoners, who enjoyed some small freedoms such as the possibility of engaging in sports activities. Hogan was saved by the Blyth brothers, one of whom, Ernest, had been one of the founders of the Vienna Cricket Club. The Blyths were two wealthy Englishmen who had obtained their freedom by paying about £1,000 to the Austrian Red Cross. They allowed Hogan to work at their property where he did various jobs including being a tennis instructor for their children, always keeping the local police informed. The fate of other athletes was not so rosy, as witnessed by the various victims that the football world mourned in those years. Some of these were Olympic athletes whom Meisl and Pozzo, employed at the front on opposing sides, had met, known and admired a few years earlier in Stockholm.

Despite the reverberations of the Great War, football did not have to start again from scratch at the end of the armed conflict: it had been played in the work camps, near the trenches and whenever the soldiers had the chance to take a break from the routine of war. Hugo Meisl was thus able to pick up his plans where he left off. Having hated his experience at the front, he now aimed to create a system that, in addition to encouraging healthy sporting competition, would act as a glue between peoples. A system that, in virtue of the increased popularity of football, would allow players to earn a living through their performances on the field of play and clubs and federations to exploit the passion of the fans for commercial purposes. This is how, in Europe between the two wars, football became the most popular sport on the continent.

Football was talked about in the streets as well as in offices and public places. In Vienna and Budapest the discussion about football took a much more intellectual turn than in England. While in London and the surrounding area everything that revolved around football was discussed in the pub, for a few minutes over a pint of beer; in the main metropolises that had been part of the Empire, football was discussed in coffee houses, places where until recently people from all walks of life had gathered to talk about music, literature, cinema and theatre. This new way of approaching a conversation about football, sitting down and taking their time, gave the participants the opportunity to delve into specific analysis of tactics, technique, roles and other related topics. The coffee houses were also places where the exploits of the first real stars – who in Vienna were called *Kanonen* – of the European football scene were extolled: true icons comparable to those of cinema and music.

But there was also another trend emerging: the football market. In fact, the first transfer of a player from one club to another recorded in Europe dates back to 1913, when Genoa secured for a few thousand lire the services of Milan defender Renzo De Vecchi, then nicknamed '*Il Figlio di Dio*' ('the Son of God'). But it was in the early 1920s that the phenomenon intensified, especially on the Hungary-Austria axis, when the wealthiest clubs in Vienna, Austria Vienna – at the time Wiener Amateur Sportverein – and Hakoah signed Hungarian champions such as Alfréd Schaffer, nicknamed 'the King of Football', Kálmán and Jenő Konrád, Béla Guttmann, Ernő Schwarz and József Eisenhoffer. Football, although still at an unofficial level, had in fact become a business and some clubs, not having the economic strength to compete, were forced to sell most of their talents, ending up in the lower positions of the league table, if not in the lower divisions.

It was clear to Hugo Meisl that all the ingredients existed for football to make a leap in quality from the amateur model to the professional one. The fear that haunted several Central European clubs was that they would not be able to cope with the burdens that this model would bring, such as salaries, advertising expenditure and expenses related to the maintenance of the playing facilities, despite the fact that their earnings would also increase due to a larger turnout at the games and the increase in ticket prices. Meisl recalled that 'the practice of paying footballers' salaries had in fact already begun during the war years', although this was done unofficially and usually as reimbursement for expenses.

The first professional league in Central Europe was created in Austria at the beginning of the 1924/25 season, one year earlier than in Czechoslovakia and two years earlier than in Hungary. However, the fears expressed by some clubs materialised almost immediately, and while the major clubs in the capital were strengthened by being able to acquire players from smaller clubs, the latter struggled to the point of bankruptcy. The football market was thus made official. An article in *Sport-Tagblatt* outlined how it worked:

'A contract can last six or 12 months. Goals and bonuses are meant to be included in the contract and the minimum monthly wages must be 500,000 kronen for the first division and 300,000 for the second division. Regarding transfers, the system is that a good portion of the sum goes to the player, although this depends largely on the number of years he has played for the selling club. The basis is ten per cent to the player, which rises by a further ten per cent with each passing year. This means, for example, that after five years of playing, 60 per cent of the sum goes to the player.'

The new system came into effect and the vehement protests of some clubs and players were to no avail. Some of them, gathered in Vienna outside the Hotel Post, protested strongly against this decision. The accusation was that a new system had been imposed without the consent of those concerned, who were now forced to choose between their profession and that of footballers. An example of this was the case with the Konrád brothers, Kálmán and Jenő. The two players, who had embarked on careers outside football, Jenő as an employee in a bank and Kalmán in the financial sector, wanted to continue playing football while earning a second income. And in such an uncertain period, dominated by financial problems, to give up a fixed and paid job to devote themselves entirely to football seemed a big gamble. The issue was not resolved and Konrád, who was sidelined for several months, was sold to First Vienna the following spring.[10] In order to resolve these

---

10 Despite the friction, Kalmán Konrád would return to the Wiener Amateur within six months and Jenő, struggling with knee problems, would hang up his boots.

issues, the first trade union in continental Europe was formed to protect the rights of footballers, headed by Josef Brandstetter, defender and captain of Rapid Vienna.

The football world was thus split in two – those who believed football should remain amateur and those who advocated the leap towards professionalism – and Hugo Meisl, who nevertheless enjoyed the support of old and new acolytes, had two competitions in mind. One would be for club sides, the Mitropa Cup, reserved for the best Central European teams, and one for national teams, the International Cup, a good antidote to heal the wounds of the previous years. The prevailing aim, however, remained of an economic nature. Meisl was inspired after watching a friendly match between First Vienna and Slavia Prague at the Hohe Warte Stadium. There were only 3,000 spectators in attendance, which was not enough for a match of that level. This is because in the years between the wars, while matches between national teams already attracted a large number of spectators, the same could not be said for those between clubs. Several football managers of the time were promoting European club competitions: first of all Henrik Fodor, president of the Hungarian federation and director of MTK, who proposed a mini-league with return matches. Meisl, who had not endorsed Fodor's proposal, because it did not include Czechoslovak teams, developed another idea: to conceive the same tournament but with a direct elimination format along the lines of the Challenge Cup but introducing – an absolute novelty – round-robin matches. This formula met with far greater approval, although some suggested further changes: Edwin Herzog, president of Hungarian side Sabaria, wanted to create a parallel competition to involve clubs from nations that had been left out, but that proposal was soon abandoned. Although the idea of an event for Central European clubs had been the result of several heads, there was no doubt about one thing: the driving force behind the new-born competition was and would be Hugo Meisl. *Nemzeti Sport*, a well-known Budapest sports newspaper, in an article published on 1 June 1927, claimed that Mitropa was born thanks to Meisl's diplomatic and organisational skills, 'capable of convincing the federations involved through figures and concrete data, making them understand the economic potential of the event'. In fact, it would be Meisl himself who would weave, manage and, where necessary, adjust the fragile relations between the forces that would participate in the tournament.

However, the plan to set up the tournament presented at the FIFA Congress in Paris in 1926 was rejected, which led its promoters to seek outside support. Between August and October of that year, Meisl met with the Hungarian and Czechoslovakian secretaries Fodor and Loos and with some members of the Italian federation, with whom relations had been frozen for a few years. On 27 October came the final squeeze: the representatives involved met again to define the birth of the tournament. All agreed except Italy, which said it was sceptical about the travel costs and the difficulties of including the matches in its calendar. The Mitropa Cup thus became a reality and the subsequent meetings were only intended to extend the invitation to other possible participants. One of the Czechoslovak representatives, Bednář, was appointed secretary of the committee, whose headquarters were established in Vienna along the Tegethofstrasse, since the organisation would be entrusted to Hugo Meisl. Between 1927 and 1940, more than half of the meetings related to the event took place here. In the first few months of 1927, several meetings took place, attended by representatives of hitherto disregarded nations such as Poland, Yugoslavia,

Romania, Italy – which was considering a change of heart – and Sweden, whose presence would probably force the organising committee to adopt the more inclusive name of the Central European Cup.

In the minds of Meisl and his team-mates there was still the hope of obtaining official recognition from FIFA, and with this goal in mind the main representatives of Central European football presented themselves at the congress that FIFA held in Helsinki in 1927. The US delegation, with whom the Central European federations had enjoyed frosty relations for years, was also present: Austria and Hungary, angry that two of the leading clubs in the USA had signed a number of Central European championship-winning players, had lodged a complaint with FIFA. Relations were then mended when Meisl decided to withdraw the complaint, and although this enabled him to gain the support of the United States, FIFA issued a second rejection. It was clear that the Mitropa Cup, at least at first, would have to be created with a private agreement between the signatory federations.

The congress for the foundation of Mitropa, which took place simultaneously with that for the International Cup, was held in Venice between 15 and 16 July. While he was in Italy, Meisl learned that the Palace of Justice in Vienna had gone up in flames: a very violent citizens' revolt had broken out that had forced the Austrian Chancellor Seipel to order the police to open fire on the demonstrators. Some 600 people were killed and more than 1,000 injured.

The congress decided the cup would have four participating federations: Austria, Hungary, Czechoslovakia and Yugoslavia. Italy, which at first seemed to be confirmed, was excluded, due to the fact that relations between Austria and Italy had cooled again: since 1926 Mussolini had been implementing a process of Italianisation that had undermined the freedoms of German-speaking minorities living in northern Italy, especially in South Tyrol. The controversy, of course, had reverberated in the newspapers, and not only on a sporting level. Fascism, moreover, had made a number of changes to the world of football: in 1926 it had introduced the Viareggio Charter which, while on the one hand marked the transition to professionalism, on the other would have first limited and then, from 1928, prohibited the use of foreign players by Italian teams, most of whom came from Austria and Hungary. For these reasons, the Austrian federation boycotted the FIFA Congress held in Rome, which Meisl, as a member of the association, had attended.

In the end it was decided that Italy, like Switzerland, would only participate in the International Cup. The Italian federation acknowledged Meisl's commitment and in September 1927 Mussolini granted him an audience at the end of which the Austrian secretary was presented with a photo of them signed by the Duce in person. Germany was excluded from both competitions: from Mitropa because of its refusal to compete with professional teams and from the International Cup at the behest of the organising federations, given that in 1924, when Austria had turned professional, Germany had asked for its exclusion from FIFA.[11]

One of the biggest problems that Meisl and his associates knew they had to live with was the calendar: it was decided to put the International Cup matches on certain weekends during the season when the national tournaments stopped, while the Mitropa Cup matches would be played in the summer after the championships, and in the years when

---

11 You have to take into account the fact that German football and its teams did not have much appeal at the time.

the World Cup would be held immediately after the latter. The winning team would receive two trophies: the cup, bearing the names of the participating federations and that of the finalists, and the Providentia, a reproduction of the fountain that stands in the Viennese square of Neumarkt.

1927 – STEEL SPARTA

The first edition of the Mitropa Cup was an unknown quantity for the entire European public. The continent's teams had faced each other on a few occasions and there were no certainties about the favourites and the relative strengths of the teams, only hints resulting from a few matches and friendly tours played over the years. However, one thing was clear: it would be an affair reserved for the teams of the main European capitals. Vienna, Budapest and Prague would compete for the trophy, with the Yugoslav teams playing the role of Cinderellas, since they were still too inexperienced to compete at the highest levels. The participating federations each established their criteria for participation: Austria decided to invite its defending champion and the winner of the Vienna Cup; Czechoslovakia the first- and second-ranked teams from its national tournament; and Hungary had opted to enrol the top two teams from a mini tournament between the top four teams in the league. This was the reason why Ferencváros were missing, as although they won the Hungarian championship with a seven-point margin, in the final tournament, they finished third.

* * *

DESPITE THE fact that at the end of the first post-war period the world of football had almost immediately recovered and the championships had restarted, the international sporting scene still suffered from some disharmony: in 1920, due to the friction between Austria and the victorious powers, Hugo Meisl's national team had not been invited to the Olympic Games in Antwerp. However, this had not prevented the British coaches who had come to Europe years earlier, particularly to the nations that until 1918 were united under the Habsburg crown, from continuing their work. If in Austria and Germany during the war political prisoners were sent to work camps, and often prison, in Prague and its surroundings the unfortunate ones had better luck: thanks to the influence of the Bohemian nationalist movement, they were able to remain free from imprisonment on condition that they did not leave the country. This is what happened to John Dick, the creator of Železná Sparta, translatable as Steel Sparta, the formidable Czechoslovakian team Sparta Prague after the First World War. The nickname '*Sparta d'Acciaio*' reflected the character of the Bohemian side: less attractive to watch but more effective, tough and blunt than their Slavia cousins.

Dick had been the first player in the history of Arsenal – at the time Woolwich Arsenal – to reach 250 appearances. He had visited Prague for the first time in 1907 on the occasion of two friendly matches that the London team had played against Slavia Prague, coached by another Scot, John William Madden, and then, in 1912, had decided to settle in the Bohemian capital. Here he was contracted in the dual role of player and coach by DFC Prag, a historical club, representative of the Jewish bourgeoisie, and played for them until the outbreak of the Great War. During the years of the conflict he remained in Prague and as soon as the hostilities ended he was employed by Sparta, and was able to make them Europe's strongest team. The club adopted the name Steel Sparta in 1919 and only the following year, when the new-born Czechoslovakia reached the final of the aforementioned Antwerp Olympic Games – the only final in the history of football to have been abandoned because of some disputed refereeing decisions[12] – Sparta supplied the national team with ten players.

The first success of the new-born Czechoslovakian football movement, which was actually a Sparta success, dates back to the previous year. Between 22 June and 6 July, the Inter-allied Games[13] – known in Prague and surroundings as the *Pershingova olympiáda,* or Pershing Olympics, after the American commander John Joseph Pershing who had strongly supported them – were held in the surroundings of Paris. They were a unofficial Olympic event involving the nations that came out victorious from the Great War.[14] The Stadion Pershing, built for the occasion, was the venue for Czechoslovakian football's first great international success, as the national team guided by Madden and composed almost exclusively of players from Sparta triumphed. Czechoslovakia eliminated, in order, Belgium (4-1), the United States (8-2), Canada (3-2) and in the final France, thanks to a 3-2

---

12 The Czechoslovakian players, unlike their Hungarian and Austrian colleagues, were known to be polemical and stormy towards both opponents and match officials. On this occasion, they did not like the expulsion of one of their players, Steiner, for having attacked an adversary, and the concession of a penalty, which they claimed was invented in favour of Belgium.

13 The football competition began on 24 June.

14 Czechoslovakia, in reality, having been under the Habsburg hegemony, was not a winning nation but it was able to recompose its political relationships at the end of the Great War when it was constituted in the form of an independent republic. At a sporting level it succeeded in maintaining stable relationships both with the ex-powers that were part of the Habsburg monarchy and with England and Italy.

comeback victory. The star player was Antonín Janda, who usually played as a forward but that day was lined up as a defender. He was moved up to the offensive line with a quarter of an hour left to play and between the 84th and 88th minutes he scored a decisive double. He was so acclaimed that at the end of the match a large group of fans, probably not French, came on to the pitch to carry him on their shoulders and celebrate his performance.

Between 1919 and 1922 Sparta won 58 out of 59 matches and four national titles. An important year was 1921: the club beat, in order, Nuremberg – winning an unofficial tournament organised by the German team – Celtic, Barcelona and Athletic Bilbao. At the end of the match against Barcelona, the Catalan management did everything they could to sign Janda. They offered him a staggering amount of money, but he refused. In Bilbao the Bohemians played two matches, winning them 3-1 and 4-1 respectively. The public and local newspapers also dwelled on some individual performances: 'Seeing Káďa, Janda, Pilát, Mazal and all these prodigious players play is for a football-lover like seeing Naples for a tourist: you have to see them before you die!' wrote *La Gaceta del Norte*. And it was probably no coincidence that in 1926 the Czechoslovak team would be invited for a tour of the United States.[15]

In 1922 Dick was tempted by a new adventure: he moved to Belgium and went to coach Beerschot. He was replaced by the Czechoslovakian Václav Špindler, who won three more national titles.[16] Then, on 5 January 1927, just

---

15 The 1920s went down in history as the Golden Age of American Football. For this reason, several European teams organised summer tours overseas and almost always managed to fill the stadiums.

16 Statistics and reports are incomplete. Many claim that Dick was still with Sparta that year, but more reliable sources say *Špindler was in charge*.

a few months before the start of the first edition of the Mitropa, the club was hit by terrible news: the 22-year-old talent Jaroslav Poláček had died of kidney failure. Shortly before his death he told his team-mates: 'Bury me with a Sparta shirt on.' No sooner said than done.

The fruits of Dick's work were clearly visible: Sparta played exactly as the coach had taught them, putting the dictates of Scottish football into practice to perfection. Although Janda and some of the champions of the past years had hung up their boots, the club had replenished its ranks with some very valuable elements and was always led by its veteran star, Karel Pešek, known as Káďa. Káďa's popularity went far beyond the playing field: Karel Balling, the famous Bohemian cabaret artist, dedicated the song 'Dneska hraje Káďa' ('Today Káďa is Playing') to him and the player received praise from all over the world. Santiago Bernabéu said he was the best player he had ever played against, while Hungarian manager Henrik Fodor, after watching him in a match, said: 'Maybe Orth[17] is slightly more technical and elegant, but Káďa is faster, quicker and more gritty. He is the soul of the team. I'm sorry to say this but I think Káďa is superior!' And every time Sparta went on a tour of Europe or South America, the home side set one condition: Káďa had to play. Káďa, who in addition to being a footballer was also an ice hockey player,[18] was considered in those years the 'strongest holding midfielder in Europe', as an article of the *Corriere della Sera* defined him. That view was echoed by *La Gazzetta dello Sport* which, in an article that appeared shortly before a match between Italy and Czechoslovakia, pointed out that

---

17 Orth, we'll see shortly, was one of the best Hungarian players of the 1920s.

18 He was present at the 1920 Olympics in two capacities: as a player in both soccer and hockey.

while in Austria and Hungary football was undergoing a profound generational renewal, in Czechoslovakia, 'the palace of Káďa,[19] the superiority of the veteran talisman was not questioned by anyone. 'Ten times he was given up for dead, ten times he was unanimously re-elected,' the *Rosea* concluded.

* * *

Sparta, who had never taken part in the Challenge Cup in the past, made their European debut against Admira Vienna, who were participating in the tournament as winners of the local league. The Czechoslovakians' participation had been in doubt until the last minute: the club's president had declared that he did not want to participate as the event evoked 'the monarchical nature of the late Austro-Hungarian Empire'. But then either he changed his mind or someone made him retrace his steps. Admira had won the title for the first time in their history, battling to the last against Brigittenauer AC, a terrible freshman team that had only arrived in the top division the previous year and had made headlines for their defence – the best in the league – and for the performances of their goalkeeper, Franz Köhler. But in the end, thanks to their greater experience, Admira had inflicted a 5-0 defeat on their rivals and secured their ticket to Europe. The leading figure of the Austrian club in those years was undoubtedly the striker Anton Schall, top scorer of the just-ended championship. And it was thanks to Schall that the Viennese fans had any hope against the Czechoslovak battleship.

---

19 Káďa's greatness is evidenced by one fact: even from 1934, the year in which he left Sparta, when the newspapers spoke of Sparta they continued to associate the club with its former captain by calling it 'Káďa's team'.

Only 7,000 spectators turned up for the first leg in Prague, partly because of the heavy rain that turned the pitch to mush. The game began with the Czechs scoring a goal: Patek forced his way in from the right and fired a torpedo that hit the underside of the crossbar before Veselý – replacing usual starter Dvořáček – slotted into the net. In the next play, Patek almost made it 2-0 but the goal was disallowed for offside. In the eighth minute, however, Veselý scored another goal from a pass by Silný. Then it was Austria's Runge who scored from a free kick after a foul by Hajný. After some wasted chances by Sparta, Admira came back and dominated the match for about a quarter of an hour. But in the 43rd minute Maloun made it 3-1 from a corner kick.

From the beginning of the second half, Admira stopped playing and Sparta took advantage to score two more goals and in the final minutes also had an appeal for a handball penalty turned down. The match thus ended 5-1 to Špindler's men, whose superiority was also evidenced by the corner count: 11-3. According to *Prager Presse*, a Prague newspaper published in German, Sparta could have won by an even larger margin: the newspaper underlined the excellent performance of Káďa and the defensive line, but it said of Veselý that he had done nothing else apart from score the two goals and of Silný that he had been inoperative for the whole first half. Admira, a side known for thrashing their direct rivals in the league, were criticised in the Viennese newspapers for not repeating that form at European level and for lacking in playmaking ability. Franzl, the goalkeeper, despite some important saves, was accused of not being irreproachable in some circumstances. The Hungarian referee, Gero, ended up in the crosshairs of some newspapers, although they all agreed that his direction did not influence the result.

In the return match, played the following week, the two teams presented the same line-ups. Sparta played with the handbrake on from the beginning and this gave confidence to the Austrians: in front of 15,000 spectators who roared their team on, Admira rose to the challenge with great intensity and, perhaps, excessive antagonism, given the several clashes with the opposition players. Also, the fans didn't help: they insulted the Czechoslovakian players for a good part of the match. However, on the field, the Austrians used their home advantage to go ahead in the 13th minute through Schall, then doubled the lead at the end of the first half with a Sigl penalty.

The second half began with Silný's goal that made the score 2-1 before Schall restored the two-goal advantage for Admira. Admira continued their attacks and first Runge, with a free kick, as in the first leg, and then Stoiber, scored to make it 4-1 then 5-1. The aggregate score was tied but the home side then lost Schall because of an injury and, with a numerical disadvantage, they conceded two identical goals from Veselý: the Czechoslovakian forward taking advantage of two Kolenatý crosses to seal their place in the next round. The end of the match was marked by the fans booing the visiting team and Kolenatý was sent off for protesting.

Apart from the Prague leg, the first official matches in history between European clubs – with the exception of the Challenge Cup matches – had met Meisl's forecasts: the stadiums had almost all been filled and the clubs had received an improved income.[20]

* * *

---

20 Some stadiums of the time, however, had limited capacity, such as those of Yugoslav clubs.

So Káďa and his team-mates reached the semi-finals where they met FC Hungária[21] who, as predicted, had defeated Beogradski in the quarter-finals – a team that was still immature, despite including several of the main stars of Yugoslav football, who would go on to play at the first World Cup in 1930. The Hungarians scored eight goals in the two legs and their progress through the round was never in doubt. In the return match, which ended 4-0, György Orth's star shone. Orth, who Jimmy Hogan had wanted to sign years before, had arrived at MTK after a few years of apprenticeship with SKI, a local team sponsored by a coffee house located on Aradi útca, and Vasas.[22] Hogan once said about him: 'He's the strongest, smartest and most versatile player I've ever seen.' But a serious injury damaged his career and from September 1925 Orth was never the same again. The match against Beogradski was a sort of swansong. In 1930 he would leave for South America and become the manager of the Chilean national team, taking part in the first World Cup in history as a coach.

Over the years the Hungarian team had also lost other talents: Imre Schlosser and Alfréd Schaffer, two of the leading Magyar goalscorers in history, had left the club in 1922 and 1923 respectively. But the club's decline coincided with Orth's injury and MTK's long-standing hegemony over Hungarian football came to an end.

The first leg of the semi-final was played in front of 18,000 spectators. Alongside Orth, Hungária fielded Ferenc Hirzer, a forward who had returned from Juventus.

---

21 Name adopted in 1926 by MTK.

22 Jonathan Wilson in *The Names Heard Long Ago* reports a curious anecdote: on the day Orth was bought by Vasas Reiner, the team's scout had gone to watch him in a match against Hungária, then MTK. Shortly afterwards MTK president Alfred Brüll had also noticed him, but did not know his name. As soon as the match was over Reiner would put him under contract.

The first goal of the match was scored by the Hungarians thanks to Opata, who took advantage of a corner kick in the 39th minute. Then, just six minutes later, Patek equalised for Sparta and it was 1-1 at the break.

The second half was definitely Sparta's, who were awarded a penalty that was then revoked for a foul on Horejs in the 60th minute. Then, in the 65th minute, they went 2-1 up thanks to Silný. It was only at that point that Hungária returned to the attack and Jeny levelled the score at 2-2, which was how it stayed. Opinions were divided on the result: Hungária manager Henrik Fodor said: 'We should have won the game as we had more chances. Sparta's midfield is better than ours and for this reason they were superior for a good part of the match.' Nathan, manager of Sparta, declared: 'We will win the match in Prague. Sparta are of a higher class and that will give us an advantage.'

The return semi-final was played in front of 24,000 spectators. The feeling among them was that Sparta were favourites, especially when it became known that Vesely and Steiner had recovered and that Hungária would play without Orth. Just as in the first leg, Braun, probably the most respected whistler of the time, was refereeing. He entered the field with the 22 players and was applauded by the public.

Sparta made themselves dangerous in the first few minutes with two shots: the first, a header by Silný, went just over the crossbar while the second was blocked by Hungarian goalkeeper Biri. Then the game slowed down and Hungária, amidst the whistles of the home crowd, started to attack. Opata and Braun had two comfortable chances but wasted them before Vesely failed to finish from a corner.

In the second half, the home side's pressure increased and both sides came close to scoring, but the goalkeepers both kept their goals intact. A tough but fair match ended 0-0 and the Czechoslovaks, including Káďa, were severely criticised; particularly the forwards, for not making the most of their opportunities. Biri was instead praised by the opposition press. The lack of verve of the home team had pushed the public, initially enthusiastic, to boo their favourites, who had given the impression of wanting to control the game.

'We played badly, Hungária did better than us. But the result is still fair,' said Káďa at the end of the match. Fodor was more explicit: 'We were clearly superior to Sparta. Regarding the Konrád case, we called a meeting with the committee.'

The 'Konrád case' had been raised by the Sparta management as soon as the match was over. Kálmán Konrád – or Konrád II, as he was called to distinguish him from Jenő – had been signed by Hungária during the competition.[23] This was against the rules laid down by the organising committee and for this reason, at the end of the meeting held on 13 October in Bratislava, it was decided that the play-off – which was to be held to determine the winner of the semi-final after the two drawn games – would not take place. Hungária were disqualified amidst the anger of their leaders, who left the meeting. Sparta thus advanced to the final without having to play a third match. The Hungarian newspapers were furious with the committee's decision and with Hugo Meisl: 'They want to destroy Hungarian football', read an article in the Hungarian newspaper *Sporthirlap*.

---

23 Kálmán Konrád, whom I mentioned earlier, moved to the United States, to the Brooklyn Wanderers, after playing in Austria, and then returned to Europe in 1927. He had a contract with MTK, but they would not be able to play him, as he arrived during the competition.

* * *

Sparta met Rapid Vienna in the final, a team that had taken the competition very seriously: they had not taken any days off after the championship and just before the Mitropa began they had signed Hans Horvath, one of the most promising talents on the Austrian scene, from Simmeringer. The Austrians had eliminated Hajduk Split with no problems, inflicting an 8-1 defeat in the first leg of the quarter-finals in Vienna and then, with more difficulty, they had defeated Slavia Prague in the semi-finals. The Czechs had held out for a long time thanks to some superb saves from goalkeeper František Plánička, who had thwarted Rapid Vienna's siege to keep the score at 2-2 in the first leg and repeated the feat in the return before having to surrender to a masterful free kick from specialist Ferdinand Wesely, one of the world's best left-wingers. The match ended 2-1 and Rapid reached the final.

In front of around 25,000 spectators and under a beautiful autumn sky, Sparta and Rapid took to the pitch for the first leg with Belgian referee Van Praag. Sparta went on the attack and in the very first minute, after a corner kick, they took the lead: Káďa received the ball and fired an unstoppable torpedo that grazed the face of Austrian defender Jellinek before entering the net: 1-0. The Bohemians then created another chance for Silný, served by Patek, but he wasted it. The Czechs and Slovaks continued to attack and Feigl, the Austrian goalkeeper, showed his skill by intervening several times. Then it was 2-0: Patek crossed, Feigl cleared the ball and it found its way to Šima, who easily put it into the net. But only two minutes later Rapid reduced the deficit: Burgr touched the ball with his hand just outside the area and Wesely scored from a free kick. Rapid, galvanised, increased their pressure and the game grew in intensity. Within two minutes, between the

33rd and 34th minutes, the scoreboard read 3-2: first Silný brought Sparta's score to three and then Wesely, this time from the penalty spot, rekindled the Austrians' hopes.

In the 62nd minute, Patek received a pass from Myclik and scored to make it 4-2. Rapid reduced their intensity and became less dangerous and Sparta made it 5-2 from a cross collected by Silný, whose shot ended up in the net again. Only three minutes later, again from a cross, their sixth and final goal came: Horejs crossed, Šima let it pass and Patek shot into the top corner. Patek, close to making it 7-2, was stopped for offside. A few minutes before the end, Rapid went a man down due to Nitsch being sent off.

The match ended 6-2, a real triumph for the Czechoslovaks. The local fans carried their favourites on their shoulders, Káďa above all, who was acknowledged by the press as having improved considerably compared to the home game against Hungária. Kolenatý was also lauded as he had had the toughest task of marking the opponents' star, Wesely. Apart from two goals from set pieces, the Austrian winger only scored once, and that was at the end of the game.

The Mitropa Cup, decorated with the flags of the four participating federations, was on display that day in a Vienna jewellery shop on Kärntnerstrasse and bore a silver plaque with the names of the finalists.

The return match, played in front of 40,000 spectators and under the direction of Dutch referee Eymers, seemed a formality given the first-leg result. Wesely tried to liven up the contest early on with a goalbound effort that was saved on the line, and then he scored, skipping past Káďa and defender Perner before unleashing a shot that crashed on to the inside of the crossbar and into the net. Rapid's fans, partially delighted by the goal, were concerned to see the scorer leave shortly afterwards with a minor injury.

However, the attacking midfielder soon returned. Towards the end of the first half Silný had an opportunity but wasted it. The first half ended 1-0.

The second half began and Sparta scored but Eymers, to the players' disbelief, disallowed it and shortly after, near Rapid's area, overlooked a charge that Czechoslovakian Horejs suffered from two opponents. Then, in the 56th minute, Rapid doubled their lead: Bauer crossed for Luef, who kicked weakly at goal but Hochmann let the ball slip and it ended up in the net.

The game became heated and the clashes multiplied: first Káďa and then Hochmann had to leave the field temporarily. Then, in the 61st minute, Eymers interrupted the match for two minutes after a clash between Perner and Horvath. Horvath was taken off in pain – he would not return – and Perner was sent off. The game resumed as ten against ten. Towards the end of the match, Sparta improved while the Austrians dropped in intensity, so Silný, in the 86th minute, dribbled past Feigl and scored the final goal, to make it 2-1.

This was the result that was always expected. Rapid, even though deserving of their victory thanks to the performance of their leader Wesely – who risked being sent off for unfair play – had to bow overall to the superiority of their opponents, and acknowledge that some of their players weren't good enough. One of those was Karl Bauer, on his debut in the competition.[24]

It was the Vienna crowd and the referee Eymers who were in the eye of the storm. The Prague press claimed that the green-and-white fans behaved even worse than those of Admira and that never before had Vienna witnessed such a

---

24 In some European newspapers there was an error: it was said that the coach Bauer, then 33 years old, had decided to play himself in attack. It was actually Karl Bauer, not Eduard who played.

violent match. At one point, due to a pitch invasion, not a novelty in those years, the police had to intervene and the match was stopped for some minutes.

At the end of the match Bednář, the chairman of the committee, handed the cup, the first in history, the plaque and the medals to the players. Káďa received the trophy and Kolenatý the plaque in front of an angry crowd that kept shouting and throwing everything on the field. Stones and objects of all kinds rained down from the stands at the Czechoslovak players and supporters. The visitors, despite police support, struggled to leave the stadium and Káďa was hit by a stone on his way to the changing rooms. While some remarked on the high attendance and involvement of the crowd, the German journalist and founder of the well-known *Kicker* newspaper Walter Bensemann was extremely critical of the organisation of the final. In reference to what happened after the match, he said he was disgusted by the fanaticism of the fans and the fact that the police had to escort the winning team. Just as Hungária had threatened to boycott the event because of the Konrád case, Sparta did the same because of the riots in Vienna. Meisl once again managed to mediate between the leaders of the two clubs and for this reason he was made an honorary member of Sparta Prague.

Josef Silný, the event's top scorer, has a curious story behind him: born and raised in the town of Kroměříž – which years later would name a street after him – the player had been pursued by Prague's leading clubs from a very young age. In a 1974 interview with Josef Pondělík, correspondent of the magazine *Gól*, a 72-year-old Silný revealed some background information about his adolescence: he said that when he was only 16 years old, the managers of Sparta, Slavia and some Brno clubs knocked on his door several times trying to convince him and his father to move to the capital. They also talked to the directors of the local club for which Silný played, Haná Slavia, but there was no solution: the boy was happy with his life and only planned to leave his hometown to take part in military service at a barracks in Olomuc. However, the interest of Sparta and Slavia did not fade and one day in Olomuc, the young man found himself in front of an officer who recited a poem in which he praised the beauty of Prague. The officer finished and revealed to Silný that he was actually a representative of Sparta who had come to convince him to join the team. He agreed and thanks to the approval of the Sparta leaders he was immediately transferred to a barracks in the vicinity of Prague. A few days later the club's emissaries went to look for him in Smichov, the town where they thought he was serving, convinced that it was finally time to sign the contract, but they didn't find him: the player was instead in Pohořelec, another town near the capital, and he had just become a Slavia player! Slavia's managers had been waiting for him at the station when his train arrived from Olomuc and an official dressed as an officer ordered him to sign a paper which was actually the contract that would bind him to Slavia.

The dregs of that episode would dissipate a few years later and in 1927 Sparta bought him from their arch-rivals for a record sum of 60,000 crowns. Silný would occupy the centre-forward position until 1930, when the Czechoslovak club signed Belgian Raymond Braine. From that moment on, Silný would be used as a winger or a centre-forward, although his goalscoring averages were excellent. On 19 October 1932 he scored his 100th goal, against his former team. The striker beat goalkeeper Plánička but as goal statistics were ignored at the time, the event went under the radar. Silný would find out many years later, in 1972, when a journalist from the aforementioned *Gól* magazine, Luboš Jeřábek, established the *Klub ligových kanonýrů GÓLU*, a ranking of Czechoslovak players active since 1925 who had scored 100 goals. Silný was the first to join the list.

A story within a story also concerned the striker. During the second leg of the final, Silný had decided that he would do anything to take the ball home. When the game ended, the player found himself with the ball at his feet. He managed to sneak it with him first to the changing rooms and then to the Hotel Post, where Sparta were staying. Here he met a Czechoslovakian fan who offered him 750 crowns to take the souvenir home: the striker accepted without thinking.

1928 – FRADI AND THE FIRST TREBLE IN HISTORY

In order to avoid further Konrád cases, a month before the start of the 1928 tournament the organising committee asked the clubs for a list of the players they wanted to register. It also decided on the distribution of the proceeds: 60 per cent to the home team and 40 per cent to the visiting team.

The format remained unchanged: it started from the quarter-finals, with two-legged ties and a knockout system. In a change from the previous year, a preliminary round was introduced but it was not played because of the refusal of the Romanian team Tmişoara Chinezul to face Beogradski.

* * *

IN 1928 Ferencváros, or Fradi, as they are still called by their fans, appeared on the Mitropa Cup scene. Born as FTC (Ferencvárosi Torna Club) they are the team of the ninth district of Budapest, have Germanic origins – the Franzstadt district was largely populated by Germans – and in those years were supported mainly by workers and inhabitants of the suburbs. They had several points of contact with Rapid Vienna, not least the fact that both sides sported a green-and-white kit.[25] There are two versions of the origins of Fradi's jersey: the first, credited as official, claims that the club's management, in order to keep faith with their patriotic identity, wanted to adopt a red-white-green jersey but had to give up the red due to the fact that this kit had already been adopted years earlier by BTC, another club in the capital. The second, more romantic, version is that the decision was taken in one of the Hungarian capital's coffee shops, the Gebauer Coffee House. According to this version, Kornél Gabrovitz, one of the founders of the club who was in a relationship with one of the owner's daughters, asked her what her favourite colours were. She chose lilac, because of a personal taste, and green, since the club was full of billiard tables. After the first washing, however, the lilac faded, giving way to the famous green and white uniform.

Among the historical teams of Budapest, Fradi were the only one to have won an international title, the Challenge Cup in 1909. That year the Hungarians – FTC at the time – had been unstoppable: besides winning the Challenge Cup they had lifted four other trophies including the championship and the Ezüstlabda, translated as Silver Ball, a forerunner of the Hungarian Cup which was finally awarded to Fradi after their fifth victory in 1909. Then, from the end of the First World War until 1926, Hungarian football was dominated by MTK and only at the end of the 1925/26 season did the green-and-whites return to lift the title, a feat they repeated the following year despite, as noted, not having the opportunity to participate in the Mitropa. No other team supplied the Hungarian national team with as many players as Fradi, with the likes of Amsel

---

25 It should be noted, however, that *Ferencváros* had a much more pronounced patriotic connotation than Rapid.

– the goalkeeper – Bukovi, Kohut, Turay and Takács II regularly appearing on the team rosters.[26] Some of these champions would go down in history: Bukovi, in particular, would become a very successful coach years later. Born as Marton Selinka, Bukovi was the Magyar alter ego of Káďa: he occupied the role of support centre and was considered the brain of the team. He arrived at Ferencváros in 1926 thanks to the will of the coach István Tóth, who immediately made him captain. The feeling between the two was so strong that Bukovi was often a guest at his coach's house to talk about football and tactics. Years later he would say in an interview: 'We spent whole afternoons sitting around the table talking about football, I can't even imagine how bored his wife was!'

József Takács, who was commonly referred to as Takács II in newspapers all over Europe to distinguish him from his brother Géza, was to become one of Hungary's greatest pre-war trikers, topping the list of scorers for five seasons. He started out as a goalkeeper and became a striker through a fortuitous coincidence: during a match, Takács II, who was playing for Vasas at the time, replaced an injured team-mate as a centre-forward and from that moment on he would never leave that position. He became the nightmare of many European defenders and goalkeepers, especially the transalpine keeper Maurice Cottenet who decided to retire after conceding six goals to the Magyar forward in a Hungary–France match that ended 13-1.

The story of Turay, another Fradi pillar, is peculiar: in 1926 Tóth was living with MTK coach Gyula Feldmann. Feldmann, who was of Jewish origin, had been disowned by his family following his marriage to Tóth's sister, who was

---

26 During the first edition of the International Cup (1927–30) Hungary alternated several coaches: Gyula Kiss, Tivadar Kiss and Janos Földessy.

not well liked as a non-Jew. One day Turay, who at the time was playing for a local team, knocked on Tóth's door. He had made an appointment with Feldmann, who wanted to sign him for MTK. But when Turay arrived, Feldmann had not yet woken up from his afternoon nap so Tóth took the opportunity to talk to the boy and convince him to sign for Ferencváros. Tóth also deserves a mention: known as Istvan Tóth-Potya, he was a real flag-bearer for Fradi, both as a player and a coach. The nickname 'Potya' – Potyka actually, but the 'k' is silent – means 'carp' and refers to the chubby appearance of the coach, once a prolific striker famous for his ability to burn defenders at speed.

* * *

The quarter-finals pitted Ferencváros against Beogradski, who qualified, as mentioned, without going through the preliminary round that they would have had to play against Romanian champions Timişoara Chinezul.

The first leg was played in Belgrade and the local public was as warm as it had been the previous year towards Hungária and enthusiastically welcomed the visiting team, one of the most feared and respected of the continent. The welcome was characterised by fair play and began with the arrival of the Hungarian players at the central station of Belgrade and then continued until the entrance of the two teams on to the field.

The match began and with it a real lesson in Danubian-style football: the exchanges between the green-and-white players worked wonderfully and it was the collective rather than the individual players that stood out. Ferencváros scored their first ever Mitropa goal in the first minute through Takács II. In the tenth minute the score was already 0-3 thanks to Turay's double. With qualification in the bag, Fradi began to play freely and scored four more times. The final score was 0-7, with three more goals from Takács II – one of them a stunning acrobatic effort – and another from Turay, and the local crowd could only applaud their opponents' performance. At the end of the match the president of BSK, Andreivić said: 'I must admit that playing against Ferencváros was an incredible experience for Belgrade, something that the public will remember for a long time.'

The return match, contrary to expectations, was not played at Fradi's home ground of Ülloi útca but at the ground of their rivals, Hungária. The reason was that the club's management, in agreement with Hungária, had decided to host both matches at the same ground as the two teams were playing on the same day and not far from each other.[27]

However, the match was a formality, since nobody, not even the most pessimistic of the local fans nor the most optimistic of the guests, expected a reversal of the first-leg result. Ferencváros repeated their performance from Belgrade and the stars of Takács II and Turay shone again, with a double and a treble respectively. The goal scored by Marjanović for the Yugoslavs was irrelevant. The Austrian referee Pressler, at the end of the match, said: 'With a greater effort, Ferencváros could have obtained an even better result. However, I must congratulate the players for their disciplined behaviour on the field. Despite the six goals conceded, the player I liked most was the Beogradski goalkeeper.' In fact, quite a few people that day had the feeling that at a certain point in the match Fradi had stopped.

* * *

---

27 Hungária beat Rapid 3-1.

The semi-finals pitted Fradi against Admira Vienna, once again the Austrian champions. The undisputed star of the Austrians, just like the previous year, was Anton Schall, who was again the top scorer in the championship. *Nemzeti Sport*, Budapest's main sports paper, pointed out that Ferencváros would face an extremely difficult obstacle. One of the reasons was that just a few months earlier, in Vienna, an Austro-Hungarian mini-tournament had taken place in which Ferencváros and Admira had faced each other with a disastrous outcome for the Hungarians: Admira had won 6-1. The stars of the match were the Austrian forwards Stoiber and Sigl, while Takács II had vainly tried to respond, scoring the Hungarians' only goal. Moreover, in the quarter-finals Admira had eliminated a strong Slavia Prague team by beating the prodigious goalkeeper Plánička six times. As a result, the Viennese team was nicknamed the '*Wunderteam*', long before the Austrian national team was given the same name.[28]

The first leg was played in Vienna and Ferencváros got off to a strong start: in the third minute Turay put his team ahead after a free kick resulting from a handball on the edge of the area. The visiting team continued to make themselves at home, and Admira were probably guilty of underestimating their opponents after the friendly match they had won in the summer. The shock for the Austrians arrived in the 21st minute thanks to Sigl's goal, as he took advantage of indecision by Amsel, the goalkeeper. From that moment until the end of the first half, Admira took courage and tried to come back but Amsel didn't get caught out a second time.

---

28 The Austrian national team was nicknamed the *Wunderteam* in May 1931, following a victory over Scotland.

The second half started along the same lines as the first with Fradi on the attack and again scoring, this time through Takács II. The match became nervy, with repeated clashes and with the referee giving the impression of having lost control of the game. In the 87th minute Sigl and Berkessy got into a fight and a local fan tried to intervene in defence of his favourite, but was stopped in time by two policemen. The game ended 2-1 to the visiting team, who therefore had a slight advantage going into the return match. A Viennese newspaper wrote: 'In the first ten minutes Ferencváros's attack reminded us of the best offensive lines in Hungarian history.' Mihály Pataki, former star player and then manager of the Hungarian club, preferred to dwell on the team spirit in containing the fearsome Admira forwards. Hungler, the Fradi captain, said, 'I am very happy with this win, we have shown that this summer's defeat was just an accident. With a little more luck we could have beaten our opponent with the same result.' This analysis, however, does not concur with the reports of the time, according to which a Hungarian victory with a minimum scoreline was the result that best reflected the match and for this reason the return leg looked like being extremely even.

The return match – the first at international level that Ferencváros played at their home ground of Üllői útca – was played in Budapest on 16 September. It was a strange match that remained in the balance for almost the whole 90 minutes, but only because Fradi, indisputably dominant, struggled to find the goal they needed to progress without a play-off. But in the 78th minute the Hungarian fans breathed a sigh of relief: Rázsó, one of the club's lesser-known players, beat Admira's goalkeeper and decided the semi-final.

It was Rázsó himself who commented on the goal at the end of the game: 'As soon as I crossed the halfway line, I saw Franzl way off the mark. My instinct told me to kick towards the goal.' The 'Little Warrior', as *Nemzeti Sport* nicknamed him, would stay at Ferencváros until 1930, scoring 22 goals in 120 games, two of them memorable. The first one is the one just described; the second one Rázsó scored the following year during Fradi's summer tour of South America. The goal was scored against Uruguay, the strongest national team of the time and winner of two Olympic gold medals in 1924 and 1928.[29]

The management of Admira, through the mouth of president Rudolf Mütz, accepted the defeat in a sporting manner: 'I can honestly say that the best team won. All my players did their part, but if the adversary is superior, nothing can be done about it.'

* * *

In the final, the green-and-whites of Budapest faced the green-and-whites of Vienna, Rapid, the previous year's beaten finalists. They were two teams with proletarian souls and origins that drew most of their fans from the outskirts of the two metropolises. The working classes were in heaven!

Rapid had not had an easy journey: they had won two play-offs at the end of a quarter-final and a semi-final that was in the balance until the very end, against Hungária and newcomers Viktoria Žižkov.

The first leg of the final was played in Budapest in front of about 25,000 spectators and in the 20th minute, thanks to a double from Sedláček and a goal from Takács II, Ferencváros seemed to have already secured the final.

---

29 Uruguay would also host and win the first World Cup in 1930.

What was impressive was the determination and the rhythm of the Hungarians with their rivals in clear difficulty. The first half ended with a three-goal difference and while the teams were in the dressing rooms the famous Hungarian pilot Károly Kaszala performed an aerial display.

The second half continued along the same lines as the first and the match ended 7-1, a clear but fair result according to what was seen on the field, determined by three more goals by Takács II and one by Kohut. What on paper was supposed to be an open and hard-fought game between two of the best European teams turned out to be a domination of one over the other.

The match in Vienna, at which Fradi arrived strengthened by the advantage acquired in the first leg, produced a splendid first half with chances at both ends. Rapid were 3-2 up at the break: for the Austrians, Kirbes scored two goals and Wesely one, while Fradi's scorers were Kohut and Turay.

In the second half, following a tremendous double strike by Rapid that brought the score to 5-2 by the 53rd minute, the Hungarians' confidence began to waver. The pressure of the Austrians continued but was interrupted in the 79th minute by Sedláček's goal. Fradi, who were down to ten[30] players, won the coveted trophy and the crowning achievement of an extraordinary season: championship, Hungarian Cup and now Mitropa! It was the first *triplete* in football history.[31]

---

30 Takács I was injured or sent off; it is not clear from the reports.

31 Ferencváros would have already achieved a treble in 1909, but the Challenge Cup and Ezüstlabda were too different to be compared to the Champions League and the Hungarian Cup.

The cup, which had been on display on the sidelines for the whole 90 minutes, was handed over by Mór Fischer[32] to the Ferencváros players who had to run to the changing rooms due to a pitch invasion by the Viennese fans. The local crowd, angry at seeing the cup slip away again in the final act, continued to boo even during Fischer's speech. The two presidents, Szigeti and Holub, then spoke. The latter, representing Rapid, had sporting words for his rivals, unlike Dyonis Schönecker, a historic Rapid manager who was not known for his diplomacy, and who expressed his disappointment with very harsh words.

The protests of the Viennese would continue in the following days: in their view, the ball used was outdated and not of the regulation size, despite the fact that both teams had given their consent days before. The feeling of many was that if Hugo Meisl, who was in Rome that day to direct his own national team, had been present in Vienna certain disorders would have been avoided.

For about a year the ball from the Budapest final was kept by Takács II. Then, during a match of his old team, Vasas, a historic club from the Hungarian capital that had recently been relegated, 'Kis Taki', or 'Little Taki', as he was nicknamed, came to the stadium with a hat and a bag in his hand. His presence did not go unnoticed by the Thököly Út crowd[33] and at the end of the match, when the opponents had left the pitch, the striker walked towards the home players and handed them the ball with which he had scored four goals in the first leg.

Kis Taki was undoubtedly one of the most famous faces of pre-war Magyar football, an extraordinary goal-

---

32 Fischer was a Hungarian engineer and diplomat who, in the years following the Great War, had organised several international meetings to bring relations between nations back together.

33 Thököly Út is the street where the Vasas stadium was located.

scorer who was attributed only one major flaw: scoring few goals in the air. In a friendly match, at the request of his fans, the striker promised to break that taboo. He waited for a decent cross for most of the match and in the end, discouraged, he decided to go on his own: he mocked the entire opponents' defence, sat the goalkeeper down, placed the ball on the goal line and, after kneeling down, headed it into the net. The stadium erupted with joy but was frozen an instant later: the referee had decided to disallow the goal for disrespecting the opposition.

1929 – CHAMPIONS IN EUROPE, BIT-PART PLAYERS IN HUNGARY

The 1929 edition of the Mitropa Cup was the first in which Italian teams took part. The Italian federation applied to join in March 1929 – after Meisl had invited it to take part in a meeting held on 3 February in Budapest – and was admitted a few months later, in the same year the Italian championship adopted the single-round system. The members of the Italian committee, some of whom would remain in office until 1940, were Giovanni Mauro, Giuseppe Zanetti, the FIGC general secretary whom the Italian newspapers called 'Maestro', engineer Ottorino Barassi and commissioner Mario Ferretti.

Making way for the Italian clubs were the Yugoslavian teams. The committee had decided to exclude the Yugoslav federation for three fundamental reasons: the trips were very expensive, the matches attracted few spectators and the teams were not yet competitive,[34] which is why Switzerland's candidature was also rejected.

---

34 Germany's candidacy was back in vogue. Although some teams were in favour of it, the DFB, the German federation, had once again vetoed it.

The format of the tournament had not changed: it started with the quarter-finals and ended with a double final. Henrik Fodor had proposed a different division of the profits – 50 per cent each to the home team and visiting team – but the idea was rejected and they remained faithful to the old rules. It was the first edition to be officially recognised by FIFA, which that year, before the tournament began, had asked the committee to send it the results of previous years so that they could be included in their almanacs. And at the end of the third tournament, the founding members of Mitropa would receive a gold medal from FIFA at a conference in Vienna.

France, in an attempt to copy the Mitropa format, would invite Luxembourg and Portugal to establish a Western European Cup and a similar idea was mooted in Northern Europe. However, neither project ever saw the light of day.

Due to tours already organised in the previous months in South America, Bologna and Turin, the winners of the respective Italian groups, could not participate in the event. So, on 12 May, the committee met in Genova and allowed Italy to invite two other participants. The Italian federation decided to organise two matches between four clubs, with the winners representing their country on the European stage. The draw, which took place that same day, established the following pairings: Genova v Milan and Juventus v Ambrosiana.[35]

---

35 Inter, following their merger with Unione Sportiva Milanese, were renamed Ambrosiana. Juventus and Genova progressed to the quarter-finals, the latter through a draw at AC Milan's headquarters followed by a replay.

Hungary also had to do without their defending champions as Ferencváros also opted to tour South America.

The committee decided that the Austrian champions would face the winner of Milan v Genova, the winner of the Czechoslovakian Cup (Sparta Prague) would play Újpest, the winner of the Austrian Cup (First Vienna) would meet Hungária and the winner between Ambrosiana and Juventus would play the Czechoslovakian champions (Slavia Prague). Referee designations were also discussed, the new edition of the International Cup, and at the end of the meeting two telegrams were sent: one to Hugo Meisl[36] to wish him a good recovery[37] and one to FIGC president Leandro Arpinati to thank him for his hospitality.

* * *

THE FIRST clubs in Budapest were formed a few years after those in Vienna. In most cases, they were sections created within sports clubs that had existed for years, and who noticed that football was beginning to acquire great popularity in the streets, gardens and suburbs of the capital. The first multi-sport club to establish a football team was the Budapest Torna Club, better known as BTC, and within a short time it was emulated by others: one of these was the Újpesti Torna Egylet, known as UTE, later called

---

36 Italian newspapers used to call him Ugo Meisl, as the Hungarian coach of Inter and Bologna was called Veisz instead of the more Hungarian Weisz.

37 Hugo Meisl had not been well and had been away from Vienna for a while.

Újpest FC.[38] In 1885 János Goll, Antal Berényi, Ábris
Szèkely-Sonnenfeld and Gyula Ugró met in a pub on Deák
ütca[39] and decided to found a multi-sports club. On 16
June of that year, the birth of UTE was made official: the
slogan 'Integrity, Strength and Understanding' was adopted
and the club's colours were white and purple, which were
also used by the football team years later, which is why
the players of Újpest FC are still nicknamed '*Lilák*', the
'Lilacs'. Újpest – now a district of Budapest – was at one
time a small town on the outskirts of the capital and an
important industrial district. It was founded by Izsák Löwy
who, as a Jew, had been denied the opportunity to open a
shoe factory in Pest.

The club, which would take part in Mitropa in 1929
due to the absence of Ferencváros, boasted neither the
tradition of Hungária nor Fradi but within a few years
would become a serious contender for the title and in the
1930s would supply the Magyar national team to the same
extent as the better-known Budapest teams.

In 1922 the first modern stadium of Újpest[40] had
been built on Megyeri ütca, and in those years Újpest
had started to occupy the top positions in the league. The
club had become famous for the '*Fogl-gát*', the 'Fogl dam',
composed of the brothers Károly and József who at that
time were the only Újpest players regularly summoned to
the national[41] team. As well as interpreting the Danubian

---

38 The main football clubs in Budapest were founded in the following
chronological order: BTC in 1897, Újpest in 1899, Ferencváros in 1900
and MTK in 1901. In 1901 the first Hungarian championship would
also take place, which is why before that date Budapest teams would
never participate in the Challenge Cup.

39 Ütca means street in Hungarian.

40 The stadium was often called Megyeri út.

41 Despite the fact that Hungarian coach Kiss also sporadically called up
striker Albert Ströck and defender László Sternberg, who years later
would also become captain.

style to perfection, Újpest boasted an attacking line with a peculiarity: three of their forwards, Avar, Wetzer and Ströck, were born in the region of Hungary which had come under Romanian control following the defeat of the Austro-Hungarian Empire in 1918. The three of them had the same story: they had started their careers in Romania and had subsequently landed on Hungarian soil. While Avar and Ströck would play for both national teams, Wetzer only played for the Romanian team and took part in the 1930 World Cup.

* * *

The draw had not been kind to Bányai's men, as the *Lilák* team were up against Czechoslovakia's Sparta, winners of the first edition of the event. Újpest would play the first leg of the quarter-final at home on 22 June, but not at their own ground, as the match would be played at Hungária in front of 5,000 spectators.

To the surprise of the onlookers, after five minutes the Hungarians were already ahead by two goals thanks to two penalties: the visiting defenders Perner and Burgr had handled the ball in their own area and on both occasions Szabó had punished them. The match continued, following the same script, but in spite of several corner kicks earned and chances created by the home team, they were foiled in most cases by the Czechoslovakian goalkeeper Hochmann, and the first period ended 2-0.

Avar was the star of the second half, scoring a hat-trick. Wetzer's goal brought the home side's score to six and four minutes before the end Jiran got one back for the Czechoslovaks. The Prague newspapers only applauded Hochmann and they were particularly angry with the midfield, weakened at the end of the first half by an injury to Kolenatý. Hajný had moved to the midfield and, as

61

injured players were wont to do at the time, Kolenatý went to occupy the wing but could not actually run any more. According to some local newspapers, Újpest had put in their best performance of the season and perhaps of their history. Hungarian president Ferenc Langfelder said: 'Sparta had declared that they were not only favourites for this match, but also for the final victory. And let's face it, we had approached the match with some concern. Even our most ardent supporters could never believe the score of 6-1 in our favour. We saw minutes of great football, something totally new in Újpest. We were better in every aspect and I think what Sparta said gave us the right boost.'

On 3 July the return match was played in the Czechoslovak capital in front of 22,000 spectators and under the orders of the Italian referee Barlassina. Sparta, after the result of the first leg, could only hope for a miracle. The match proved balanced in the early stages with both teams going close to scoring. Then, in the 42nd minute, the game came alive when Patek was brought down on the edge of the area and Haftl crossed for Silný, whose header was cleared by the keeper before Madelon scored.

In the 60th minute Silný was injured after a collision near the Hungarian area and was out for about eight minutes. In the meantime, Barlassina dismissed Fogl III for a foul on Haftl. Silný then returned to the pitch but because of the injury he moved to the wing. In the 77th minute Madelon doubled the score in a scrum after Sparta's third corner. Újpest were able to defend well in the final stages and a match well refereed by Barlassina, who seemed impervious to protests and reactions from the crowd, ended 2-0. With the exception of Silný, who had just been injured, and Madelon, who scored both goals, the Prague newspapers criticised the offensive line's lack of bite.

The Hungarian goalkeeper Acht and Újpest's defensive duo were particularly praised.

It had been a tough, nervous match and at the end of the game the Hungarian players had run off to the changing rooms while being chased by home fans intent on kicking and beating them. President Langfelder had also risked his own safety but fortunately he had managed to leave the field through a side door. However, it was the Hungarians who went through to the semi-finals.

* * *

In the semi-final, Újpest faced an equally tough opponent, a rival eager for revenge as in both of the first two editions they had missed out on victory in the final: Rapid Vienna. Just like Újpest, Rapid had secured their qualification in the first leg by giving Genova a footballing lesson. The match ended 5-1 and the return leg 0-0. The Italian newspapers had lavished praise and respect on the Viennese team. They wrote that Austrian football – embodied by Rapid – was superior to that of any other European movement and they praised some players, including Horvath, defined as 'the long-lived phenomenon', Wesely and the Austrian national team members Smistik[42] and Schramseis. They also recalled past champions such as Brandstetter and, above all, Edi Bauer, then coach of the green-and-whites, defined as 'the finest player Austria has ever had'. And although Vienna was famous for the phrase 'Austrian teams show how goals are scored, Hungarian teams … make them!' *La Gazzetta dello Sport* underlined how Rapid had the 'bite of a Latin team'.

---

42 Smistik played as a defensive midfielder, but compared to Káďa and Bukovi he was more of an interdictor and less of a playmaker.

With these credentials, on 21 August the Austrians would face Újpest in the first leg of the semi-final. In reality the match was in danger of being postponed: a few hours before it was due to start it was discovered that the referee was unavailable. Although the Italian federation had made the problem known days earlier through a telegram, no one had opened it. An emergency solution had to be found even though it was against the rules: to assign the match to a local referee, Majorszky.

The match, played in front of 10,000 spectators, was close from the very beginning. Hungarian Köves opened the scoring in the 17th minute with a shot from the edge of the area after receiving a pass from a corner kick. Just two minutes after the start of the second half Kirbes equalised for the Austrians but in the 80th minute Ströck scored the winning goal for the *Lilák*.

The Vienna match was attended by 22,000 spectators, double the number who had supported Újpest four days earlier. From the very first minute, luck seemed to help the Viennese, who immediately took the lead through Wesely: the Austrian left-winger made the most of Horvath's assist without the opponents being able to touch the ball. After Avar's solo strike finished high above the crossbar, the home side doubled their lead through Kirbes, who anticipated the goalkeeper's actions and scored with his head.

In the second half the Hungarians reduced the deficit thanks to a powerful Avar free kick before Horvath scored to make it 3-1. The final goal, scored again by Avar, took the two teams to a play-off.

The match had ended amidst the protests of the Magyars, motivated, according to them, by a penalty not granted, which would have meant their immediate progress to the final. The day after the match Rapid presented a complaint to the committee in which, citing as a reason the absence of a neutral referee in the first leg match, they asked to be assigned a 3-0 victory. Initially the committee said it intended to award a 0-0 result, which would have benefited the Austrians, victorious in the return leg, but in the end, it went back on its decision and left the result unchanged. The play-off was therefore confirmed and Rapid, who at first had threatened to withdraw from the competition, decided to continue.[43]

The decisive match was played exactly one month later on the neutral ground of Prague. In front of 15,000 spectators, regulation time ended with the score at 1-1: Austrian Wesely's shot from distance was answered by Avar's goal, taking advantage of a cross from the wing. The match was decided by Avar once again, as he scored two more goals in extra time before tempers flared. The Austrians, Kirbes and Ceijka, were both sent off by Italian referee Carraro, whose performance was described by *Prager Presse* as one of the best ever seen in Prague. Avar, at the end of the match, talked about a deserved victory and praised the assistance received by his team-mates, in particular by Wilhelm, Spitz and Szabó, providers of the three assists. The Prague public, initially inclined to support Rapid, had been pleasantly surprised by the Hungarians' game and some of the fans started to support Újpest. Acht, the Hungarians' goalkeeper, who had put in a great performance, was carried off by his team-mates and fans, as well as József Fogl and Borsányi. Rapid, due to the young Kaburek's injury, had brought back the veteran Kuthan, who appeared to be out of shape.

A crowd of about 500 supporters continued to cheer on their Hungarian favourites until the team bus had

---

43 In their complaint to the committee, Rapid's management also claimed that Ströck's goal in the first leg had been scored after he had crossed the goal line.

left. Some *Sporthirlap* reporters had even stood on the bus to thank the crowd for their warm encouragement. As soon as Újpest set foot in their hotel, the players received congratulatory telegrams from Ferencváros and Hungária. After defeating the champions of Czechoslovakia and Austria, the *Lilák* had earned their place in the final.

* * *

Újpest thus reached the final against Slavia Prague, a remake of the 1927 quarter-final. The Czechs had met Juventus and First Vienna on their way to the final and had struggled in both cases, but with a warm welcome from the crowd when playing at home, they made it through to the final.[44] The home match against Juventus was played in circumstances that would be unthinkable today: a few hours before the start, a tremendous downpour hit Prague and continued throughout the match. So, when the game started, the two goalkeepers had a hard time and several players found themselves mired in mud.

The first leg between Újpest and Slavia, refereed by Austria's Braun, was played in Budapest in front of 16,000 spectators and was lively from the start: both sides had good chances before the match was suspended for 60 seconds in the 40th minute to commemorate the death of Károly Iszer, president of Hungarian club BTC.[45] The goals started to come in the following minutes: first Spitz scored, thanks to Szabó's cross and the next minute Puč, assisted by Junek, levelled the score.

---

44 A characteristic trend in the first editions of the Mitropa Cup was the importance of home advantage. Between 1927 and 1929, a total of four away victories were recorded, two of which were against Yugoslav sides.

45 Iszer had been among the co-founders in 1897 of the first Hungarian football federation. He had also founded *Sportvilág*, the first Hungarian sports publication.

The deadlock was broken in the second half when the Hungarians scored three goals in the first 25 minutes. Avar converted a disputed free kick from the edge of the area before Ströck, assisted by the unstoppable Avar, made it 3-1. Just a minute later it was 4-1 when Borsányi, having advanced with the ball at his feet, served Ströck, whose cross was headed into the net by Spitz. According to some, Plánička, usually blameless, could have done more.

Slavia came back but to no avail. In the 75th minute the final goal came: Avar outmanoeuvred a few opponents and gave way to Szabó, who put the ball into Plánička's net, who this time was innocent.

At the end of the match Borsányi said he was happy with the advantage he had gained ahead of the Prague match and that the Budapest team had shown that day that Plánička could also be beaten. Plánička, who was criticised in the local press, claimed that the goals were unstoppable as they all came from close range. He added that in his opinion the Czechoslovaks had spent all their energy in the first half of the match and that this had penalised them in the second. Madden, the Bohemians' coach, justified his team's performance by pointing out that Slavia had not played badly, especially in the first half, but that Újpest had the merit of exploiting some situations to their advantage. Tusch, president of the South German Football Federation, said: 'Újpest played real football today, Slavia's academic football is a thing of the past.'

The return leg was played in Prague two weeks later. The outcome of the competition seemed a foregone conclusion to many, although some Slavia fans still seemed to believe in their team's chances, to the extent that some of them, just outside Wilson station, hung a huge green flag reading '6-0!'. Just below the hoped-for result it read that the 5-1 win in the first leg would not be enough for the

Hungarians and that the four-goal deficit was recoverable. Similarly, a local jeweller named Mann promised to give the man who scored a hat-trick a gold Omega watch.

The match, played with thousands of fans crowded on the sidelines,[46] started with Slavia on the attack. In the first minutes only the imprecision of the Czechoslovak forwards and a penalty that the Hungarian Acht parried to Junek in the 20th minute prevented Slavia from breaking through but then, in the 29th minute, Junek himself scored. Ženišek sent back a ball that went towards Joska and Junek and the latter, after controlling, shot weakly but because of the clumsy intervention of Acht the ball went in. The stadium came alive and shortly afterwards, in the 38th minute, they were on the verge of cheering again: Joska had run towards Acht's goal but slipped badly when he finished.

In the 57th minute there was a second penalty and this time Acht could not stop Kratochvíl's shot. The crowd, seeing the comeback coming closer, started to get excited. But it was Újpest who grew in intensity: Plánička foiled one goal attempt with a terrific dive but then, within two minutes, the Hungarians equalised through Szabó and Ávár, both coldly beating Plánička from close range. The 2-2 final score meant that the cup would remain in Hungary, moving from the capital's ninth district – Ferencváros – to the fourth – Újpest.

The *Prager Presse*, who critiscised of Slavia's forwards, especially Junek, for wasting several chances, praised Újpest, writing: 'Hats off to the Hungarians!' The *Lilák* were surrounded by their own supporters who hoisted them on to their shoulders and carried them in triumph before they could reach the changing rooms.

---

46 The Czechoslovak newspapers pointed out that the capacity of the stadium was inadequate to host such an event.

Coach Bányai was delighted with his team's performance and the fact that Hungary had retained the cup. Langfelder would echo him: 'Despite the two penalties against us, I am not dissatisfied. The fact that we beat teams like Sparta, Rapid and now Slavia means that we deserve the Középeurópa Kupa, or Central European Cup, as they call it abroad.'

That same evening the awards ceremony took place. Mór Fischer, the president of the committee that year, presented a consolation cup to Slavia and then gold medals and the cup to the Újpest players and their president. Goalkeeper Acht received a letter that made him jump with joy as much as the gold medal. The letter read:

'Dear Jancsi,[47] I am overjoyed to learn of your great success which is a success for the entire Hungarian sports movement and its federation. I hope that this is but the first triumph of your career between the posts. Keep it up! A warm greeting, Károly Zsák.'

Zsák[48] had been an icon of Magyar football, a goalkeeper who not only set the standard for his style between the posts but was also known for his ability to shoot penalties – he scored around 40 in his career – and Acht, after thanking his older colleague, decided to frame that letter and keep it in his room.

It was a special achievement by Újpest, perhaps unique: their first European triumph had preceded their first national title, but that accolade would not be long in coming anyway.

---

47 Jancsi is the nickname for János, the name of the Újpest goalkeeper.

48 Zsák had long remained in the ranks of the Hungarian national team. However, due to the fact that he did not play in one of the capital's top teams, he was not very prominent and was called up as a reserve at both the 1912 and 1924 Olympic Games. Around the early 1920s he continued to play despite an amputated finger until, in 1927, the doctor who operated on him ordered him to stop.

1930 – THE RAPIDGEIST

Hugo Meisl had finally recovered and had returned to his duties. He had received a telegram from Budapest from the Hungarian federation which read:

'Thank you very much for your valuable and invaluable service in dealing with the matter between our federation and the Czechoslovak federation in the interests of peace. We were sure that your valuable and esteemed person and your intervention would have routed the matter towards a peaceful solution. Now that the case has been resolved, on behalf of the entire Hungarian sports movement we express our gratitude. We will never forget your kind help.'[49]

1930 was a special year as the first World Cup was to be played, and one of the issues on the table for Meisl[50] and colleagues had to do with the World Cup: if none of the participating federations went to Uruguay then the fourth edition of Mitropa could be held as usual. Meisl also argued that the federations should commit

---

49 The reference is to the previous year's return match between Újpest and Sparta and the problems caused by the Prague crowd.

50 Meisl in the meantime had recovered and had also returned to full-time involvement with Mitropa.

themselves to promoting the participation of
their best teams, and in the end they all agreed.
Hungary, Italy and Czechoslovakia nominated
the winner of the championship and the runner-
up, while Austria nominated the winner of the
championship and the winner of the Vienna
Cup.[51] Once all the federations had refused
FIFA's invitation to take part in the World Cup,
the fourth edition of the Mitropa Cup was made
official. It would be one of the longest with the
quarter-finals held in June and the two-legged
final in November, due to the need for several
play-offs and the escalation of problems such as
protests, boycott threats and postponements.

* * *

RAPID VIENNA were the most successful team in the
Austrian capital in the early post-war years. In all of the
early editions of the Mitropa Cup, they had established
themselves as one of Europe's leading clubs, a reputation
that was recognised both at home and abroad. In the
then young history of European competitions, the only
thing missing was the final piece of the puzzle: winning
the Mitropa Cup. After two lost finals and a semi-final
that went up in smoke amidst the controversy, the green-
and-whites appeared on the European scene once again
in 1930 as favourites. The club, which had sprouted on
the outskirts of Vienna and was popular with the working
and proletarian classes, managed to combine the refined
and elegant style of play typical of Danube clubs with
an uncommon fighting spirit better known in Vienna as

---

51 From 1935 onwards, the competition would be renamed the Austrian
  Cup.

Rapidgeist. This concept was well described in an article in the *Illustriertes Sportblatt* in 1927:

'Rapid's players never let their supporters down, because they don't give up until the final whistle. Rapid's roots are the local population, and those roots have never been disowned. The Green and Whites are a proletarian formation in the best sense of the word.'

The rivalry that Rapid fans felt most strongly about was that with Austria Vienna. It was a derby that not only had sporting, but also social and identity connotations. The club's successes in the years after World War I were largely linked to the figure of Josef 'Pepi' Uridil, nicknamed *'Der Tank'* ('the Tank'), a boy who more than anyone else embodied the Rapid player archetype: he was born in the suburbs of Ottakring and like several other players and club officials was of Bohemian origin.[52] He exploded into football at the end of the First World War as soon as the championships resumed. Rapid's then centre-forward, Richard 'Rigo' Kuthan, was considered by many to be missing. He had fought in Romania, on the Piave, on the Isonzo and then ended up in Verdun. From that point onwards his trail had been lost until he reappeared 28 days later at a green-and-whites' training session in a physically impaired condition. Uridil would replace him more than worthily and only a few months later, when Kuthan had recovered, the two formed an irresistible attacking pair.

Uridil's fame reached an unprecedented level that went far beyond the Hütteldorfer, the neighbourhood where Rapid are still based, so much so that two well-known

---

52 The Bohemian presence in Rapid's ranks was also widespread at technical and managerial level. Inside the Rapideum, Rapid's museum, a panel underlines the multi-ethnic nature of the club: while in the inter-war years the line-up included several members of Bohemian and Moravian origin, in more recent years several Austrian players of Turkish origin have played for the club.

Viennese songwriters of the time, Robert Katscher and Hermann Leopoldi, wrote the song 'Heute spielt der Uridil!' ('Today Uridil is playing!') which soon became a stadium chorus sung by Rapid fans Sunday after Sunday and a song known throughout the capital.[53] Because of his origins and the humility he preserved in spite of his fame – which, as he will tell in an interview, with the passing of the years had started to weigh on him – many Rapid fans considered him one of them. Those who had seen him play asserted that the 'Tank' was almost unstoppable when he advanced with the ball, culminating most of the time with the striker, the ball and one or two opponents inside the opposition's net. The decline of this iconic striker of Bohemian origin coincided with a temporary collapse of Rapid, whose best result between 1924 and 1928 was a fifth place. From 1928 onwards, with the help of a revamped team, Rapid were once again triumphant at local level and were now aiming to fulfil the dream of their figurehead, Dyonis Schönecker, of becoming the continent's strongest team.

* * *

Fate had once again put the Austrians in front of Genova. Unlike the previous year, however, Genova's participation in the competition was not by chance: De Vecchi's men (he had hung up his boots and become coach of the Ligurian club) had fought to the last for the title with Ambrosiana, earning second place in the standings and consequent access to the Mitropa Cup. The first leg would be played in Genova under the orders of referee Stefanovsky, who had taken charge of Genova–Rapid the previous year. The favourites, for obvious reasons, were

---

53 As noted, it was 'Heute spielt der Uridil!' that inspired the song that Karel Balling had dedicated to Káďa.

Rapid, who took to the field with eight members of the Austrian national team.

The match opened with the home team to the fore: Levratto splendidly met a cross by Banchero but the ball finished high. A few minutes later Rapid responded and from a corner a weak shot by Weselik hit the post. The game went from end to end: the Italians almost scored on a couple of occasions but in both cases Bugala, the Austrian goalkeeper, said no to the red-blue forwards and after a prodigious intervention he received Levratto's handshake. A convulsive and chaotic phase followed, full of hard tackles and fouls: Levratto and Banchero were in turn pushed to the floor by their adversaries. Schramseis, in particular, didn't seem to want to pay compliments to the Italian forwards. In spite of the continuous attacks of the two teams – the last chance came from the Austrian Kaburek, whose shot was parried by Bacigalupo – the first period ended in a draw.

The second half started with a bang: in the fourth minute Banchero, the 'Mud Man',[54] after having beaten his marker, shot a bolt from close range that hit the inside of the crossbar of the Austrian goal and went in. It was 1-0! Genova threw themselves into the search for the second goal, but Rapid found the equaliser: the specialist Wesely took a free kick, which Bacigalupo saved with his fist between the feet of Luef who, from a few steps, scored.

The closing stages of the match were full of excitement. First Levratto almost scored after having taken the ball out of Bugala's hands, then Rapid went close to the goal

---

54 Elvio Banchero owed his nickname to his time at Alessandria. They played on a very poorly maintained ground and for this reason it was nicknamed the Mud Factory and Banchero, being the main goalscorer, became known as the Mud Man.

on three occasions: Bacigalupo made two sensational saves and Wesely hit a post, for the second time in the match.

So, the game ended in a draw and everything would be decided in Vienna. The large crowd at the stadium was disappointed by a performance that was not up to expectations. Genova seemed to be afraid and Rapid seemed to be content. The newspapers, however, gave the home team the merit of having stood up to the Austrians. They highlighted the positive performances of Levratto, who thanks to his sharp dribbling was often able to elude the marking of the Viennese defender Schramseis, and Casanova, defined a 'very fine distributor and excellent tactician'.

In the pre-match exchanges between the managers of the two teams, a tug of war arose: Rapid had asked for the postponement of the return match because they were engaged in a tour of Scandinavia[55] but Genova had not accepted, using the fact that they had to cancel some equally remunerative friendly matches in Barcelona to keep their Mitropa Cup commitments. The final decision was then placed in the hands of the committee itself, whether to accept the request of Rapid or automatically assign the qualification to Genova.[56] At the end a solution was found: the match in Vienna would be played on 3 September.

Genova faced the return match with a change of coach: De Vecchi had been replaced by Etienne Szekany-

---

55 The Viennese team would take the train at 6.25am the day after the first leg.

56 In a marginal paragraph, *La Gazzetta dello Sport* dedicated a few lines to the results of the opening day of the World Cup, which had begun the previous day in Uruguay.

Cicagne[57] who increased the number of Hungarian coaches in charge of Italian teams. Szekany, who was present at the Marassi on the day of the first leg of the match, had had an uninspiring career as a player. He wore glasses due to an eyesight problem and as a result a few years later, when he applied to become a referee, the refereeing panel rejected his application.

The precedent of the first leg – as well as predictions on the eve of the match – was not in favour of the Italians, but they hoped Rapid might be exhausted due to the 17 matches that they had played in 40 days between Scandinavia and Holland.

The match, officiated by the Swiss referee Ruoff, started with a sudden *coup de théâtre*: Levratto scored with a shot in the first minute, surprising the opposition goalkeeper, who had not yet positioned himself in front of the goal. From that moment on, however, the Austrian siege began: first Kirbes equalised from Wesely's assist and then Luef, with Genova momentarily down to ten because of Burlando's injury, turned the scoreline upside down. Rapid's pressure continued and towards the end of the first half, following a clash between Bacigalupo and Weselik, the Genoese goalkeeper was forced to leave the field. He returned with his face bandaged and his vision reduced. Luckily Barbieri, who had stood in as the last defender, remained between the posts for just a few minutes.

In the second half, the Viennese completed their domination: they scored four more times through Kaburek, a double from Wesely and one from Weselik. Wesely,

---

57 Born with the Hungarian name of Géza, Szekany acquired the name Etienne after working as a physical education instructor for various institutions in Belgium, where he also coached the Union Saint Gilloise team for years, winning a league title at the end of the 1922/23 season.

33-year-old veteran of the green-and-white team,[58] turned out to be the best player on the field, thanks to the goals and the assists he provided for his team-mates. Bacigalupo also deserved a mention, without whom the loss could have been even greater. The Italian team had some justification for the defeat: in addition to Bacigalupo's injury, they had played with some injured players and others out of position, probably because of the tactical instructions given by the new coach. In the end, Rapid, once again, had demonstrated a clear superiority.

* * *

The quarter-finals, with the exception of the return match between Rapid and Genova, had been fairly even. The main surprise was Ambrosiana's success over Újpest, who were not only reigning champions but had just returned from Geneva with another title in tow, the Coupe de Nations. In the final they had beaten Slavia 3-0 thanks to a hat-trick from striker Köves. Above all, the Hungarians' numbers were impressive: the line-up was not only known for Fogl's dam – on the contrary, Fogl II and Fogl III hardly appeared in the starting eleven – but especially for its forward line: in Geneva the Hungarian forwards had scored 16 times and the full-backs had only scored once.

Surprisingly, however, an unexpected obstacle stood in the way of the Magyar team: the sensational exploits of the young Ambrosiana ace Giuseppe Meazza, nicknamed *'Peppin'* or *'Balilla'* in Milan. Meazza, who a little over two months earlier had enchanted Budapest with a splendid hat-trick in a Hungary–Italy match that ended 0-5 and was part of the International Cup, amazed the Italian and

---

58 Wesely was considered by foreign newspapers to be Rapid's most well-known player, as evidenced by the fact that Rapid was often referred to as 'Wesely and Co'.

Hungarian crowds in the four matches which made up the quarter-final tie.[59] Indeed, the battle between Árpád Weisz's men and Újpest only ended in the 90th minute of the second play-off and Meazza scored in all four matches. Three times he showed off his calling card, the 'goal on invitation'. It was a solo effort that began with a serpentine movement, followed by a slight braking aimed at making the goalkeeper move – the invitation, in fact – to sit him down before *Peppin* could freely put the ball in the net or enter the goal with it. On all these occasions, including the match between Italy and Hungary, the goalkeeper was Acht who, as Meazza himself would remember years later, 'Shortly after that umpteenth defeat retired to private life, perhaps demoralised by the many goals conceded to me or more likely for his own reasons.'[60]

In the semi-final, however, the music was different. In the first match, the 20-year-old Italian talent endured close marking by Káďa[61] and in the return match the Italian team lost 6-1.

In the first match, among other things, one of the problems already seen in previous years, namely the violent clashes between fans, reappeared. For this reason, Mussolini initially said he was against allowing Ambrosiana to take part in the return match, but later withdrew his decision.

* * *

In the semi-final Rapid met Ferencváros who had eliminated Slavia in the quarter-finals, first drawing in

---

59 In the first leg in Budapest, after the opening goal of the home team, the Hungarian fans, eager for a rerun of the cup match, repeatedly chanted '5-0! 5-0!'

60 I thank Federico Jaselli Meazza for the information.

61 The *Gazzetta* would once again praise Káďa's performance, calling him an 'institution of continental football' and 'the athlete who knows no sunset'.

Prague and then, in their home match in front of the Ambrosiana players present at the stadium that day, winning 1-0 thanks to a penalty at the end of a not very exciting contest. The expectations were for a balanced match, a challenge between two teams that respected and feared each other.

The teams took the field in front of about 17,000 spectators and after a few minutes the Austrian forward Kaburek, following a run by Wesely, scored with an accurate shot. The same Kaburek doubled the lead in the 14th minute after a move orchestrated by Skoumal, Wesely and Kirbes. Then, in the 30th minute, after having tricked an opponent, Wesely brought the score to 3-0.

In the second half the game changed completely and Fradi became dominant, but despite this, Kirbes scored again in the 66th minute, after the ball hit the crossbar. Three minutes later Kohut scored the first goal for the Hungarians at the end of a fine solo run. The Hungarians threw themselves into the search for a second goal but in the 80th minute Rapid scored again, through Wesely. The match ended 5-1.

The whole Austrian team, especially the midfielder Rappan,[62] were praised while the Hungarian newspapers, disappointed, said they regretted some wasted opportunities in the second half that could have made the defeat less bitter. At the end of the match the home players received compliments from Hugo Meisl, who declared: 'What a game! Well done! Well done! I like this kind of match. But I'm sorry for Ferencváros, 11 gentlemen who despite the result continued to play sportingly until the last minute and who, although only at times, showed they didn't deserve

---

62 Karl Rappan is a figure who will reappear throughout this book. Although history remembrs him mainly as a coach, at the time he was one of Austria's most respected midfielders.

such a severe punishment. I also applaud the Hungarian public that despite the result of 5-1 cheered their players until the end.'

At the Üllői út, exactly one week later, the return match was played, for many a pleonastic event given the result of the first leg, so the attendance at the stadium was only around 10,000. However, Ferencváros started with great determination and were rewarded in the 23rd minute with a goal by Takács II from Lyka's assist, before Bugala – named by many as the best player on the field along with defender Schramseis – saved the Austrian goal several times. The Hungarians' pressure continued for about an hour, after which Rapid's quality emerged. The result remained locked at 1-0. The prevailing feeling among the Ferencváros fans was that the qualification had been trashed in the first leg, in which the team had not performed at their best. Budapest, who had held the cup for the last two years thanks to victories over Ferencváros and Újpest, saw all their teams leave the tournament.

* * *

In the final Rapid met Sparta Prague and thus had the opportunity to avenge the final lost in 1927. Sparta, however, were once again in good shape: in the quarters they had beaten First Vienna twice and in the semi-finals they had eliminated Ambrosiana by virtue of the match in Prague, which ended 6-1.

In the Czechoslovakian dugout, in the meantime, John Dick had returned, the Scottish coach and icon of Prague football who years earlier had created the legend of *Sparta d'Acciaio*. Johnny hadn't lost the winning habit: during his interlude in Belgium he had won four championships in six seasons and then, aware of the fact that football at the highest level was played along the Danube, he had decided to return to Prague.

And that wasn't all: just a few days before the start of the competition Sparta had signed Raymond Braine. The first Belgian footballer to get a professional contract, Braine had decided to leave his home city, Antwerp, when a scandal came to light. The Belgian federation did not allow footballers who owned a business to receive game from their club. They could be paid as long as they played in the reserve team but Braine, the owner of Café Matador on the Brederodestraat, also received a second income from his managers. The issue became public knowledge and the federation decided to exclude the player from the national team for years. So, Braine, undisputed star of Belgian football, skipped the World Cup in Uruguay and decided to move abroad. He was on the verge of signing for the English team Clapton Orient[63] but the transfer fell through at the last minute due to bureaucratic issues. So, the player repaired to Prague. Here there were no contractual problems: Czechoslovakian football had been professional for six years and Braine signed a one-and-a-half-year contract that included the payment to the player of 25,000 crowns for the transfer, a monthly salary of 1,500, a residence bonus of 100 and other incentives such as 1,000 crowns for each title won. Braine had proved his worth right from his debut by providing an assist for Silný's quarter-final goal and scoring the second from 25 metres. He

---

63 Clapton Orient were at the time a club in the Third Division South, one of the two leagues in the English Third Division. Although Braine was in fact one of the best footballers in continental Europe, there was a prevailing view in England that British football was still far superior, and First and Second Division clubs were hardly interested in foreign players. One of the few exceptions to this is Rudi Hiden: the Austrian goalkeeper was very close to moving to Arsenal in 1932.

repeated his performance in the return semi-final against Ambrosiana, scoring a double.

The first leg of the final was played in Prague in front of 26,000 spectators, fewer than had seen the match against Ambrosiana. The Danish whistle-blower Hansen, who had also refereed the first semi-final between Rapid and Ferencváros, was in charge of the match. The game was immediately heated: a cross from Káďa was not reached by Patek and shortly afterwards a shot from Viennese winger Wesely was parried by Czechoslovakian Bêlík. In the eighth minute the Czechoslovak striker Junek missed a penalty kick and a minute later, from an excellent corner by Wesely, Luef put Rapid ahead. The Austrians continued to attack and the Sparta team looked nervous for a few minutes. Then, in the 13th minute, the Czechoslovaks went close to the equaliser: first Bugala parried Patek's shot and then, from a corner, Hejma shot but, with the goalkeeper beaten, the Austrian Vana cleared the area with a header. Sparta's dominance continued with two clear opportunities for Braine, who first from a favourable position was denied by Bugala and then, wide open after a rebound off the Austrian goalkeeper, could not capitalise because of the intervention of the Austrian defender Czejka. Sparta ended the first half on the attack but to no avail: the score was 0-1.

The second half began exactly as the first had ended, with Sparta on the attack: Košťálek hit the crossbar from a corner but then, after Srbek was injured and moved to the flank, Rapid took control. In the 53rd minute, however, Austrian Czejka intercepted a ball with his hand and Hansen awarded a penalty. But as Braine was preparing to place the ball on the penalty spot, Káďa signalled to Hojer to take over. The mistake was telling: Hojer missed and Rapid preserved their lead.

In the 57th minute, Luef beat Madelon and Burgr and shot from a great distance to surprise Bêlík, making it 0-2. Sparta threw themselves forward desperately, Patek hit the crossbar and Schramseis, Rapid's defender, saved a dangerous situation. The match ended amidst Sparta's futile attacks and with both teams on their heels. The clear feeling on both sides was that the Austrians had guaranteed their victory. The performance of the referee Hansen was praised as well as the sportsmanship of the Prague public, also acknowledged by Rapid's management. Johnny Dick was criticised, guilty of having changed the formation that had done so well against Ambrosiana. The *Prager Presse* wrote: 'As the English say, you can't change a winning team.'

On the day of the return match, the Hohe Warte[64] amphitheatre was packed to the rafters with 40,000 people supporting the home side. The two teams took the field once again under Hansen's orders. Sparta, amidst strong gusts of wind, attacked immediately, creating two clear opportunities that they didn't take advantage of and then, on the first initiative worthy of note from the Austrians, capitulated to Kaburek's goal from Luef's assist. The advantage of the Austrians was short-lived: three minutes later Košťálek equalised after Podrazil's cross and at the end of the first half Košťálek, after a goal by his team-mate Hejma, shocked the Viennese public. Sparta took the lead and the outcome of the tournament was put into question.

The second half began in the same vein as the first: the Czechoslovak goalkeeper remained more or less redundant and Sparta, led by Káďa and their dangerous forwards, continued to attack. Then Rapid had a burst of pride: they

---

64 The reports often refer to the Hohe Warte as an amphitheatre and not as a stadium: this is because it is uncovered and stands on a hill, but has the capacity of a real stadium.

came close to equalising with Weselik and Wesely before Smistik scored to make it 2-2. Pure oxygen for the local public. Victory seemed a done deal, but it was Košťálek again who scored: Braine shot, the Austrian defender Schramseis blocked and the Czechoslovakian striker was quick to deposit the ball into the net.

There was no more time and Rapid were finally able to lift the cup after three attempts, thus realising Schönecker's dream. Árpád Kenyeres, the secretary of the Hungarian federation, said at the end of the match that despite the victory, and the three goals scored, Sparta could have won the Mitropa for the second time in their history if they had taken their scoring chances.

1931 – THE YEAR OF
THE FIRST TIMES

The committee meeting, which had been planned for mid-May, was brought forward to 27 April. The reason was that in May, the FIFA congress would be held and some representatives of the Central European federations could not be absent. The Mitropa Cup pairings were established with an unusual formula: the top two Italian teams would meet the top two Czechs and the top two Austrians would face the top two Hungarians. All the representatives expressed their satisfaction except for those from Czechoslovakia, whose request for a rethink was refused since the rules of the committee were clear: it was possible to go back on a decision already made only if the participants agreed unanimously. In reality, Hungary were at a disadvantage, but for completely different reasons: their main teams, winners of two previous editions, Ferencváros and Újpest, had already left for South America that summer. In their place, Hungária and newcomer, Bocskai would play.

* * *

THE FIRST two teams from the Austrian capital, First Vienna and Vienna Cricket and Football Club, were founded more or less simultaneously, as both submitted their articles of association on the same day, 22 August 1894, making it a key date in the history of European football. Both wanted to include the word 'First' in their names. The former club was made up of the gardeners of Baron Rothschild, who had for some time been competing in football matches at the Kuglerwiese, the field that the Baron had set up so that his employees would not spoil the lawns of his mansion; while the latter were the members of the Vienna Cricket Club, English emigrants who had decided to incorporate football into their disciplines. The dispute about the right to the word 'First' was won by the gardeners, who took the name 1894 First Vienna. On the same day they designed the logo[65] and chose their team colours, blue and yellow, the same as the Rothschilds. Both the logo and the colours have remained unchanged to this day.

That day marked the beginning of a fierce rivalry between two clubs who, as well as battling in the courts to get their names recognised, would battle it out on the pitch with two distinct identities. While Vienna Cricket and Football Club had an all-English eleven in its early years, the more inclusive First Vienna featured a hybrid line-up of both British and Austrian players. The trend would change within a few years, however, and Vienna Cricket and Football Club would also start to involve local players.[66]

The yellow-and-blues, who in those early years established themselves as one of the most successful teams of the Austrian capital, being champions of Austria and winners of two national cups, did not continue to boast a

---

65 The logo was designed by William Beale, one of the club's first players.
66 One of the first was Hugo Meisl, although his career as a footballer was short-lived.

role of honour as rich as that of some of their rivals: they added just two Challenge Cups won in 1899 and 1900, to their trophy cabinet. But the triumphs of the late 1920s definitely raised Hugo Meisl's regard for the 'Döblingers',[67] and from 1929 onwards the Austrian coach had started to call up First Vienna players more regularly to the national team's ranks.

This was the case with Chrenka, Kurz and the forwards Seidl and Gschweidl. The latter, nicknamed *'Der lange Fritz'* ('The Tall Fritz') had played a leading role in the club's recent successes: in 1929, when Döbling's club had lifted the Vienna Cup for the first time, Gschweidl had scored the winning goal in the final against Rapid, which ended 3-2, and the following year he repeated this by scoring the only goal in the final between First Vienna and Austria Vienna. Gschweidl, who in those years was competing for a place in the national team with the more famous Matthias Sindelar, finally managed to coexist with the Austria Vienna star thanks to Meisl's intuition: the coach decided to deploy Sindelar as a centre-forward and Gschweidl as a right-half-back. The combination paid off, also because 'The Tall Fritz', as *La Stampa* once recalled, was a 'fine technician' who also had the ability to serve the team and send his team-mates in on goal. What's more, thanks to his size, he was very difficult to mark in the penalty area. He arrived at First Vienna at the age of 24 and immediately carved out a leading role for himself in one of his city's historic clubs. It was largely thanks to him that the *Döblinger* team got a ticket to Europe.

* * *

---

67 'Döblinger' is the nickname of the First Vienna players. It comes from Döbling, the district of the Austrian capital where the club originated.

First Vienna, making their second appearance on the Mitropa Cup stage, found themselves facing freshmen Bocskai, the first Hungarian side not from Budapest to take part in the event. Bocskai – now defunct – were the team from the city of Debrecen, a few kilometres from the Romanian border.

The first leg was played on 27 June in Vienna under Czechoslovakian referee Krist. Bocskai, for many an expected sacrificial victim, were also unlucky: they lost their star player Jenő Vincze during the warm-up and had to revise their plans. The match was hard-fought in the first half: even though Gschweidl's initial goal seemed to have paved the way to a comfortable victory for the Austrians, shortly afterwards the Hungarian Teleki[68] surprised everybody by overcoming two defenders and sitting down the opposition goalkeeper but then, from two steps out, he incredibly shot wide. In the 40th minute, 'The Tall Fritz' scored again. The home crowd rejoiced but then, for some unknown reason, some troublemakers invaded the pitch, preventing the visitors from going back to the dressing room for a few minutes. Bocskai were not only unable to collect their thoughts, but also had no opportunity to quench their thirst, as the home team had not provided their rivals with bottles of water.

In the second half, the Viennese, after a badly wasted chance by their opponents, rounded off the result thanks to Hoffmann. The margin of advantage ahead of the return match was considerable. Meisl, who was present at the stadium, spoke of a poorly played match from both sides and praised the Hungarian striker Teleki, despite the missed goal.

---

68 Pál Teleki, the namesake of a former Hungarian prime minister, would later be called up for the 1934 World Cup.

The hours leading up to the return match in Debrecen involved a misunderstanding: both teams wanted to wear their standard yellow-and-blue kits and First Vienna had not brought a second strip with them. So, it was Debrecen who had to give up: they decided to wear the white-and-green kit of the city's railway station employees.

It was the first Mitropa Cup match a Hungarian team had played outside the capital and the din was deafening. The local fans kept chanting 'Huj huj hairá!', a generic chorus that Hungarian teams used to address their idols. It would be banned after World War II when Hungary came under Soviet influence; officially because the word 'huj' was used in the Soviet Union to refer to a male member. The issue, apparently of little importance, had begun to worry the Soviet authorities since the two national teams often played each other. In order to discourage the use of the chant, the secret police were called to patrol the stadiums, hunting down violators. A change was imposed: from 'Huj huj hairá!' to 'Rá rá hairá!', a version that was less controversial.

The match began in a general uproar and under torrential rain. In the 20th minute, Austrian Tögel's goal effectively sealed qualification. Then, towards the end of the first half, the talented Teleki, served by Mátéffy, overcame a defender, shot cleanly but found the Austrian defender Blum on the goal line to foil the threat. According to the Hungarians, the ball had gone in, as proved by the fact that the Hungarian Ormos[69] stopped instead of comfortably scoring from Blum's rebound. The second half was much less of a story and First Vienna beat Debrecen 4-0.

---

69 Ormos, also known as Opata, was a coach/player at Bocskai.

* * *

In the semi-finals, the Viennese met another newcomer to the competition, Roma, who had finished second at the end of the 1930/31 season in Italy, ahead of the more famous Ambrosiana, Bologna and Genova. One of Roma's outstanding players was striker Rodolfo Volk, nicknamed '*Sciabbolone*', who was the league's top scorer with 29 goals. They were an interesting team: they were coached by Englishman Herbert Burgess, who years earlier had replaced Jimmy Hogan at the helm of MTK, and they also included Fulvio 'Fuffo' Bernardini, an excellent all-rounder who was mainly employed as a centre-forward, and the two native-born players Chini Ludueña and Lombardo.[70] Roma, who had got the better of Slavia, had been the main surprise of the quarter-finals. '*Sciabbolone*' Volk made a decisive contribution once again: first he scored in the 1-1 draw in Prague and then he repeated the feat in the match in Rome which Roma won 2-1.

The first leg of the semi-final between Roma and First Vienna was played in the Italian capital, at Campo Testaccio, in front of a huge crowd. The home team gained a very early lead when, after less than three minutes, Chini Ludueña received a long ball from Lombardo and hit a low shot past the Austrian keeper. The Viennese didn't lose heart and, thanks to Roma's reluctant attitude, began to dominate the game, developing play down the wings. The main disappointment was the performance of 'Fuffo' Bernardini, who was far below his usual standard.

First Vienna took control of the midfield and the home side's defence fell apart. The visitors displayed one

---

70 The phenomenon of '*oriundi*' spread during the years between the two wars. Although the Viareggio Charter prevented the registration of foreign players, it allowed clubs to acquire foreign-born players of Italian origin. Many of these came from South America.

of the qualities that Italian newspapers had recognised in the days leading up to the match, namely their excellent technical play. The Austrian team as a whole made a very good impression: the two defenders, Blum and Rainer, the midfield, led by Hoffmann, and the forwards. Between the 34th and the 36th minutes, they exerted their superiority with goals from Marat and Blum. Marat scored after Adelbrecht's shot was deflected by D'Aquino and Blum scored after a free kick caused by Bernardini's foul on Gschweidl. The 2-1 scoreline at the end of the first half didn't reflect how much Vienna[71] had dominated after Roma took the lead.

In the sixth minute of the second half, Gschweidl was on hand to meet Brosenbauer's cross from the right and make it 3-1. It was then that Roma gained a foothold on the game and began to attack. A few minutes later the home side's pressure bore fruit: Costantino Lombardo's free kick was headed home by Fasanelli, to narrow the gap. Vienna retreated defensively and Roma began to collect corner kicks, but they didn't turn into goals. Horeschovsky, the Viennese goalkeeper, turned away shots from Bernardini and Lombardo before Masetti denied Gschweidl on a Viennese break.

Vienna took the train that same night aware of having shown a little superiority. At the end of the match, Frithum, the Austrian coach, talking to the Italian journalists, said he was satisfied and declared that he would not change his formation for the return match. Two days before the decisive clash, *La Stampa* featured an article about First Vienna entitled *Il Miglior Undici Austriaco* (The Best Austrian Eleven) and wrote of Gschweidl that the striker was capable of 'playing the part of the virtuoso perfectly

---

71 In Austria, First Vienna are commonly called Vienna.

but also of merging with his team if the collective action demanded it'.

The Vienna match was played despite bad weather. At first the committee had considered postponing the game due to the incessant rain. However, there was a logistical problem: two days later Roma were due to play a league match in Trieste and would be travelling to the city by train directly from Vienna. Vienna agreed not to postpone the match and Roma, as a gesture of thanks, decided to forfeit the money they were owed. To tell the truth, the gate receipts were rather meagre, given that there would only have been around 1,000 spectators due to the weather conditions.

The game began with Roma at the mercy of their opponents. The first chance for the Austrians came in the first minute and was averted by a good save from Masetti before a scuffle broke out between D'Aquino, Brosenbauer and Marat, forcing the referee to send off the first two. The goal for the home side came in the ninth minute thanks to Marat, who scored from a few steps after Gschweidl's assist. Vienna then had another chance from a free kick before tempers frayed again: Adelbrecht bickered with the referee in the 12th minute and the crowd stood up for their player. Roma finally stepped up to the plate and created a chance in the 25th minute but shortly afterwards, on the counter-attack, Bernardini fouled an opposing attacker in the box and Blum made it 2-0. A few minutes later the score was 3-0, thanks to a second for Marat.

The second half began with the pitch, if possible, in even worse condition than the first. The rain had continued to fall and the pitch had become a quagmire. The ball no longer bounced and the Austrians, who were more at ease than the Romans in those weather conditions, dominated the first quarter of the second half. Then it was Roma, spurred on by Volk, who repeatedly came forward. He created two chances that were foiled by the Austrian defence and then, with the third, Volk managed to score from a precise pass by Bernardini. The ball was back in the Austrians' hands with Marat, who came close to scoring his hat-trick: Masetti managed to intercept his shot but fell back and was slightly injured, which is why the match was suspended for a minute. The game continued but the final phase had only one protagonist, the rain, because of which Fasanelli was forced to leave the field momentarily. The pitch had given its verdict: First Vienna deservedly qualified for the final and Roma, despite the double defeat, could return to Italy with their heads held high. Roma had beaten Slavia in their European debut match and at times had been on equal terms against one of the best teams in Austria.

* * *

The 1931 final was the first time that two teams from the same country had faced each other in the competition. In order to be European champions, First Vienna had to beat Wiener AC, another team from the Austrian capital, better known as WAC, who had qualified for the Mitropa as winners of the Vienna Cup. They were the only side to win the Tagblatt Cup, the forerunner of Austria's first league between 1900 and 1903, they had lifted the Challenge Cup on three occasions – the only team to win it three times – and in 1909 they became the first Austrian outfit to beat an English side, when Sunderland came to Vienna on tour. It was the advent of professionalism that threw WAC into the abyss: as early as 1921, at a time when the first football market movements among the Central European teams were taking place, the WAC directors had declared at a meeting that they wanted to remain faithful to amateur football and were not in the least bit interested in the 'black market football'. In 1924, when the league became professional, the club had been forced to divest itself of some of its best talent and would not duel for top positions for a few years.

WAC were the third debutants the 'Döblingers' had met on their way and they had had the great merit of eliminating two teams that were superior on paper: in the quarter-finals WAC had got the better of Sparta Prague and in the semi-finals Hungária, by virtue of a 5-1 first-leg win and a return leg characterised by fierce controversy and protests from their opponents.[72] The most outstanding player was undoubtedly goalkeeper Rudolf 'Rudi' Hiden, a pillar of the Austrian *Wunderteam* coached by Hugo Meisl, whom Herbert Chapman wanted at Arsenal. Hiden, who only two years later moved to France and became 'Rodolphe' for everyone, had arrived from Graz amid general scepticism: his debut was marred by a huge mistake which cost his team a goal. It is said that Karl Sesta, a defender and companion of Hiden, a few seconds after the error, exclaimed: 'Only a Styrian can concede a goal like that!'[73] Hiden had climbed the hierarchies of the Austrian national team and was noted, in particular, for his ability to come out of his goal and tackle a striker, establishing himself as one of the most respected goalkeepers in Europe.

Besides the already mentioned Sesta, a tough defender considered one of the best full-backs of the pre-war period, WAC could count on the forward Heinrich Hiltl, who, in

---

72 Hungária, through the president of the Hungarian federation Fodor, had complained about an alleged punch that the forward Barátki had received with the ball far away, a debatable penalty given to the Austrians and a goal that WAC had scored when offside. Hugo Meisl had agreed on the latter episode, claiming that the goal should have been disallowed.

73 Graz, Hiden's home town, is and was the capital of Styria.

the quarter-finals and semi-finals, scored seven goals, and Walter Hanke, probably the first German player in history to obtain a professional contract.[74]

For the 1931 final, an innovation was introduced: one of the two legs would be played abroad. The reason why it was decided to hold a European final on a neutral pitch, as is the case today, was of an economic nature: First Vienna and WAC, despite representing the *crème de la crème* of European football at the time, did not have as large a fan base as Rapid or Austria Vienna. What's more, the Vienna crowd had already seen the two clubs play each other four times during the season, twice in the Winter Cup[75] and twice in the league. In order to attract a wider audience, it was decided to host one of the two finals outside of Austria in the hope of reaching more than just local audiences. The choice, after a ballot between Geneva and Zurich, fell on the latter.

The event began at 1pm with an opening game, the Swiss championship match between Grasshoppers, the home team, and Biel FC. At the end of the challenge – won 4-1 by Grasshoppers – the two finalists made their entrance to the applause of the Swiss public.

The match started under the orders of the Italian referee Mattea with a more aggressive First Vienna, although it was WAC that struck first: the '*Rossoneri*'[76] scored through Hanke, whose left-footed shot was unstoppable for the goalkeeper. The 'Döblingers' insisted on creating problems for the opposition defence, but on several occasions they

---

74 The first, in fact, was Max Seeburg. It should be noted, however, that Seeburg was in fact English, having arrived in London from Leipzig as a child. Hanke was probably the first German player to be bought by a professional club. It has to be taken into account that Germany – West Germany – would only abandon the amateur model in 1963.

75 Provisional name of the Vienna Cup.

76 WAC's kit was black and red, so this was their nickname.

had to deal with Hiden. The Austrian *Wunderteam*'s goalkeeper stopped more than one cross coming from the wings despite the repeated charges of his opponents.

The game opened up and WAC went close to doubling the score with Braun's shot that hit the post. In the 19th minute, the Swiss fans gave a round of applause to the WAC goalkeeper who came out of his goal perfectly to stop the striker. WAC also developed their game on the wings and after a move down the left side, the centre-forward Müller doubled the score. In terms of the balance of play, the 2-0 scoreline seemed tough on First Vienna, who started to attack again, forcing three corner kicks in a few minutes and then, at the end of a splendid move, scored through Tögel. Hiden's protests, signalling an offside call, were ignored by the referee.

The first quarter of the second half was well balanced: both the teams went on the attack but without creating big problems for their adversaries, thanks to some imprecise play. Then, in the 63rd minute, the ball arrived at Gschweidl's feet, he found Adelbrecht and the forward struck a terrific shot that hit the inside part of the crossbar and slipped into the net, with Hiden motionless.

First Vienna began to attack with more insistence and WAC retreated into defence, ready to act on the counter-attack. Hiden intervened again on a couple of occasions and WAC wasted some precious counter-attacks. Finally, in the 88th minute, from First Vienna's umpteenth corner kick, the turning point of the match arrived: in an attempt to clear the ball, the '*Rossoneri*' (red-and-black) defender Becher kicked it into his own net. WAC's final attacks, well contained by the opposition's defence, were to no avail. The '*Gialloblu*' ('yellow-and-blues') would go into the return match with a one-goal advantage. The decision to hold the first game in Switzerland proved to be a winning one: the total takings amounted to 45,000 francs of which 20,000 went to Grasshoppers and the rest of the money was equally divided between the two finalists.

The return leg was played under the orders of an Italian whistler, this time Barlassina. Just as in the first leg, the match produced a goal in the first few minutes. It was scored by First Vienna's forward Erdl from Adelbrecht's pass. Unexpectedly, WAC struggled to react. This allowed Vienna to control the match and then, in the 43rd minute, to score a second time through Erdl, who took advantage of Braun's mistake.

In the second half, WAC's pride emerged and Hanke reduced the deficit to 2-1 (5-3 on aggregate), but in spite of their numeric superiority – Erdl had to leave the field because of an injury – they couldn't find the goal needed to draw the game, which would still have represented a poor consolation. Lawyer Mauro, who was elected president of the committee that year, awarded the cup to the winners and medals to both teams. In addition to the trophy, from that year on, the winner would receive a further prize: a black marble slab with a relief of the cup adorned with a silver crown bearing the colours of the four participating federations.

It was the year of the first times: the first time that two teams from the same country – and city – faced each other, the first time that a final was played on a neutral ground and the first time that a team won the coveted trophy by winning all the matches they played.

1932 – BOLOGNA, A WALKOVER VICTORY

The conference for the Mitropa Cup was held on 20 and 21 February at the Albergo Savoia in Trieste. It was decided to maintain the same format and the same number of participants per country, despite the fact that the various federations had presented some plans for changes. The Italian federation had proposed the Zanetti Project, endorsed by Czechoslovakia, which provided for the participation of three teams per federation. Hungary, through the Kenyeres Project, had submitted a proposal similar to that of Italy but which also provided for the presence of Swiss teams and Austria was in favour of the inclusion of Swiss teams but not the enlargement to three teams per federation. With a unanimous agreement impossible to find, the format of the previous years was maintained. It was decided, in order to make the competition run more smoothly, to organise the fixture list from the outset and not to accept complaints of any kind. A registration fee of 500 Swiss francs was also set. Finally, a telegram was sent to the president of the FIGC (the Italian Football Federation), Leandro Arpinati, thanking him for his hospitality.

* * *

THE ITALIAN teams, within the European football scene of the time, had not yet reached their apogee. The editions of the cup played up to that moment had illustrated the substantial superiority of Central European football. However, Italian football was unique: contrary to what happened in the former powers of the Austro-Hungarian Empire, where titles and international trophies were the exclusive prerogative of the clubs in the capital cities, Italian football was a decidedly more widespread phenomenon. Between 1929 and 1931, Italy entered teams from as many as four different cities in the competition and 1932 marked the appearance of a fifth city on the Mitropa Cup scene, Bologna, whose team would have a considerable impact in the years to follow, both nationally and internationally.

At the end of the Great War, football in Italy had restarted exactly as it had done along the Danube and within a few years had become the most popular sport in the country. For this reason, in order to be able to contain the increased enthusiasm of the crowds, several Italian clubs had renovated or built from scratch more spacious and equipped stadiums. The Stadio Littoriale, now known as Dall'Ara, was at the time considered a futuristic facility like few others on the continent. Construction work began in 1925 and the inauguration took place on 29 May 1927. In the meantime, on 31 October 1926, when the works were finished, Benito Mussolini had visited the stadium. He made his entrance on horseback and that same afternoon, on his way back, he had survived an attack: the bullet shot by Anteo Zamboni, a boy little more than 15 years old, had grazed him and Zamboni had been executed on the spot.[77] The first to stop

---

77 The episode became a pretext for the regime to tighten its reactionary measures: nine days after the incident, 120 opposition parliaments were removed and shortly afterwards the Special Tribunal was established.

the attacker had been Carlo Alberto Pasolini, lieutenant and father of the more famous Pier Paolo.

Jules Rimet, the father and founder of the World Cup, compared the architecture of the Littoriale, which had a capacity of around 50,000 spectators, to that of a Roman circus. In 1929 a majestic tribute to Mussolini was erected inside the stadium: a neo-Renaissance-style statue of the Duce on horseback, a clear reference to his entrance a few years earlier. Across Italy, only the Mussolini Stadium in Turin was larger.

Bologna had won two national titles, in 1925 and 1929, which is why the Bologna team should have made its debut in the event well before 1932. But as we have seen, Bologna and Torino, the winners of their respective groups in 1929, had already organised tours in South America and Italy had to represent itself at the starting line-up with two replacement teams.

In 1932 Bologna had earned their place in the Mitropa thanks to their second place the previous year at the end of a two-horse race with Juventus, which had seen the two teams leave their rivals far behind. There were a number of red-blue stars: the flag-bearer Angelo Schiavio, nicknamed 'Anzlèn', top scorer of the championship that had just ended, along with the Uruguayan Petrone; the *oriundi* Sansone and Fedullo, often called Sansullo and Fedone because of the frequency with which they exchanged positions; Carlo Reguzzoni, a promising Italian footballer who arrived from Pro Patria; and Eraldo Monzeglio, a national team defender and close contact of the Mussolini family.[78] Lelovics, the coach who arrived that same year, whose original name was

---

78 He was a friend of the Duce's sons, Vittorio and Bruno, and sometime later became Mussolini's tennis instructor.

Lelowichnak,[79] gave continuity to the tradition of Austro-Hungarian coaches, which had begun with Hermann Felsner under whose aegis Bologna had won both of its championships. Lelovics had some experience as coach of Iberian teams – Sporting Lisbon and Las Palmas – and, probably because of his ability to impose himself on foreign stages, he wrote important columns in the Hungarian sports magazines *Nemzeti Sport* and *Sporthirlap*.[80] Moreover, as reported by the Hungarian football historian Béla Nagy in his work *Fradi Futballmúzeum*, in January 1928 Lelovics had taken part with other present and future Hungarian coaches in a course for trainers[81] and then, in 1930, he had been contracted by Bologna after a period as assistant to Felsner himself.

There are two possibilities: either Lelovics was a genius as a coach and had been able in a year and a half to move up the ladder by securing a contract with one of the most important clubs in Italy, or the role of the coach at the time was very different from today. I'm leaning towards the latter hypothesis: Lelovics was neither the first nor the last coach who landed at a major club without first working his way up the ladder. This was because at the time the public's expectations fell mainly on the players and, also, the coaches were selected thanks to the approval of their predecessors.

---

79 I would like to thank Mirko Trasforini, manager of the TIMF Archive blog, for the precious information.

80 Years later, Lelovics, together with Istvan Mike, a Hungarian striker who would play for Bologna in the 1940s and '50s, would discover the future club legend Giacomo Bulgarelli.

81 The course probably had two aspects: it was aimed at aspiring coaches but was also open to experienced coaches, as evidenced by the names of some participants including Istvan Tóth and Imre Schlosser.

The fact of having beaten teams such as Ambrosiana, Genova and Roma in the table meant that the red-blue club could now have their say in the international arena, despite the fact that the draw was anything but easy: on 19 June Bologna would make their debut against Sparta Prague.

* * *

In the days leading up to the match at the Littoriale, the Italian newspapers had predicted a sell-out. The tickets, costing from 10 lire and with discounts for season-ticket holders, were selling like hot cakes despite the fact that most of the Bolognese had already left for their summer holidays. On the eve of the match there was an unforeseen event: Sparta, who had announced they would arrive at 10am and then postponed it to 10pm, had finally arrived at the San Marco Hotel at 11.20pm, thus having little time to rest before the match. Bologna, on the other hand, were in excellent condition: Reguzzoni and Sansone, victims respectively of a knee problem and tonsillitis, had recovered in time and the club had given rest in the previous weeks to Schiavio, as Bologna had not been called upon to face particularly formidable teams.

The match, played under the eyes of Pozzo and Arpinati, started at 4.40pm, ten minutes later than the pre-announced time and under the orders of the Austrian Miesz, who had to replace the unavailable Majorszky at the last minute. In the centre of the pitch there was a coin toss between Schiavio and Burgr, who had become captain of the Czechoslovak club since Káďa, now 37, had been confined to the bench.

Bologna started out against the sun but were aggressive from the off and were immediately rewarded by Reguzzoni's goal; his left-footed shot, strong and precise, slammed against the inside of the post before going in. Bologna's defence was also shaky and on two occasions Gianni, the red-blue goalkeeper, denied the Czechoslovakian forward Nejedlý. After ten minutes, the home team regained control of the game. From a corner by Sansone, Maini scored to make it 2-0. The third goal was a photocopy, with Maini scoring his personal double after Reguzzoni's cross from the left. Then 'Anzlèn' came to the fore: first he hit the post and then, after an attempt by Sparta, he made it 4-0 thanks to an assist by Sansone. The first half ended on that score, to the delight of the local fans, who were visibly thrilled with their first Mitropa Cup match.

The beginning of the second half seemed to take a different turn: in the first minute Podrazil had an opportunity to reduce the lead but Gianni, always present when called upon, said no. Then, before a long shot from Gasperi finished just too high, the Austrian referee sent off Braine for repeated protests against his decisions.[82] Some inconclusive attacks followed one after the other and the only noteworthy highlight of a second half decidedly more nervous and less amusing than the first was Bologna's fifth goal. It was scored by Baldi, nicknamed for his elegance 'the centre-forward in tails', with a free kick from 40 metres.

It was a convincing win. Never before had an Italian team won a Mitropa Cup match by such a margin. If the Italian newspapers spoke of a fully deserved result, the Sparta management, who had also complained about a handball by defender Martelli in the penalty area, claimed that 4-2 would have been more in line with what was seen on the pitch.

The return leg was played on 28 June in Prague. Bologna started with a five-goal lead but also had two

---

82 The Bologna crowd, probably eager to see one of Europe's biggest football stars with their own eyes, disapproved of the referee's decision.

important absentees: Schiavio, who had suffered a knee injury, and Baldi, who was getting married in the capital that day. There were also important changes in the Sparta ranks: the disappointing away match in Bologna had induced the coach of the Bohemians to replace pillars like Perner and Silný and not to pick the idol of the Prague fans, the now elderly Káďa. Braine would occupy the inside-left position.[83] The atmosphere in Prague was as fiery as it had been in Bologna. Outside the Hotel Parigi the Bologna players had crossed paths with some Czechoslovakian fans who had signalled 'ten' with both hands, as they wished for an unprecedented rout.

The early stages of the game disappointed onlookers: Bologna began as aggressively as they had done in the first few minutes of the first leg and in the sixth minute Maini hit the post. The visitors' dominance continued for half an hour before the game took an unexpected turn: Sparta were awarded a penalty after Braine was brought down in the box and Nejedlý made it 1-0 from the spot. A minute later the lead was doubled when Donati's own goal revived the home side.

The 2-0 scoreline seemed harsh on Bologna, who began the second half once again on the attack, but as had happened in the first half, it was Sparta who made it happen: Podrazil scored direct from a corner kick, marking one of the first official 'Olympic goals' in the history of European football.[84] Sparta were desperate to get forward but their attacks were contained by a Bologna side who

---

83 As on other occasions, Braine was allowed to play the match on payment of a fine.

84 A goal direct from a corner kick, especially in South America, is often called an Olympic goal. It is so called in homage to Cesareo Onzari, who in 1924 scored directly from a corner against Uruguay, who had recently been crowned champions at the Olympic Games in Colombes.

were punished harshly by the result, as all of Sparta's goals had come from set pieces. Bologna's qualification for the semi-finals seemed well deserved.

* * *

In the semi-final Lelovics's men found an equally formidable opponent: defending champions First Vienna, who had eliminated Újpest in the quarter-finals. They had not been very convincing: they had won the Vienna match 5-3 after the first half had ended 2-3 in favour of the Hungarians and the second half, according to the visiting team, had been characterised by a series of fouls committed by the Viennese that were not punished by the referee. Hugo Meisl had espoused the superiority of the Hungarians underlining, however, their clear decline in the second half.

In the return match the Austrians held their opponents and the 1-1 result meant they went through to the semi-finals.

The 'Döblingers' relied once more on their excellent backbone composed of the goalscoring defender Blum, the supporting centre Hoffmann and 'The Tall Fritz'. One of the flaws of the Austrian team, described by most as a defensive formation and as such in contrast to the style expressed by the Danube clubs, was the lack of rhythm and speed, something that often translated into a lack of bite.

The first leg of the trip was held in Bologna on 10 July in a climate cooled by the rain that had fallen on the city over the previous two days. For this reason, First Vienna had holed up in the Hotel San Marco instead of going sightseeing. Both teams were at full strength and at 5pm the Czechoslovakian whistle-blower Cejnar began the hostilities with the omnipresent Arpinati in the stands.

Bologna approached the test against the reigning champions in the best possible way: the first save by the opposing goalkeeper came in the sixth minute. Then the pressure of the '*Rossoblu*' generated four corners from the ninth to the 15th minutes before Kaller, one of the visiting team's defenders, managed to stop Schiavio's shot with the goalkeeper beaten. Gschweidl, left to his own devices, seemed to be almost uninterested in the game, as his team-mates were all busy in defence. Schiavio, on the other hand, was repeatedly encouraged by his team-mates and in the 26th minute he again went close to scoring with a nice shot from outside the area that was deflected wide by the goalkeeper. The Bologna striker missed another chance before the teams went back into the changing rooms.

The second half began with a livelier First Vienna and attacks from both sides. In the fifth minute the visitors came close to scoring and at times kept possession for long periods, perhaps because Bologna were tired from the energy expended in the first 45 minutes. Paradoxically, after a first half spent constantly in the opponents' half, Bologna went ahead on the counter-attack: Reguzzoni crossed from the left and Maini headed the ball into the net. A phase of nervous play began, characterised by skirmishes between the players: Blum, Maini, Schönwetter and Montesanto were all arguing. The game remained tense and Bologna maintained their lead thanks to a great save by Gianni from Gschweidl's shot. Then, in the 44th minute, Sansone scored from a free kick taken by Montesanto, with the ball finding its way into the net through a crowd of legs. It was an important goal that gave Bologna a significant advantage ahead of the return leg on 17 July.

On the day of the return match the atmosphere was tense, and not because there had been any particularly important events in Bologna, but because of the clashes between fans that had characterised the match in Prague between Slavia and Juventus. For this reason, the Hohe Warte stadium was on high alert and because of the downpour that fell on Vienna, there were not many spectators.

First Vienna approached the match nervously, with some players seemingly caught up in the frenzy to immediately overturn the result. Gschweidl, usually the central point of reference, played a more decentralised role than usual and the two wings, Brosenbauer and Schönwetter, showed little incisiveness. The game seemed to be balanced from the beginning, with Bologna wanting to play attacking football. In the 15th minute the game opened up after Monzeglio's handball in the penalty area. Schönwetter converted and the public regained confidence – confidence that grew a few minutes later when Blum went close to making it 2-0 with a shot from distance. Then Bologna took hold of the game: in the 26th minute Schiavio was stopped at the last moment by Blum when he was about to score and the 'Döblingers', now on the ropes, started to set up some counter-attacks. Although the first half ended 1-0 to the Austrians, some Italian newspapers claimed it was one of the best performances by an Italian team at European level.

The first 20 minutes of the second half were less exciting, with the two antagonists battling with corner kicks, but without any appreciable results. First Vienna, needing to find at least a second goal, increased their pressure and some of their players started to get more involved. Brosenbauer, who hadn't played during the first half, was noticeable for some raids down the right wing that created many problems for Gasperi, the full-back in charge of marking him. The home side had two more opportunities, but always on the counter-attack: Bologna's attitude of attacking their opponents even when they could have defended their advantage was atypical for an Italian team and this made them the most Danubian of Italian teams.

Part of the credit certainly had to go to the Austrian and Hungarian coaches who had made and were making club history. The match ended exactly as it had begun and how it had continued: end-to-end play that could have brought a goal for either side, but actually brought neither. Lelovics's men more than deservedly qualified for the final. They had got the better of a powerhouse like Sparta and now, in a show of strength across the first leg and the return leg, they had eliminated the title holders. It was the first time that an Italian team had not only reached the final but had given the impression of being the strongest team on the continent.

* * *

On the day of the match in Bologna, Juventus and Slavia faced each other in the return leg of the other semi-final. The first leg had ended 4-0 to the Czechs and had been marked by controversy and violent clashes between fans. The atmosphere had been heated right from the start, with the noisy 28,000 local spectators cheering their own players and booing their opponents in the pouring rain at Letná Stadion. Even the Slavia players didn't hold back: in the first minute of the game, an Italian player, Bertolini, was forced to seek medical help from the Juventus staff.

The game was open until the 25th minute of the first half and both teams repeatedly came close to scoring. Then, Slavia took the lead and minutes later had doubled their advantage. The clashes went on for the whole 90 minutes: after a hard contact between Puč and Cesarini, Sloup-Štaplík, the Czechoslovak coach who had succeeded

Madden two years before, went on to the pitch to protest and Cesarini, not liking it, moved threateningly towards the coach. Cesarini then took it out on the referee, guilty, according to him, of not having punished a foul on Sernagiotto.[85]

The disagreements between the referee, Braun, and the Italian players had actually begun a few days earlier: Braun had also taken charge of the return match of the quarter-finals between Ferencváros and Juventus and had awarded three penalties to the Hungarians.[86]

But let's go back to the facts of Prague: a first pitch invasion took place, followed a few minutes later by a second one, caused by yet another foul by Cesarini. Some Juventus players, in particular Orsi, Varglien, Vecchina and Caligaris were attacked and, notwithstanding the intervention of the police, had to defend themselves from the kicks and punches of the home fans. Cesarini was sent off before the game could resume. Referee Braun was also hit in the melee, and had to leave the field for ten minutes. When the match resumed the *'Bianconeri'* were down to eight players: apart from Cesarini, who was sent off, Varglien and Vecchina were still recovering from their blows. It was in that phase of the game that Fiala scored Slavia's fourth goal from a penalty kick.

The match ended in controversy, a controversy that would inevitably flare up in the newspapers and within the individual federations. A few hours after the events in Prague, the FIGC requested a report from Juventus, the

---

85 Pedro Sernagiotto, nicknamed *'Ministrinho'*, was born in Sao Paulo and was part of the group of players who arrived in Italy from South America at the beginning of the 1930s.

86 The penalties were scored by György Sárosi, who was making his first appearance on the international stage that year. At the end of that match he was defined by Juve coach Carcano with one word: 'Extraordinary'.

Italian Legation in Prague and Hugo Meisl about what had happened. The Italian newspapers hoped that the following Sunday, when the return match was to be played, Juventus would teach a lesson 'to the uncivilised fools of Prague'. The FIGC, wanting to show solidarity, decided to punish Cesarini for his unsportsmanlike conduct by fining the player 2,000 lira, the same measure Sparta had taken against Braine after the match between Bologna and Sparta. At the same time, however, the federation asked Hugo Meisl about the sanctions imposed by the Czechoslovak federation.

The return match in Turin was fixed for 10 July and it would be played in a decidedly overheated atmosphere. As soon as they arrived in Turin, the Slavia players were attacked by a group of Juventus fans, then blocked by the intervention of the police. Near and inside the stadium, the police patrolled every corner in order to quell any signs of violence. The game had not even started when the first incidents occurred: on the touchline, before the coin toss, Combi refused to shake hands with Ženíšek, captain of Slavia, and Plánička, who had just positioned himself in front of the goal, was hit by some pebbles coming from the upper tribune. It is not easy to clarify the extent of the damage to the Czechoslovak goalkeeper. The events relating to the double confrontation between Slavia and Juventus should be analysed by listening to both camps, proponents of two diametrically opposed versions. What is certain was that Plánička was hit, that he remained on the ground for a few moments and then got back up amidst vehement protests from his team-mates.

It was only then that the Austrian referee Miesz began the match and the Italian fans, who seemed to have calmed down, began to support their favourites with chants of encouragement. Juventus took the lead in the 15th minute through Cesarini after Plánička had made three crucial saves to deny the Torino side an advantage. That didn't change and in the 40th minute Plánička conceded again, thanks to Orsi's penalty – a penalty, according to the Prague newspapers, awarded due to pressure from the local crowd. As the first half drew to a close, Junek, the visiting forward, picked up an object from the stands and threw it at one of the opposition. The blatant gesture was noticed by Combi, who immediately told the referee. The result was an incredible skirmish that required the intervention of the police before the players could reach the changing rooms. The Czechoslovakian newspapers accused Caligaris of approaching threateningly the area reserved for the Czechoslovakian radio commentator Josef Laufer. Puč, who would go on to become the Czechoslovak national team's all-time leading scorer and who was present on the pitch that day, would recall years later: 'We felt like prisoners, escorted by police off the pitch. In order to protect us, it was even forbidden to sell bottled drinks. And at the end of the match, when we returned to the hotel, police cordons had been set up along the streets in the neighbourhood.'

Early in the second half, after a run by Sernagiotto on the wing had been halted by a visiting defender, Plánička fell to the ground again, probably because of another stone coming from the stands. The day after the match the Italian newspapers were sceptical: according to them Plánička had pretended to have been hit but then, as the doctors on the pitch didn't find any marks on the back of his head, he had said he had been the victim of sunstroke. The Italian newspapers also hypothesised he might have collapsed due to an illness caused by ice water drunk during the interval. The Czechoslovak version was quite different: Plánička, following the blow received, had suffered a psychological trauma that prevented him from continuing the game. In any case, the Slavia players dragged their goalkeeper off and never returned to the pitch.

So, the match lasted 45 minutes and 50 seconds. The Italians were unhappy, as the referee could have invoked the use of a technical time of ten minutes allowed to replace a goalkeeper with an outfield player.[87] The result remained pending and the two teams went on holiday waiting to hear the decision that the committee would take. If the committee had judged that Slavia's abandonment of the pitch was due to *force majeure*, they would probably have punished Juventus by automatically excluding them from the competition. Otherwise, the '*Bianconeri*' would have been awarded a 3-0 victory, a result that was pointless given the outcome of the first leg.

The whole question revolved around Plánička and the extent of his injury. Had he been the victim of an illness? Had he put on a show? Or had he actually been hit repeatedly by the Juventus fans? The affair escalated in the days that followed. From Prague they declared that 'Slavia and its leaders were victims of the barbaric behaviour of the Italian fascists', while referee Miesz claimed that Plánička had not been injured and that the game could have gone ahead. Two Hungarian newspapers, the *Uj Nemzedek* and the *Nemzeti Ujszag*, pointed the finger at the Czechoslovaks' misconduct in the first leg match. According to the Czechoslovak newspapers, however, their Italian colleagues had insulted the players and fans of Slavia with epithets such as 'pigs' and 'Bohemian cockroaches'.[88] The FIGC even considered cancelling the match between

---

87 Slavia could have deployed a player in goal in place of Plánička, but as substitutions were not yet available they would have had to continue the match with 10 against 11.

88 I haven't been able to verify this claim by the Czech papers.

Czechoslovakia and Italy that was scheduled for the International Cup on 28 October. The concern of the Italian federation was that the stadiums in Prague were not fenced off and that on too many occasions the local public abused the freedom they were given.

The committee, which had at first considered the possibility of organising a play-off on a neutral pitch, met in Klagenfurt on the morning of 16 August. After four hours of intense consultations that also involved the referees from Prague and Turin, as well as the Italian and Czechoslovakian representatives Zanetti and Pelikan, president Gerö ordered the interested parties to momentarily leave the room while the federations that were not involved in the matter – the Austrian and Hungarian ones – made a decision. When Zanetti and Pelikan returned they learned from Gerö that both teams had been disqualified: they had been found equally guilty of the disturbances between the first leg and the return leg. Slavia appealed in the following days but the appeal was rejected.

A diatribe within a diatribe arose: the Czechoslovak federation declared its intention to boycott the referee Miesz, guilty, in its opinion, of having drawn up a false report that damaged Slavia's claims, while the organising committee, supported by the Viennese board of arbitrators, backed the referee, claiming that if Miesz's boycott was not withdrawn the various federations would have the right not to accept Czechoslovakian referees.

On 7 November, the committee made its final decision: the cup and the gold medals went to Bologna, the first Italian team to win a European club competition. This joy was tempered by the fact that, as Bologna could not play in the double final, they would have had to forgo a hefty income. The fact that Bologna's victory was made official on 7 November led to a misunderstanding: according to various sources, the coach who won the 1932 Mitopa Cup was József Nagy. Nagy was, in fact, the coach in charge at that time, but it was Lelovics who had been in charge for the Mitropa matches, but who had moved to Livorno the day after the victory.

1933 – MATTHIAS SINDELAR AND THE COFFEE HOUSE TEAM

The proposal to have four participants per country and to invite other countries was repeated in the autumn of 1933: the Austrian clubs in particular were pressing for an increase in their presence. Meisl did not agree. He had nothing against the enlargement to include other teams and nations in principle, but he feared that doing so would multiply the problems already observed in previous years, the last one in particular: namely the violence in the stadiums and the constant threats of boycotts. The format therefore remained the same. A change in the distribution of the proceeds was discussed: the Italian teams, however, who were the ones with the highest proceeds, vetoed it and the division remained the same: 70 per cent to the home team and 30 per cent to the visiting team.

The 1933 edition promised to be open to all possibilities: with Bologna's victory the previous year, all the participating federations had won at least one trophy between 1927 and 1932. European football, a year after the World Cup, the first to be hosted on the Old Continent, had become more competitive than ever.

* * *

AUSTRIA VIENNA, who in the early years of their existence had mainly competed with First Vienna, found Rapid later became their closest rivals. Austria Vienna and Rapid were two antithetical teams from every point of view: while Rapid were the most popular team in the suburbs, Austria Vienna ruled in the city centre, and while Rapid were seen as the team of the working class, '*Die Veilchen*', 'the Violets', as Austria Vienna were nicknamed, were the bourgeois and Jewish team of the capital, whose supporters were mostly bohemians, lovers of the good life and regulars in the cafés of the centre. Here, it was said, they used to meet in the evening to squander their money on gambling. This diversity in terms of origins and social identity was the basis of the frequent clashes that occurred every time the derby was played.

However, Rapid and Austria[89] had not always duelled for the title: under the name Vienna Cricket and Football Club, Austria had twice lifted the Challenge Cup at the turn of the century, in an era when Rapid were far from the standards they would reach only a few years later.[90] From 1911 – the year that marked the birth of a proper Austrian league – it was Rapid who had established themselves as the country's best side. Austria Vienna only managed to stop the green-and-whites' ('*Grün-Weiss*') hegemony in the 1923/24 season, thanks mainly to the arrival of some top players from Hungary. It was from this point on that the rivalry between Austria Vienna and Rapid was revived due to the strength of both teams.

---

89 In colloquial terms Rapid Vienna and Austria Vienna are known to everyone as Rapid and Austria.

90 Rapid had competed in the Challenge Cup on four occasions but only on one of those occasions did they make it past the first round.

Not that Austria and Rapid were the only two title contenders: the Austrian scene featured other top teams such as Admira, First Vienna, WAC and Hakoah, although the latter only lasted a few years; but no rivalry aroused the enthusiasm and passion of the fans like the one between '*Die Veilchen*' and '*Grün-Weiss*'. It was such a keenly felt dispute that it often ended up involving even the top management, first and foremost Rapid's manager Dyonis Schönecker. As Karl Geyer, a former Rapid player, recounted years later, every time the 'green-and-whites' had to face Austria, Schönecker would address his players with the following words: 'Be good boys, today we are playing against the Jews. You know what you have to do, give them a good lesson! Then they'll go back to where they came from.' Even the sports newspapers of the time, often inclined towards certain political positions, did their bit to exacerbate this rivalry. The *Illustriertes Sportblatt*, which used to praise Rapid and its working-class roots, described 'the Violets' as 'a team of football mercenaries stunned by the suffocating fumes of the coffee houses'.

However, there was also some common ground between the two clubs: just as Austria Vienna's eleven consisted of several players from the capital's suburbs whose families were of foreign origin, Rapid Vienna had had some Jewish managers: Leo Schidrowitz, for example, author of one of the books on the early years of football in Austria that you will find in the bibliography, had been manager at the Hütteldorfer club for a few years from 1923.

If Austria Vienna were able to maintain their position at the top and lift more titles after the two Hungarian stars Schaffer and Konrád had packed their bags, it was mainly due to one factor: the explosion of Matthias Sindelar, nicknamed 'The Paper Man' because of his slight build, who would become one of the greatest players of the 1930s and one of the most important in the history of Austrian football. He was signed by Austria in September 1924, won the Vienna Cup at the end of the same season and the following year won both the cup and the championship. His consecration, however, coincided with a decline in the team from the Viennese suburb of Favoriten, which did not prevent him from winning yet another Vienna Cup in 1933 and making an essential contribution: six goals in five matches. This victory led to participation in the Mitropa Cup, the first in the history of the Vienna 'Violets'.

* * *

Austria were drawn against Slavia, a team smarting from the events of the previous year. Managing the Viennese was Josef Blum, a recent acquaintance of Austrian and European football, a former defender and hero of First Vienna who had won the Mitropa two years earlier. Despite the fact that Austria were newcomers to the competition, there were more than 20,000 spectators in the Letná Stadion at 6.30pm on 21 June. This was mainly due to Sindelar's presence, his recent exploits with the Austrian national team and his origins: 'The Paper Man' was born in Iglau, a small town halfway between Prague and Brno. The Prague newspapers did their utmost to promote the event and bring as many people as possible to the stadium. Sindelar, predictably, was showered with applause.

Slavia started to attack but at the first counter-offensive of the visitors the home crowd fell silent: the captain Ženíšek, in an attempt to clear the ball, scored an own goal. Nevertheless, the pressure of the Czechoslovakians started again and in two minutes, between the 27th and 28th, Slavia turned the scoreline around thanks to Kopecký's goal after a pass from Joska – who was playing in place of the injured Puč – and Svoboda.

Joska's goal in the fourth minute of the second half made the score 3-1, but the home team seemed to feel that was too close, as they continued to attack. For Austria, the two-goal deficit represented a margin that they thought could be recovered, especially as it was from an away game – a sentiment backed up by other results in the short history of the competition. Sindelar, author of a good individual performance, was subjected to tough marking and had to leave the field for a while after suffering a blow.

Hugo Meisl said at the end of the match: 'Slavia's victory was not undeserved; maybe with a bit of luck Austria could have scored another goal, but hardly reach the victory. Sindelar showed off his strengths and weaknesses, such as the finishing phase. For this reason he was not able to surprise Plánička.'

The day before the return match Sindelar warned the Viennese public, through a local newspaper, to 'get ready for a fight without quarter'. The match began and only two minutes after referee Barlassina had blown the whistle, 'The Paper Man' had a chance: his lob flew past Plánička, but just before it went in, an opponent managed to stop the danger acrobatically. The tussle was now in full swing: two minutes later Plánička had to intervene at Mock's feet to prevent a 1-0 scoreline before the Czechoslovakian goalkeeper won another duel with Sindelar with a spectacular dive. But Plánička was powerless minutes later when Stroh put his side ahead on the stroke of half-time. The enthusiasm of the crowd was slightly dampened by the stadium announcer telling them Ambrosiana were leading First Vienna at half-time.

The second half was described as a real 'The Paper Man' show: in the 48th minute the striker inspired an attack foiled at the last minute by Puč with a deep defensive retreat and in the 58th minute he helped Viertl score the second goal. The third goal, resulting from a defensive error, bore his signature. The Viennese public was in raptures as much as the newspapers would be the next day. *Sport-Tagblatt* described it as 'an incredible day for Viennese sport', while *La Gazzetta dello Sport* wrote: 'Except for Rapid's performance against Glasgow Rangers, no other match can compare in beauty of play to that provided by Austria in the Municipal Stadium.' The 4-0 defeat of First Vienna had faded into the background.

* * *

The semi-final pitted Austria Vienna against Juventus, who had got the better of Újpest. Austria's comeback in the second leg of the quarter-final had averted a huge risk: that of a rematch between Juventus and Slavia, an event that would have been difficult to manage in terms of public order given what had happened the previous season. On a sporting level, the Italian public were unable to establish whether Austria's victory was good for the '*Bianconeri*': while Slavia boasted a greater international tradition than the Austrians, it was also true that Austria Vienna – and Sindelar – were emerging as one of the European teams to beat.

Both Italian and Austrian newspapers showed mutual respect. In Vienna there was a clear conviction that they were up against the strongest team in Italy, while on the Juventus side the feeling was that, although they had finished fifth the previous year, 'the Violets' were the best Viennese team at the time. Austria Vienna president Emanuel Schwarz, who along with Sindelar, Hugo Meisl and other Austrian players had greeted the '*Bianconeri*' at the train station, had declared that he feared Juventus to the point of feeling that a return leg tie lead to play-off would be a good result. Meisl appeared more confident:

'If our players play as they did against Slavia, we will not have worries,' he declared. Sindelar, asked by journalists about his condition, answered: 'Am I okay? Perfectly! In Prague, after our mediocre performance, many thought I was finished. "Sindelar", those smart guys said, "is now a footballer of the past." And, convinced that they had buried me, they were stunned when they learned that, without wishing to boast, it was in fact largely me who had destroyed all the Czechs' rosy hopes.'

The '*Bianconeri*' were just as carefree on the eve of the match: the public's reception had been warm and that same evening the Turin team had gone to the theatre to watch Fritz Kreisler's opera *Sissy*, a classic based on the love between Emperor Francis and Elisabeth. Rarely had a match been so eagerly anticipated: everywhere in Vienna and in Turin people were talking about the imminent challenge. In this turbulence of sensations and emotions, marked by great sportsmanship and mutual respect, two of Europe's strongest teams would face each other on 9 July in the bedlam of the Prater.

Although the capacity of the Prater was around 46,000, more than one of the following day's reports put the attendance at 50,000. The 50,000 – or 46,000 – spectators were soon rewarded for their anticipation: in the third minute Sindelar, following a free kick taken by Nausch, put his side ahead with a superb shot from 20 yards which curled in under the right-hand crossbar of Combi's goal. The match resumed with the teams attacking in turn and both Juventus and the Austrians came close to scoring. Austria Vienna were more effective and Sindelar had two more chances, first with a shot that hit the post and then with an effort that the Italian goalkeeper blocked. In the 43rd minute, amidst Italian protests, the referee gave the Austrians a penalty after contact between Bertolini and

Molzer on the edge of the area. Both players fell down but the referee saw a foul by the Italian player. Orsi tried in every way to annoy his opponent by running around the penalty spot and probably succeeded, since Molzer hit the post with his spot kick. The two teams went to the changing rooms with the score at 1-0.

The second half began with Juve moving forward and Austria more wait-and-see. But in the seventh minute Sindelar, engaged in a tussle with Rosetta, drew half the Juventus defence to him before serving Viertl who, from a distance, beat Combi for the second time. The Italians thought it was an offside call, but referee Klein, who pointed to the centre circle, did not.

Juventus tried to reduce their disadvantage by attacking: several times the Austrian goalkeeper Billich had to come out or dive to deal with the danger. The game was evenly matched until the 85th minute when Monti was making a run with the ball and Sindelar pounced on him from behind. The Italian kicked Sindelar, who remained on the ground in pain for a few minutes, and Klein sent off 'Doble Ancho' (this was Luis Monti's nickname, which translates roughly as 'double wardrobe)), although according to the Italians their opponent's star player deserved the same sanction.

A few moments later Spechtl shot past Combi from 15 yards out and the final score was 3-0, which seemed excessive in terms of the balance of play, although, as Meisl pointed out at the end of the match, Juventus were not very effective when they had scoring chances.

The following day La Stampa wrote: 'Austria had an artist in Sindelar. If they play like this in the return leg, Juventus will be in pain.' Other Italian newspapers, while accepting the superiority of the Viennese and underlining some negative performances among the 'Bianconeri', instead complained about Klein's supposedly biased refereeing.

Klein was accused of having overlooked fouls by home players and of having excessively punished those committed by the Torinese. Sindelar was accused of having prompted Monti's expulsion by faking injury and the Vienna crowd of behaving in an unsportsmanlike way.

The return leg, which was as eagerly awaited as the first leg, was played exactly one week later. The Austrian players, greeted with great enthusiasm by their own supporters before their departure, were warmly welcomed by their rivals. Juventus arrived at the match without one important player: Monti, their only natural centre-forward, banned after his sending-off the week before. He had also been fined 1,000 lire by Juventus, as had happened the year before to Cesarini.

The match started and Sindelar, as in the first leg, had a chance in the first few minutes: this time, however, his shot finished just over the crossbar. That woke up the Italians and they started to attack: in the 21st minute they took the lead through Ferrari, who was able to deposit into the net a ball which had escaped from the Austrian goalkeeper Billich's hands. The home team's attacks went on for the whole of the first half. In the space of five minutes, between the 28th and 33rd, Billich was rescued twice by his goalposts, as Ferrari and Cesarini both shot from corner kicks.

The second half, however, went in the opposite direction: in the 48th minute the Austrian midfielder Gall hit a post from long distance and Austria took charge. Sindelar, marked in turn by Caligaris and Varglien II, led the way, but couldn't make as telling an impact as he had in the first leg. The day after the match *Sport-Tagblatt* reported on the 'attentions' that the Italian defenders had reserved for the Austrian star and also the Italian newspapers reported an elbowing that Sindelar had received off the ball from Varglien II with the Czechoslovakian referee Cejnar's back turned.

However, Molzer's equaliser, contested by the Italian players who claimed that the Austrian right-winger had crossed the goal line before shooting, sealed the deal. While the Austrians played a cautious game and thus qualified for the final, Juventus had to rue the many chances they wasted in both legs. Austria Vienna repeated the feat achieved by Bologna the previous year, qualifying for the final in their tournament debut.

The competitiveness of the 1933 tournament was evidenced by one fact: the four winners of the respective national competitions had been eliminated. This meant that the champions would be one of Matthias Sindelar's Austria Vienna and Giuseppe Meazza's Ambrosiana, two real outsiders.

* * *

Giuseppe Meazza and Matthias Sindelar, two boys whose fathers were killed during the Great War, are still considered by football historians to be the most important European footballers of the pre-Second World War period. Two authentic icons of their respective football movements; two champions whose popularity went far beyond the playing fields: both had become ambassadors for various international brands and their faces were associated with all kinds of products. While Meazza had become the symbol of fascist football, an image that would become even stronger after he played in the World Cup, Sindelar in Vienna was considered a sporting extension of the greatest local artists: he was compared to Mozart and in every corner of the city his sporting exploits were loved and praised.

The two had other things in common: they were leaders of teams that struggled in their respective leagues and both occupied the position of centre-forward in an atypical way. Not possessing the physique and stature of the classic English goalscorers, they made speed and technique their best weapons. Friedrich Torberg, a Viennese writer of the time, nicknamed Sindelar 'Wafer' because of his lightness, and Alfred Polgar claimed that Sindelar played football like a chess master moving his pieces through an incredibly broad mental concept. If Sindelar was known for his elegance, his ability to fake and send his team-mates through on goal, Meazza stood out for his individual virtuosity: since appearing on the Italian and European football scene he had repeatedly displayed his trademark, the famous 'goal on invitation'. The defenders, worried by his serpentine movements, often tried to create human cages to contain his talent.

Ambrosiana had now truly established themselves in the competition. The first time they appeared on the Mitropa stage, in 1930, they defeated reigning champions Újpest, and in the 1933 edition they eliminated the more experienced First Vienna and Sparta Prague in the quarter-finals and semi-finals, avenging the 6-1 defeat they had suffered three years earlier. On two occasions the fans of Austria Vienna had heard the results of Meazza and his team-mates over the speakers in their stadium, and if the defeat of First Vienna was booed due to mere parochialism, the exploits of the Milanese team against Sparta Prague aroused surprise but also fear. In addition to Meazza, Ambrosiana, coached by the Hungarian coach Árpád Weisz, boasted other excellent players such as the national defender Allemandi, the *oriundi* Frione and Demaría and the forward Levratto, who had made his debut in the competition years earlier in a Genova shirt.

The Austrians, in order to avoid the usual crowds around the station, had left Vienna at 7.45pm the night before,

together with Meisl and president Schwarz. The teams
took the field under the orders of the Hungarian whistle-
blower Klug[91] on 3 September at the Arena Civica in front of
about 35,00 spectators. Austria started as the favourites and
the Austrian forwards created good chances several times
without ever hitting the goal. The best attack was a solo
effort by Sindelar who, after having freed himself with three
body feints, launched a powerful shot that went just wide.

Then the game switched from end to end and
Ambrosiana went close to the goal with Frione. In the
11th minute, after a Ceresoli save from a shot by 'The Paper
Man', Levratto was injured after contact with the Austrian
Graf. He left the field for a few minutes and then came
back, even if visibly sore and limited in his movements.
After one of Viertl's shots, Levratto hit the post and the
same forward, in the 20th minute, didn't manage to score
after Frione's shot was cleared by Nausch.

In the 35th minute, the 'Nerazzurri' fans exploded
with joy after Frione, from Meazza's assist, beat Billich.
But Klug disallowed the goal: he had spotted a forward
offside. Five minutes later, after a corner kick, Meazza put
the Austrian goalkeeper's short rebound into the net and
finally the public could really rejoice. Only one minute
passed and Levratto, from a stationary spot, scored from
a corner kick to bring the 'Nerazzurri' to 2-0 up. Austria
looked like a beaten boxer and almost capitulated for the
third time in four minutes but Frione's shot hit the upper
part of the crossbar. The teams headed into the changing
rooms with the score at 2-0.

In the second half the Austrian team began to
weave their magic but without creating major dangers:

91 Austria had not accepted the candidacy of referee Ivanicsics, claiming
that he was a friend of Weisz.

Ambrosiana played a careful game and managed not to give great opportunities to the opposition. Faccio, the *'Nerazzurri'* centre-half who was marking Sindelar, took Monti's place, trying to follow the Austrian as much as possible. The first part of the second half was a real siege with the ball hitting Ceresoli's crossbar several times. After a save by the Austrian goalkeeper from a Demaría shot, Austria's pressure paid off: Spechtl took advantage of a good pass from Sindelar and from an off-centre position made the score 2-1.

The final 13 minutes passed without any particular excitement and the result in Milan left both teams happy: Ambrosiana, who, apart from the quarter of an hour in which they scored the two goals, had not been brilliant, and Austria, who knew they would play the second leg on their own ground. The respective clubs could also say they were satisfied as they would share the generous takings of 300,000 lire. Never before had a sporting event hosted at the Arena Civica generated such profits.

The two teams dined together after the game in a restaurant in Milan city centre and, a few days before the return match on 8 September, Austria Vienna returned the hospitality by meeting the Italians at the station and taking them to the Hotel Meissl & Schadn. Several Italian fans also went to the hotel and Sindelar, who had greeted the guests along with his managers, was caught chatting with Meazza in the lobby.

The two teams both had some absentees from their final line-ups: for the Italians, Levratto was the victim of a muscle strain suffered during the first match, and Demaría was also out. The Austrians had to do without Gall, victim of an injury, and Spechtl, the latter due to a tactical choice: even though he had been the scorer in Milan, Blum had surprised everyone by deciding to bet on one of the emerging talents of Austrian football, Camilo Jerusalem. If the match in Milan had recorded record takings, the one in Vienna did too: 58,000 spectators filled the stands, a turnout never seen at the Prater until that day.

The beginning of the first half was quite even and both sides had scoring chances; Ambrosiana, the slight underdogs, confirmed how dangerous they were and created a good chance in the fifth minute, but three of their shots were stopped by the opposition defence. The match went from end to end and in the 44th minute Austria went ahead with a penalty kick after Viertl was fouled by Agosteo. Referee Cejnar whistled for the penalty, despite the Italian protests, and Sindelar beat Ceresoli, despite the Italian goalkeeper having guessed the trajectory.[92]

At the beginning of the second half Ambrosiana's equaliser froze the enthusiasm of the home fans: Nausch lost a ball that Meazza, after advancing at great speed, crossed for Frione to head into the net. But the linesman's flag was raised and the Italians' exultation was dampened, once again giving rise to protests. The match became heated and in the 65th minute Allemandi, after having given Stroh a stomp, was sent off. Only a few minutes later Ambrosiana found themselves two men short: Cejnar sent off Demaría for another foul. The Milanese, whose morale was visibly affected, found themselves in obvious difficulties and Sindelar scored the second goal with a flying shot from Molzer's cross.

Everything seemed to be turning out for the best for the Austrians until, in the 83rd minute, Meazza collected a cross and beat Billich, making it 2-1. With the aggregate score tied, Ambrosiana entrenched themselves in defence

---

92 According to *Corriere della Sera*, the granting of the penalty had caused surprise even among the Austrian players.

but two minutes from the end they committed a fatal error: they forgot about 'The Paper Man', who received another cross from Molzer and completed a hat-trick.

The match ended with the Austrians happy, their joy embodied by the dazzling smile of captain Nausch as he lifted the cup, while the sadness of Ambrosiana was reflected in the tears of Meazza who, critical of the referee's actions, is said to have defined the match as 'a sports scandal'.

Josef 'Pepi' Blum, the young Austrian coach, achieved an unprecedented record: he was the first to win the Mitropa both as a player and as a coach. The Italians allegedly lodged a 20-page complaint about the refereeing by Cejnar, whom *La Stampa* described as 'the fat dictator of whistle blowing', also complaining that the Austrians had changed the match venue. But it was all in vain: Matthias Sindelar and Austria were at the summit of European football.

1934 – BOLOGNA, ITALY'S MOST DANUBIAN TEAM

In the days leading up to the 1933 return final, two proposals were evaluated: converting the competition format into a mini championship and extending participation to more teams. In the end, only the second change was made. In a photo showing the members of the organising committee, Meisl, who on several occasions had said he was against an increase in the number of teams, appeared tired and discontented, in clear contrast to the smiles of his colleagues.[93] Now four teams from each federation would participate in the event, which presupposed a draw that would also include the round of 16. As always, the selection criteria were at the discretion of the individual federations and, with the exception of Austria, all opted to enter the tournament with the top four teams from their

---

93 On several occasions Meisl had not hidden his opposition: for example, on 7 September of that year, two days before the return final, *Littoriale* reported an interview given by Meisl to the Czechoslovakian newspaper *Ceskie Slovo* in which he underlined his feelings about the number of teams invited, claiming that not all of them benefited economically. The *Littoriale*, for its part, said it hoped that the number of clubs would remain unchanged, since it would benefit the sporting and competitive nature of the competition.

respective leagues.[94] However, some concerns did not seem unfounded: that year the Mitropa Cup would be played at the end of an exhausting season and only a week after the World Cup Final, an occasion that would have sucked up an enormous amount of physical and mental energy. At the beginning of the second edition of the World Cup, a curious anecdote occurred which testifies to the importance the players attached to the Mitropa. FC Wien's Johann 'Hansi' Horvath decided to skip the first match of the World Cup with his national team in order to take part in the second leg of a final between his club and Floridsdorfer, which was a qualifier for the Mitropa. He reached Italy a few days later and was picked by Meisl to play in the quarter-final against Hungary.

If, on the one hand, the World Cup competition showcased the main stars of the European firmament, on the other hand it rekindled some sporting, political and diplomatic rumblings that had been dormant for some time. The relations between Italy and Austria had been decidedly strengthened only a few months earlier: Benito Mussolini, following the attack that had caused the death of the Austrian Chancellor Engelbert Dollfuss, had deployed his troops on the Brenner Pass to protect against an eventual invasion by the National Socialist Party of Germany and had declared his closeness to the Austrian people. But in the years between the two wars

---

94 Austria decided to enter their top three teams and the winner of a mini tournament between the fourth, fifth, sixth and seventh-place teams in the league into the Mitropa. The tournament was won by Floridsdorfer.

the relations, following the events of the First World War, had mostly remained uncertain and the newspapers not infrequently threw petrol on the fire. The events that took place during the World Cup certainly did not help: Vittorio Pozzo's Italy, winners of the tournament, met Austria in the semi-finals and Czechoslovakia in the final. Both matches were characterised by vehement controversies about the refereeing and the organisation of the event. All this contributed to poisoning the atmosphere around the upcoming edition of the Mitropa.

* * *

THE DECISIVE goal in the World Cup Final between Italy and Czechoslovakia was scored by Angelo Schiavio, winner of the Mitropa two years earlier and still the undisputed star of a Bologna team who had changed coaches once again: Lajos Kovács, who had succeeded Lelovics, was the fourth coach from the Danube region to sit in the '*Rossoblu*' dugout. Bologna had not really excelled in the championship: they had finished fourth, meaning they had been able to enter the event under the new rules. However, the names of their players remained high profile: although Baldi had retired the previous year, the Bolognese had kept their very best players, such as Sansone, Fedullo, Reguzzoni and Monzeglio, as well as the already mentioned Schiavio.

It was impossible to say who the favourites were this time: as well as reigning champions Austria Vienna, the tournament featured Ferencváros, led by an emerging György Sárosi, Meazza's Ambrosiana, Admira Vienna, who were double champions of Austria – league and cup – and the usual feared teams from Prague. Rapid also had a

new-look team: that year the 'green-and-whites' presented
a very young, attacking line-up made up of Bican, Binder
and Kaburek, three players who would make people talk –
especially the first two.

* * *

In the days leading up to the round of 16, the Italian press
was more downbeat than usual. Napoli – newcomers to the
competition – seemed to be doomed on paper, given that
they had to face Admira, one of the favourites, while the
other teams from 'the boot' would take on three teams with a
modest international tradition: Ambrosiana against Kladno,
Juventus against Teplicky FK and Bologna against Bocskai.
In the last three cases victory was taken for granted. In the
case of Bologna, the Italian newspapers were even worried
about the size of the victory, which should have allowed the
'Rossoblu' to face the return leg without any worries.

The first leg between Bologna and Bocskai was
played at the Littoriale on 17 June. The referee was
Czechoslovakian Krist. The first half was a total 'red-
blue' domination: Reguzzoni, making his first Mitropa
appearance of the year in that match, exactly as he had
done two years earlier, scored in the opening minutes
after receiving a weak rebound from the goalkeeper from
a Schiavio shot. The undisputed Bolognese hegemony led
to Schiavio scoring the second goal on the half-hour mark,
thanks to a low shot into the corner that left the Hungarian
goalkeeper motionless at the end of a collective attack.

The second half was much harder-fought: Bocskai took
courage, created several opportunities, especially from the
right flank, and protested that a Teleki shot, aimed at the
top corner, had crossed the goal line. According to the
referee it had not and he ordered the game to go ahead.
Then, a few minutes from the end, the Hungarians had a

second opportunity to halve the deficit but Dóczé's shot hit the crossbar. The match ended 2-0. A convincing first half had been counterbalanced by an underwhelming second half, as coach Kovács pointed out at the end of the match. In any case, the 2-0 win was a decent margin for Bologna ahead of the return leg.

The teams met again in Budapest exactly a week later. The beginning was similar to the first leg: Bologna showed an undoubted superiority and the Hungarians could hardly contain the Italian attacks. Then Bocskai came to the fore and in the 18th minute a cross from the right by Markos found Hevesi, who beat Gianni. The Hungarians continued to attack in search of a second goal, but to no avail.

At the beginning of the second half Bologna equalised: Maini dribbled round the goalkeeper and passed to Reguzzoni, who scored the easiest of goals. Bologna entrenched themselves in defence in an attempt to preserve the result but in the 66th minute the Magyars took the lead again with a scrambled goal, scored by Vincze. Monzeglio, who had been injured during the action and was visibly recovering, was confined to the right wing although he was no longer able to run.

Bologna, who had not impressed in either the first or second legs, managed to preserve their advantage and qualified for the quarter-finals.

Given the large crowd, something never seen before in Debrecen, the directors of the Hungarian club proposed the creation of a mini consolation tournament between teams eliminated from the Mitropa Cup that would be held in Debrecen. However, the idea never came to fruition.

* * *

This time Bologna's opponents would not be a Cinderella team; on the contrary, the Italians faced one of the most significant clubs of that era (notwithstanding the fact that team had not participated in the last three editions of the Mitropa). Rapid Vienna had qualified for the quarter-finals at the end of a double challenge against Slavia. An away win in the first leg, followed by a draw in the return leg. The 'green-and-whites' had shown their attacking qualities thanks to the duo Bican–Binder, both rookies in the competition and authors of three goals in total against Slavia.

The first leg was played in Bologna on 1 July in front of a large crowd. The turnout was helped by the fact that Bologna, despite the importance of the match, had decided to keep ticket prices unchanged. Before the game began, Monzeglio, who would not play due to the injury suffered against the Hungarians, and Schiavio received an award which their fans had instigated: a gold medal for their exploits at the World Cup.

Bologna's line-up included the debutant Perazzolo, arrived on loan from Fiorentina. The Duce's sons Bruno and Vittorio were also in the crowd.

Bologna began by attacking and after a first chance was foiled by goalkeeper Raftl, they went ahead in the 20th minute: it was Perazzolo himself who gave Bologna the lead with a shot that finished a move started by Maini and continued by Schiavio. Schiavio provided the assist again when Reguzzoni doubled the score, but it was in vain as the referee frustrated the enthusiasm of the crowd by signalling an offside. The same situation occurred in the 36th minute, when the referee disallowed a second goal from Reguzzoni.

After that, Reguzzoni and Schiavio swapped roles and the Bologna striker made it 2-0 in the 40th minute. A minute later, however, Rapid scored from one of their attacks: Binder took advantage of a penalty kick for a hand-ball in the box by Maini and beat Gianni. Shortly before the end of the half, Bologna also got a penalty for a foul by defender Jestrab, but Reguzzoni kicked the ball at the goalkeeper. The first half, despite the clear domination of the home team, ended with Bologna 2-1 up.

In the 52nd minute, Reguzzoni, served by Fedullo, made up for his penalty miss and scored to make it 3-1, and that was followed by the fourth goal for Bologna, scored by Fiorini, supported by a rampaging Schiavio.

Bologna's pressure continued to bear fruit and in the 69th minute Reguzzoni and Schiavio combined for the fifth goal. Finally, Reguzzoni, who had put in a sumptuous performance despite the mistake from the penalty spot, put Fiorini through to score the sixth goal three minutes before the end. The match, which everyone expected to be balanced, turned out to be a triumph for Kovács's men: with a five-goal advantage, a comeback from Vienna looked unlikely.

The return match was played at the Prater and even though the odds were not in favour of the Austrians, the green-and-white fans came in large numbers. They made themselves heard right from the start and supported their favourites with every legal and illegal means, according to the Italian newspapers of the following day, which reported repeated throwing of bottles from the stands towards the visiting players. According to the Italian newspapers, the fiery atmosphere also influenced the refereeing of the Czechoslovak ŽENÍŠEK.

Franz Binder, nicknamed Bimbo, scored in the first minute: he put the ball in the net at the end of a melee that injured the Bologna goalkeeper Gianni. The crowd became even more excited, but were disappointed by a couple of saves by Gianni from two shots by Binder.[95] But

---

95 Binder was known for his extremely powerful shooting, so much so that he was often drawn by cartoonists of the time with a cannon instead of a leg. The day after the meeting, *La Stampa* described him as a 'master marksman'.

then they fell silent: Reguzzoni received a pass from Maini and equalised.

The match came back to life because of a violent episode in the 65th minute: Pesser kicked Montesanto and Monzeglio, who rushed to his team-mate's defence, was sent off after a fight with the Austrian. With eleven against ten, the result was a foregone conclusion: between the 71st and the 80th minutes, Binder scored three more times, in the first two cases with penalties. But despite the controversy surrounding the refereeing and the riots in the stands, Bologna deservedly kept their place in the competition.

* * *

In the semi-final Bologna found another team that had not excelled in the Mitropa in recent years: Ferencváros, winners of the 1928 edition. They had reached the semi-finals by eliminating two newcomers: first Floridsdorfer and then, with a few more headaches, the Czechoslovakian club, Kladno. The Hungarian team had qualified for the Mitropa as champions of Hungary and their rebirth was mainly linked to one name, that of György Sárosi. Sárosi had been impressive in the previous year's tournament; he had amazed the Hungarian and the Italian public with a great performance against Juventus. He had recently been moved from centre-back to centre-forward, the result of which, if possible, was even more surprising. On 1–2 April, the Easter Cup was held in Budapest, a tournament in which 'Fradi', Hungária, Rapid and Austria Vienna participated. Ferencváros dominated both matches against their Austrian rivals – 6-2 and 9-5 – and György Sárosi scored nine goals. Then came the World Cup, a bitter one for Hungary in which Sárosi scored just once, from a penalty kick.

The Bologna players had received an unusual offer from their management: if they qualified for the Mitropa final, they would earn a free holiday in Rimini. Monzeglio, banned after being sent off against Rapid, had to miss his second match of the competition and four of his team-mates – Reguzzoni, Montesanto, Gasperi and Gianni – were trying to recover from injuries suffered during the battle in Vienna, and went to a sports medicine centre for treatment as soon as they arrived in Budapest. Schiavio would join his companions the following day, but eventually they would all take part in the match.[96]

The match was played on 15 July under the orders of Austrian referee Braun, on a rather unusual pitch: it was almost entirely without grass. Bologna approached the match with an unusually defensive attitude, leaving the initiative to the home team who began to press right away. In the ninth minute Toldi gave Ferencváros the advantage thanks to a header from a throw-in by Táncos. But a few minutes later Maini equalised on the counter-attack. The plot remained the same: Ferencváros were proactive and Bologna were a breakaway side who were dangerous on the counter-attack. In the 30th minute Schiavio had a goal disallowed for alleged dangerous play – very alleged, according to the Italian newspapers – and in the 33rd minute the Bologna striker was brought down by Bán in the penalty area. The referee pointed to the spot, but Schiavio kicked more at the ground than the ball and goalkeeper Háda saved comfortably.

In the second half 'Fradi' intensified their pressure with some chances for Sárosi and Polgár but without scoring any goals. The performance of Fiorini was particularly

---

96 Angelo Schiavio did not always travel with his companions. Sometimes he would go earlier or later, depending on the commitments he had to carry out for the family business, Schiavio-Stoppani.

praised, for containing an outstanding player like Sárosi. In spite of a performance which really only shone from the defensive point of view, the *Felsinei*'s (Bologna's) coach said they were optimistic: they hoped to repeat last year's home performances and reach the final.

The return match in Bologna was played in a fiery atmosphere, both from a human point of view – despite the summer, the crowd was still very large – and from a climatic point of view, as the barometer registered 40°C. The game was exciting from the very beginning and Bologna, as usual, threw themselves forward and found the lead in the fourth minute: Perazzolo collected a rebound from Reguzzoni's shot and beat the opposing goalkeeper. Two minutes later Sárosi, left unmarked, took advantage of a cross from the right and levelled the score. The game became hard-fought, with both teams trying to take charge. '*Fradi*' seemed to be on the ball more and shortly afterwards they went close to doubling the score: after a throw-in, Gianni dropped the ball and it was picked up by a Hungarian player, who found Sárosi, but his shot was stopped thanks to a miraculous recovery by the Italian goalkeeper.

However, Bologna proved to be more dangerous and thanks to Maini, who took advantage of a scramble in the area, scored a second goal. The first half ended 2-1 and the Hungarian players went into the locker room but came out a second later: it was so hot in the tunnel they were better off on the pitch and more than one of them, exhausted, collapsed on the field waiting for the match to start again.

If the first half had been enjoyable, exciting and hard-fought, in the second half the Hungarians definitely seemed to be worn out by the weather and their rhythm dropped. Bologna took the initiative and in less than 20 minutes guaranteed their victory thanks to Schiavio and a double from Reguzzoni. While the Hungarians' manager

Klemens spoke of an excessive winning margin and blamed too many defensive errors, Vittorio Pozzo from the pages of *La Stampa* did not hide his satisfaction with Bologna's performance and pointed the finger at some unsportsmanlike attitudes from the visitors, in particular the striker Toldi, described as 'a fine player if he didn't lose his temper so often and so easily'.

That victory took Bologna to the final, giving them the chance to repeat the success of two years earlier, but this time with a victory on the field. First, though, they would take a well-deserved holiday in Rimini. Entirely at the company's expense.

* * *

A little over a month later the double final was played. Bologna faced Admira, a team that were antithetical to them: if Bologna had shown a marked aptitude for the cups and for the European showcase, Admira until that moment had only asserted themselves at national level. But in 1934, for the first time, the Viennese seemed to be competitive on the international front as well. In the round of 16 they had got rid of a combative Napoli, who were making their debut in the European competition by scoring the first goal in their history at international level thanks to Attila Sallustro,[97] one of the many foreign-born people of Italian origin who arrived in Italy between the two wars. Then Admira had eliminated giants such as Sparta and Juventus, which is why the two-legged final looked like being extremely balanced.

The first match was held in Vienna on 5 September. Curiously, the two finals were entrusted to two English referees, Walden and Jewell, despite the fact that the

---

97 Sallustro was born in Paraguay of Italian parents.

British federation was not taking part in the event. The day before the match the Bolognese – who had Sansone back after an injury, but had arrived in Vienna without the injured Schiavio – had paid a visit to the tomb of the former Austrian Chancellor Dollfuss. Among the Admira ranks, Anton Schall, the historic striker and talisman of the Viennese team was back, after recovering from a back injury suffered during the World Cup.

In front of 50,000 people, the first leg started. Spivach, Schiavio's replacement, lived up to expectations and scored the first goal of the match in the seventh minute. The score remained 0-1, because in the 12th minute Schall's shot from inside the penalty area went wide. The lack of clinical finishing by the home team was again punished by Bologna as they doubled their lead in the 25th minute with a splendid finish from distance by Maini. The match went on in alternating phases and with a few too many clashes, so much so that the centre-back Donati left the field momentarily due to injury. At the end of the first half Bologna were deservedly ahead by two goals.

The second half was a different story: Admira went on the attack and Bologna, believing they could hold on to the lead, were pegged back by their opponents. In the 52nd minute the Viennese were awarded a penalty – Sigl was brought down in the box – but Humenberger had his shot saved by Gianni. Then, between the 56th and 60th minutes the hosts scored through Stoiber, Vogl and Schall. With a 3-2 lead, at that point the Austrians entrenched themselves in defence of the result and some important interventions by Austria's national team goalkeeper Platzer[98] prevented Bologna from levelling the scores. Both referee Walden

---

98 Platzer, since Hiden had moved to France in February 1933, had become the starter for the Austrian 'Wunderteam'. It was he who had defended his national team's goals at the 1934 World Cup.

and Meisl praised the Italian team, talking about 'first class football' while Schiavio, who was absent that day, announced his presence for the return leg and said he was optimistic about the final outcome.

On 9 September, in front of around 30,000 spectators, including Bruno, Vittorio and Vito Mussolini, the teams met at the Littoriale in scorching weather. Bologna began the match as they had done in the first leg, beating their opponents and having a goal disallowed. But in the 21st minute Maini opened the scoring with a sliding shot after passing his marker. The reaction of the Viennese produced several corner kicks and from one of these, earned a penalty for Montesanto's handball. Vogl equalised from the penalty spot. But Bologna came forward again and in less than a minute took the lead: served by Schiavio, Reguzzoni outwitted two opponents and after sneaking into the box, beat Platzer: 2-1 to Bologna, with the home crowd in a frenzy. The third goal came from the Bologna left-winger, who was once again unstoppable for the Austrian defence: after having beaten a half-back and a defender he scored twice, taking advantage of the goalkeeper rushing out. The first half was about to end when, from a new attack by the Felsinei, Fedullo scored the fourth goal, his first in the competition, with a violent right-footed shot. The teams headed for the dressing room with Bologna decidedly confident and refreshed.

The second half confirmed the substantial superiority of the red-blue team: even more so because after the Austrian Hahnemann was injured in the 79th minute, Bologna scored once more, with three minutes to go, through Reguzzoni, after another attack down the left side. Reguzzoni, whom Hugo Meisl had once defined as 'the strongest winger on the continent', was the competition's leading player and became the top scorer, with ten goals. For some reason, probably due to the presence of a champion like Raimundo Orsi first and Gino Colaussi a few years later, during an era in which the Bologna winger was no longer at his best, Vittorio Pozzo never gave him the space he deserved.

Bologna, undoubtedly the Italian side with the greatest international reach between the wars, were certainly an atypical team: they embodied the same style as the best teams on the Danube thanks to the influence they had received since the Felsner era. The Mitropa Cup win was a well-deserved success that brought down the curtain on an exceptional year for Italian football. Josef Gerö presented the medals to the players and the cup to president Dall'Ara. Hugo Meisl said at the end of the match: 'It was a shame that Bologna only won 5-1. The fairer score would have been 10-1.' The competition was also a success from another point of view, the economic one: it recorded a total of 505,000 spectators, 161,000 in Austria alone.

1935 – RAYMOND BRAINE: OUTCAST IN ANTWERP, KING IN PRAGUE

Europe was becoming an increasingly unsafe place. On 26 February 1935, Hitler announced the foundation of the Reich air force, the Luftwaffe,[99] appointing Hermann Göring as commander and openly defying the prohibitions of the Treaty of Versailles; then, three weeks later, he reintroduced compulsory military service. However, European football seemed impervious to the threats that raged across the continent.

Due to the success of the previous year, it was decided to maintain the format of the Mitropa Cup with matches starting in the round of 16, despite Hugo Meisl's opposition. In March 1935, Meisl, convinced that the competition was in need of reform, proposed to transform it from a direct knockout tournament to a championship between European clubs. The teams, divided into two groups, would play on Wednesday and Thursday and the two winners would face

---

99 The project had actually begun secretly years before, but was made official on 26 February 1935.

each other in a two-legged final. But despite the strong support of some local managers such as Dyonis Schönecker, the proposal, presented at two conferences held in March and April 1935 in Vienna and Milan, was not ratified. The format therefore remained unchanged.

In Vienna, it was also decided to do away with the appeals committee and to stop using a neutral ground for the play-offs, a decision that was withdrawn the following month. At the April meeting, which took place at Ambrosiana, the committee rejected the Swiss federation's application for membership due to organisational difficulties, but promised to accept it in 1936.

In the 1934 edition, a similar case to Konrád's in 1927 had occurred: the Czechoslovakian Faczinek, for whom Sparta had not yet paid Zurich the full transfer fee, was deployed in Sparta's play-off win against Hungária. As the striker was not officially a Sparta player the committee had invalidated all three matches. Once Zurich received the money, the committee agreed to play a second play-off which ended 1-1. This resulted in a coin toss and the Czechs went through. To avoid such situations recurring, Henrik Fodor, a member of the Hungarian delegation, demanded and obtained a renegotiation of the rules regarding the presentation of the players' lists. It was established that the teams could field players contracted after the beginning of the tournament provided that their presence was notified 24 hours before the match.

* * *

IF THE years following the Great War had marked the emergence of Sparta Prague, or '*Sparta d'Acciaio*', in the early 1930s the Bohemian club had not achieved as many triumphs. They had won just one national title compared to Slavia's four and had not reached the Mitropa Cup final since 1930, when they lost to Rapid Vienna. The only survivor of the 1927 winning team was defender and talisman Burgr. Káďa, the club's most iconic player, had packed his bags. His love affair with the garnet shirt had ended as badly as it could have: Sparta had sued Káďa and family for 500,000 kkronen! The reason? The year Káďa was contracted by Sparta, his mother, Miss Peškova, had obtained a licence from the club to run a canteen inside the stadium. Exactly 21 years later Sparta realised that the terms of the lease had not been met, especially in the last year, after the stadium and its interior had been rebuilt following a fire. In the end Káďa and his family won the case and the player, burnt by the incident, chose to spend what was left of his career with a minor club. But the affection of his fans remained undiminished: when Káďa returned to Letná with his new team-mates the tickets sold out immediately.

The team was handed over to Ferenc Sedláček,[100] a young coach and former Ferencváros striker, winner of the Mitropa in 1928, who took over John Dick's heavy inheritance. The undisputed strength of the Bohemian team was the attack line thanks to the presence of Oldrich 'Olda' Nejedlý, finalist and top scorer at the World Cup, and the Belgian Raymond Braine. The hegemony of the two main Prague teams guaranteed Sparta the chance to play in the Mitropa Cup every year and both teams, facing much inferior opponents in their domestic league, could

---

100 In Prague he was commonly called František.

often rest their players ready for the challenges against the most famous European teams. The enlargement of the Mitropa entry to four teams from each nation also guaranteed the European limelight to other clubs, such as Kladno and Teplicky, the first two Czechoslovakian teams not from Prague to play on the continental stage. But in spite of Kladno's unexpected victory against Ambrosiana the year before, they were in fact two Cinderellas, light years away from Sparta and Slavia.

* * *

The draw for the round of 16 pitted Sparta against First Vienna, two teams who had already won the competition but had struggled to raise their heads for years. While the Czechoslovak championship was a two-horse race at the start, the Austrian championship was much richer in contenders and the *'Döblingers'* had the merit of having won a title in 1933. In the 1934/35 season, however, First had disappointed: they finished third, 13 points behind Rapid. According to most, the Czechs were the favourites.

The first leg was played in Vienna on 18 June after the other title contenders had taken to the pitch in the previous days. Italian referee Sassi was in charge in front of 7,000 spectators. The first half ended 1-0 to First Vienna thanks to Holec's goal in the 35th minute. Before and after taking the lead, the Austrians wasted several chances and hit the post twice, which could have meant a bigger lead.

In the second half, the match became more competitive and soured in terms of discipline, with both teams suffering the consequences and one player on each side being sent off, Machu for the Viennese and Bouček for the visitors. Nejedlý restored parity in the 69th minute with a fine shot from distance before the home side, just a minute later, had a goal disallowed for offside. The final few minutes were tight, although the spectacle offered by both sides did not satisfy the crowd. The frustration, however, was felt more on the pitch than in the stands: despite a seemingly flawless performance the Italian referee was almost attacked towards the end of the match by the Viennese goalkeeper.

The return match was played at the Letná Stadium four days later. Fischer, the Viennese striker, silenced the Prague crowd with a goal after only eight minutes. However, thanks to the crowd's support, Sparta started to attack and earned a penalty which Zajíček scored. From that moment on, an extremely intense, nervous and hard-fought match took place. Late in the first half and early in the second, the teams scored four more times, the Czechs through Braine, Nejedlý and Zajíček again from a penalty kick and the Austrians through Pollack. The challenge continued unabated, and in the 71st minute Pollack made it 4-3, this time from the penalty spot. First Vienna then threw themselves forward in desperate search of the goal that would have resulted in a play-off, but Zajíček completed his hat-trick and closed the discussion with a 5-3 win that sealed Sparta's passage to the quarter-finals.

* * *

There, Sparta found Fiorentina, a team making their debut in the competition and who had the merit of eliminating the much more experienced Újpest by imposing a double defeat on the Magyars. Lajos Kovács, the former Bologna coach who had been in Budapest for the first leg, praised the performance of 'the Violets'.

Sparta and Fiorentina met on 30 June in Prague for the first leg. The match, refereed by the Hungarian Ivanicsics, was influenced by an episode in the very first minutes: Comini, the Fiorentina right-wing, was forced to leave the field with an injury, leaving his team down to ten men for the rest of the match. From that moment, Sparta started to bombard the goal defended by Amoretti: several times Nejedlý and Braine went close to scoring. Fiorentina had a boost around the 20th minute with a shot from Gringa, but it missed the target. In the 24th minute, from an assist from Braine, Faczinek passed Amoretti and deposited the ball into the net to make it 1-0. In the 40th minute Sparta doubled the score: the dynamics were the same as the first goal, but this time it was Nejedlý who got past the Italian keeper before scoring.

Fiorentina, in obvious difficulty, tried some sorties in counter-attack and at the beginning of the second half were rewarded: from a wide position Gringa shot a cannon that brought the score to 2-1. But the theme remained the same: Sparta resumed control of the race and, strengthened by the numerical superiority, wove spider webs of low passes that soon created danger. Between the 53rd and 60th minutes, Braine, Kalocsay and Faczinek all scored to bring the result to 5-1. They were three individual goals, facilitated by a Fiorentina crippled and out of energy. In the 79th minute the Czechoslovakians scored a sixth goal and in the 85th minute Faczinek, served by Nejedlý, beat the opposition's goalkeeper for the seventh time.

The Italian newspapers partially justified the debacle of 'the Violets', underlining the differences between the Italian championship and the Czechoslovak one: they claimed that except Slavia and Sparta the Czechoslovak tournament was composed of small teams and that the participants, and consequently the games, were inferior. This was to the advantage of the main teams from Prague who could rest more.

Meisl said at the end of the match: 'It's too much, too much for the value of Fiorentina that I know well. But

Sparta have won well and the big advantage is unlikely to be regained on Sunday in Florence.'

And in fact, Sparta would not be overhauled in the second leg, despite a burst of pride from a Fiorentina, back at full strength, who came out of the Berta Stadium, now Artemio Franchi, winning 3-1.[101]

* * *

In the semi-final Sparta met another Italian team, Juventus. There was a precedent between the two clubs, that of 1931, a 'duel to the death' which was resolved in the play-offs with the Czechs going through. Four years later there were nine survivors of that triple-header and some of the players who would play – Ferrari, Bertolini, Monti, Čtyřoký, Košťálek and Nejedlý – had taken part in the fiery World Cup Final the year before. The double challenge promised sparks, and sparks there were.

The first leg was played on 16 July in Prague at the Stadion Masaryk. The Masaryk had recently been refurbished and years later would be converted into the Stadion Strahov, one of the world's largest venues, capable of holding 250,000 spectators. Although the Masaryk was not as large at the time, 40,000 spectators would recreate the same atmosphere the 'Bianconeri' had found every time they travelled to Prague. Before the match began, the flags of Italy and Czechoslovakia were flown at half-mast as a sign of mourning for the death of Agnelli, Juventus's president, who had died just two days earlier.

Under the pressure of their home crowd, Sparta began aggressively, forcing Juventus to drop back. In the 43rd minute, after a solo break by Braine, Faczinek found

---

101 Two goals from penalties by Viani and a goal by Negro. Zajicek scored for the Czechoslovaks.

himself alone in front of Italian goalkeeper Valinasso – successor to the legendary Combi – and put his side ahead. The final minutes of the first half saw Juventus attack but to no avail.

Their attacks continued in the second half and in the 66th minute, the decisive episode occurred: the Austrian referee Beranek punished a foul in the box by Rosetta on Braine and gave Sparta a penalty kick. Zajíček converted in the right corner and Monti, angry like all the Italian players, was sent off for protesting. This meant that Juve would have to face more than 20 minutes down by two goals and a man.

In spite of everything the '*Torinese*' tried to halve the deficit, but without results. The first leg thus ended 2-0 to the Czechs.

The day before the return match, Budapest hosted a meeting of the committee during which the Italian delegates, complaining about the penalty awarded to Sparta – a decision that had perplexed even the Prague newspapers – tried to get Monti's dismissal reversed. Against all odds their appeal was upheld and the '*Bianconeri*' did not have to revise their tactical plans.

The pre-match in Turin was also dedicated to the memory of Edoardo Agnelli: the Juventus players played with black armbands and the captain of the Czechoslovaks brought a wreath of flowers to the grandstand.

Juventus took an immediate lead: Prendato, who had made his debut for Juventus in the first leg, collected a cross from Cesarini and scored. Juventus continued to attack and in the 28th minute Borel, after cutting through the defence, was tripped. 'Penalty!' they shouted from the stands, but referee Ivanicsics waved play-on, and the whistle blew. And so Juventus ended the first half in total control of the game, but with only a one-goal lead.

The second period began along the same lines as the first, and Borel, who was unstoppable that day, finished a three-way exchange with Monti and Ferrari, discarding two or three opponents and depositing the ball in the net. That goal meant absolute parity with still more than half an hour to play. Just five minutes later, however, the Czechs took advantage of their only chance and, thanks to Nejedlý, regained a one-goal lead in the overall tally. Dazed, Juventus began to succumb to their opponents' repeated attacks and came close to drawing level on more than one occasion. Then, in the 84th minute, the 'Bianconeri' had a huge chance: Cesarini hit the post and Borel was again brought down from close range. This time, too, the penalty seemed obvious, and this time, too, the referee overlooked it amid the anger of the crowd. A few minutes later, incredibly, he gave a penalty that was defined as non-existent by the sports newspapers all over Europe, but Monti kicked it straight at the goalkeeper and the score remained 2-1.

However, when the crowd was about to leave, Juventus mounted their last offensive. A shot from distance by Monti hit the post and Borel, positioned near the goal, headed the ball into the net. Once again, as in 1931, Juventus v Sparta would be decided in a play-off, with the players having to postpone their summer holidays.

The decisive match was played at 6pm on 28 July, at a neutral ground, the Nordstern in Basel. Sparta started with the wind in their favour and immediately imposed a clear supremacy that resulted in a couple of chances, foiled by goalkeeper Valinasso. However, he could do nothing when Nejedlý, after a solo run, appeared in front of the goal and scored. The game came alive when Cesarini hit the post in the 35th minute and Sparta doubled and tripled their tally in the space of two minutes. Kalocsay made it 2-0 with a seemingly innocuous shot which was deflected by Monti and caught Valinasso off guard. The third goal came from Braine, who hit an unstoppable shot.

In the second half Juventus reacted and first Cesarini and then Borel challenged the giant Czechoslovak goalkeeper Klenovec, who could do nothing about Foni's penalty kick in the 72nd minute. However, it was just a flash in the pan as Sparta continued to dominate and between the 83rd and 85th minutes they scored again through Braine, who hit a spectacular volley, and Kalocsay. The match finished 5-1 and Sparta were in the final.

At the end of the game, Valinasso pointed out Braine as the strongest player he had ever seen and the English referee Fogg opined that no British team had a striker of that level.

* * *

In the final Sedláček and his team found Ferencváros, the team with whom the Czechoslovak coach had won the 1928 event as a striker. 'Fradi' and Sparta had been the first two sides to lift the trophy, but over the years they had been unable to do so again. The Hungarians had eliminated an unrecognisable Austria Vienna in the semi-finals: Matthias Sindelar had given one of his worst performances of recent years and captain Nausch, playing in the unusual position of central support because of the absence of a team-mate, had not been up to the task.

The first leg of the final was held on 8 September in the Hungarian capital. The start, under the direction of the Englishman Walden, was characterised by strong gusts of wind and was completely to the home sides's advantage, as they scored through Toldi – Sedláček's former team-mate – who, according to the Czechoslovaks, had controlled the ball with a touch of his hand. Kiss doubled the score with an assist from Sárosi.

In the 69th minute Braine, with a free kick from the edge of the area, reduced the gap and kept his side's hopes alive. The Czechs played the last seven minutes of the game with an extra man due to Sárosi's injury, but could not equalise.

Meisl, Fischer and the linesman, the Dutchman Boas, all expressed themselves along the same lines: if the first half had seen '*Fradi*' dominating the tie, in the second half, thanks to a slump by the midfielders, the Hungarians had got into difficulty and had struggled to contain their rivals' attacks. The Hungarians criticised some of Walden's decisions. Walden, on the other hand, had criticised the conditions of the pitch as he had sprained his ankle during the match. The 2-1 scoreline left the door wide open: the history of the Mitropa competition showed that home advantage played a significant role, especially considering that the Hungarians had lost all their away matches in that season's competition, even against less famous teams such as Roma and Židenice.

The eve of the return match brought a bit of apprehension in the Ferencváros ranks: Sárosi had left the field during the last minutes of the match in Budapest and was therefore in doubt, but in the end he was able to play.

In front of 56,000 spectators the teams took to the field under the orders of referee Fogg. '*Fradi*' maintained a dominance in the first 20 minutes, which was followed by only one chance, for Toldi, who shot narrowly wide. Then, in the 26th minute, Sparta took the lead thanks to a superb effort from outside the box by Faczinek. In the 33rd minute Braine's impressive 30-metre effort rounded off the first-half scoring.

In the second half '*Fradi*' repeatedly came close to scoring, but to no avail. It was Sparta who found the target, again through Braine, whose shot, deflected by Hungarian defender Korányi, put the Magyar goalkeeper off balance. The match ended 3-0 and Burgr, the Czechoslovak captain, lifted the second Mitropa Cup in Sparta's history, an honour shared only with Bologna. The Hungarians, for their part, rued several wasted chances by their forwards and a last-gasp goal at a time when they were under great pressure. After Blum, Sedláček became the second – and later the last – coach to win the competition both as a player and as a coach.

Newspapers all over Europe agreed on one fact: the absolute star of that year's competition was Braine, whom *La Gazzetta dello Sport* described the day after the final as 'a striker of inexhaustible vitality, more of a juggler than a Chinese' (meaning he could do difficult tricks). Comments such as the one from *La Rosea* testified that, although he went down in history as a great scorer, Braine was actually much more: an extremely technical and versatile striker capable of commanding the whole attack. On the same wavelength Jean-Norbert Fraiponts, one of the main historians of Belgian football, would say of him many years later: 'He knew how to do everything, both in terms of play and finishing. He was the pre-war Di Stéfano and the best striker Belgium ever had.' It was probably no coincidence that Braine, some three years later, would captain the Rest of Europe selection in a friendly against England.

1936 – AUSTRIA VIENNA, EUROPE IN THE DNA

On 20 July 1935, while the semi-finals were in full swing, the committee met in Budapest. A number of decisions were taken to ensure greater safety and better maintenance of grounds: more than one club, especially the Italian ones, had complained in previous years about the lack of barriers in the stadiums in Prague and the fact that some pitches were lacking grass. The participation of the Swiss teams was confirmed, although their presence was conditional on passing a preliminary round.

At a second meeting on 10 April 1936, a few months before the start of the new Mitropa competition, the draw was made: the four Swiss teams would play against the fourth-placed teams from Czechoslovakia and Hungary and the winners of the Italian and Austrian Cups. The Swiss newspapers had something to say about this: they claimed that they deserved the same treatment as the other federations and that Switzerland, not only in sporting matters, was only consulted when it was convenient, such as when finals and play-offs had to be organised on neutral[102] grounds. In any case, all four Swiss teams were eliminated in the preliminaries. At the suggestion of Italy, the involvement of Romanian and Yugoslav teams was also considered. The decision, which was initially postponed until a later date, was taken in the following months: Yugoslavia and Romania would be able to participate with their national champions from 1937 onwards.

* * *

AUSTRIA VIENNA and Austrian football in general were not sailing in the calmest of waters. Since 1933, the year the 'Violets' won the Mitropa Cup, the Viennese teams had been left empty-handed. None of them had played in another international final and Meisl's men (besides being a member of the Mitropa committee, Meisl was also the coach of the national team) had lost both the World Cup and the International Cup to Vittorio Pozzo's Italy.[103] The entire Viennese football movement was undergoing a profound change which made exceptions for no one, not even a legend like Matthias Sindelar. Meisl had started to cut back on his use of Sindelar in favour of his main protégé, the emerging Josef Bican, who made up a young attack of enormous potential with Rapid Vienna star

---

102 In this regard, however, it should be remembered that it was Switzerland that applied to host the 1931 final between First Vienna and WAC.

103 Italy also beat Austria in the final of the Olympic Games in Berlin. However, Olympic football was a different story: only players with amateur status took part, which is why Hogan, then coach of the Austrian national team, went to Germany with a line-up of semi-unknown players. Pozzo used another stratagem: if a player was registered as a student at a college or university, they could play, which allowed him to pick some players who were already established at high levels.

Binder, 'Gitano' Hahnemann,[104] Matthias Kaburek and the more seasoned Karl Zischek,[105] a right-winger who had taken part in the World Cup.

Unlike in the national team, Sindelar's leadership remained intact and undisputed at Austria Vienna. The club, which had once again qualified for the Mitropa through victory in the Austrian Cup, defeated Austrian coach Rappan's[106] Grasshoppers in the preliminary round. Rappan and his team had been in a bad way: during the journey to Austria for the first leg of the match, the train on the Paris–Vienna route had derailed. Luckily for them, no players were injured.

Jenő Konrád, who had replaced Josef Blum the previous year, took over as coach of Austria Vienna. Konrád had started his coaching career at the Favoriten club[107] after hanging up his boots. During the following years he toured Europe, coaching in Romania, Germany and Czechoslovakia before returning to Vienna. In addition to 'The Paper Man' and captain Nausch, Austria Vienna had retained cup-winning players from 1933, such as Stroh, Mock, Viertl and the now matured Jerusalem, and had newcomers such as goalkeeper Zöhrer and the rock-solid national defender Sesta, a 1931 WAC finalist.

---

104 Hahnemann was born in Vienna to Viennese parents: however, teammates and fans called him 'Gitano' (Gypsy) because of his dark features.

105 Although Zischek was one of the best wingers in the world at the time, he never played in the Mitropa Cup. This was due to the fact that his club, Sportclub Wacker, never qualified.

106 Rappan, who years earlier had been a footballer and had played a few games in the national team with some players of Austria Vienna, is considered by many sources as the inventor of the 'Catenaccio' system of defence, although there are many who refute this, claiming that 'Le Verrou', his formation, is actually a forerunner of the 4-2-4.

107 Favoriten is the tenth district of the Austrian capital where Austria Vienna play their home matches.

* * *

The match was certainly not a good one: as winners of the Austrian Cup, the 'Violets' had to face Bologna, newly crowned Italian champions and the only team, together with Sparta, to have lifted the trophy twice. In the Italian dugout was Árpád Weisz, an institution in Italian football who is credited with the development of Giuseppe Meazza and who, three years earlier, at the helm of Ambrosiana, had faced Sindelar and his team-mates in a two-legged final full of controversy. This time, however, the odds were in his favour.

The first match, in Bologna's impregnable fortress in front of 20,000 spectators, was played in the typical summer weather that had characterised previous years' matches in the city: 44°C, which did not deter Italian fans from coming to the stadium. Bologna started aggressively and almost immediately found the way to the goal with a precise header from Maini before Schiavio, following a solo run by Reguzzoni, scored again for the Italians in the 22nd minute.

In the second half Austria, who had appeared soft in the first half, increased their efforts: Sindelar forced his way into the red-blue defence and when he was about to shoot he was brought down. Viertl converted the penalty kick and reduced the deficit. There were 23 minutes to go but the Austrians' attempts to score again were in vain. Despite Bologna's victory, Vittorio Pozzo argued after the game that a one-goal lead against a team like Austria was nothing and that 'The Paper Man' and his team-mates were favourites for the return leg. *Sport-Tagblatt* was not of the same opinion: they wrote a column in which they praised the class of the Italian team and expressed concern about the challenge in Vienna.

Austria Vienna fielded the same team, but Bologna arrived at the match without Schiavio and with two question marks: the presence of Fiorini and Corsi, both coming back from injury. Of the two, only Fiorini would play. The atmosphere at the Prater was not so different from that of Bologna: 32,000 spectators had occupied the stands convinced of a possible comeback.

After only 11 minutes the Austrians took the lead. In the seventh minute, Sindelar had hit the crossbar from a distance but four minutes later, Jerusalem scored from a free kick on the edge of the area. A few minutes passed and the situation repeated itself: Jerusalem earned and took another free kick from the same distance but this time the crossbar said no. With the aggregate score in perfect parity, the home team sought the advantage with greater insistence, taking advantage of the brilliant form of 'The Paper Man'. In the 30th minute, Stroh turned a corner-kick scramble into the net to make it 2-0 to the Viennese before, late in the first half and early in the second, Zöhrer repeatedly denied Bologna's forwards the joy of scoring. Between the 88th and 90th minutes Sindelar and Jerusalem converted two more easy chances and the 4-0 final score left little room for argument.

* * *

A week after the match against Bologna, the Prater was once again packed for the first leg of the quarter-final between Austria and Slavia, a team that could not count on forwards Svoboda, Sobotka and Puč, all coming back from injuries sustained at the end of the championship.

The first half ended in a disappointing 0-0, underlined by boos from a crowd resigned to an unsatisfactory scoreline ahead of the trip to Prague. The biggest thrill was a spectacular acrobatic save by Plánička from Matthias Sindelar's 16th-minute shot before Zöhrer prevented a Czechoslovakian striker from scoring.

György Sárosi, the main star of the Ferencváros team which won the Mitropa Cup twice

Josef Bican, Slavia's centre-forward, in ordinary clothes

Giuseppe Meazza never won the Mitropa Cup but was unanimously regarded as one of the key players of inter-war football

Karel Pešek, better known as Káďa, the first captain who lifted the Mitropa Cup

Béla Guttmann has gone down in football history for having won the European Cup twice. However, the first international trophy he won as a coach was the Mitropa Cup in 1939

Angelo Schiavio, two-time winner with Bologna (1932/1934)

Matthias Sindelar, one of the most influential players of the period, in action
Bezirkmuseum Favoriten

Comité de la Coupe de l'Europe Centrale am Como See (Lago di Como)

Cav.Gaudenzi   Signesi   Cav.Barlassina

Dr.Fodor Ing.Fischer,Gen.Sekr.Petru,Hugo Meisl,Major Tesar,Commendatore
Avv.Mauro,Dr.Ing.Barassi,OLGR Fikeis,Dir.Valousek,Zoppini

Martha Meisl,Cav.Coppola,St.A.Dr.Gerö,Prof.Dr.Pelikan.

Hugo Meisl gathers with the Committee of the Mitropa Cup by Lake Como
Hugo Meisl Archiv Hafer

The pressure from the Austrians increased in the second period: Karl Sesta came to the fore and, thanks to Slavia's reluctant attitude, as they were now intent on defending the draw, he moved up a position and became an additional midfielder. Austria took the lead in the 61st minute when Riegler took advantage of a perfect combination between Sindelar and Stroh. Seven minutes later Jerusalem kicked the ball weakly towards goal, but fortunately for him it reached Stroh who once again found the back of the net. Slavia increased their attacks and were denied two goals, both for offside, by Vytlačil and Vacek, the youngest player in the competition at the time, aged only 16. The third goal for the Austrians was scored by Jerusalem with an assist from Sindelar.

The return match, refereed by the Italian Scorzoni, was played in a typical Prague atmosphere: a large crowd, despite the rain, supported Slavia without interruption for the whole 90 minutes. From the start, the match followed the opposite script to the first leg: Slavia were on the attack and Austria were entrenched at the back. Bradáč, the Czechoslovaks' best player, came close to scoring several times, but Zöhrer was able to save on more than one occasion. In the 67th minute the striker at least scored one consolation goal: Vytlačil went down the wing, crossed and Zöhrer, who had first deflected the ball out of the box and then saved Kopecký's shot, could do nothing about the Bohemian striker's rebound. But that goal was not enough: Austria Vienna went through to face Újpest in the semi-finals.

* * *

Újpest were recent acquaintances of the Austrians, as they had met two years earlier. On that occasion the Hungarians had qualified for the round of 16 after a fierce double-header: four penalties were awarded in the first leg, some of which were highly disputed, and towards the end of the game Austrian Viertl and Hungarian defender Seres were sent off for fighting. The away match in Budapest was reportedly attended by a number of Austrian fans who took advantage of a promotion by Schenker & Co. offering trips to the Hungarian capital for only 25 schillings.

Újpest started on the attack and took the lead through Kállai in the fifth minute. The Hungarians continued to attack but the Austrians, thanks once again to their goalkeeper, managed to hold out. Fear swept through the fans and the Austrian players when, towards the end of the first half, Zöhrer collided with Sesta and was injured for a few minutes. Referee Barlassina gave the nod to continue after the Austrian goalkeeper had received treatment from Dr Schwarz, the club's president and doctor. As he was leaving the field, Schwarz was attacked by the Magyar striker Kocsis, who was convinced that the opponents' president was trying to waste a few minutes. Sesta came to Schwarz's defence and the police, who had intervened on the pitch following an invasion by Hungarian fans, managed to break up the melee.

In the second half Sindelar and his team-mates reacted by finding the equaliser through Stroh[108] and then the winning goal through Viertl ten minutes from the end, despite the Hungarians having complained about a handball before the forward flew towards the opposition's goal. Ferenc Langfelder, Újpest's president, pointed the finger at the lack of strength of his forwards, especially Pusztai, who he said was guilty of kicking an easy ball into Zöhrer's hands. Nausch, captain of the Austrians, said that

108 Some reports of the time attributed the goal to an own goal by the Hungarian goalkeeper Hóri: Stroh's shot hit the post and then, after being deflected on to the goalkeeper's head, ended up in the goal.

in his opinion the return match was open to any result. Barlassina also spoke at the end of the match. He pointed out the Hungarians' bad luck in the first half and justified his decision to give the second Austrian goal by claiming that the Viennese's touch was unintentional.

The return match was played under the orders of Czechoslovak Krist and in front of a large crowd, as 50,000 Austrian fans filled the stands of the Prater, confident of a successful outcome. However, after a shot from the Austrian striker Stroh had hit the post, Gyula Zsengellér, the rising star of Hungarian football, gave Újpest the lead with a great solo goal. After that, Camilo Jerusalem took the initiative, first hitting the post with a free kick and then scoring the equaliser.

The second half began with no team dominating. Újpest went 2-1 up with another Zsengellér goal before Austria took control of the game: Sindelar equalised in the 52nd minute with a solo effort and then, after a violent clash between Zsengellér and Zöhrer, Jerusalem, Sindelar – with one of his well-known splendid shots from distance – and Stroh brought the result to 5-2 between the 56th and the 69th minutes. The Austrians went on holiday with high spirits, conscious of the fact that in September another appointment with history would be waiting for them.

* * *

In the final Austria found the reigning champions Sparta, a team who had once again established themselves as one of the strongest on the continent, thanks in large part to their attack: Braine, Nejedlý, Zajíček and Faczinek had scored a total of 17 goals. *Sport-Tagblatt* claimed that the match between Austria and Sparta represented the *crème de la crème* of European football: Sindelar and Braine were mentioned as the strongest forwards on the continent, while Mock and Bouček were considered the best centre-halves. Bouček, interviewed by Austrian journalists as soon as Sparta arrived in Vienna for the first leg, answered a question about Sindelar: 'He is a great player for whom I have great respect. The last time I faced him he played very well in the first half, but then spent himself in the second half. I wonder if he'll be able to hold out for the whole game this time.'

A total of 42,000 spectators filled the stands when the Italian Scarpi blew for the start of the match. It was a hard-fought game right from the start and the two most admired champions, Sindelar and Braine, lit up the contest. The first chance fell to the Belgian who, after an individual breakaway, was stopped at the last moment by Nausch. Then Austria and 'The Paper Man' switched on: the Austrian centre-forward and Adamek were close to scoring three times, but partly due to bad luck – Sindelar hit a post – and partly due to the skill of the imposing Bohemian goalkeeper, the first period ended with a draw.

In the second half the first goal came from the Czechoslovak captain, the veteran Burgr, a player who had played in the Mitropa every year and who had the chance to crown a wonderful European career with a goal in the final. Unfortunately, however, his double shot hit the left post both times. In the final minutes, Sparta's goalkeeper Klenovec took centre stage. The 0-0 final score seemed to be in favour of the Czechs. Although Austria were dissatisfied with the result, they were delighted with the 200,000 schillings they received, 11,000 of which went to First Vienna, who had given up their league game that day to allow the final to take place.

Exactly one week later the decisive match was played. The Masaryk Stadium crowd of 60,000 spectators was so large that the police had to intervene to move everyone back a few paces, otherwise corners and throw-ins could not be taken. Despite expectations, Austria were in control in the first half, but several opportunities created by Sindelar and his team-mates were foiled by the Bohemian defence.

The second half began with the Austrians showing more pace and they scored in the 56th minute through Stroh, but his goal was disallowed for offside. In the 67th minute, Riegler escaped down the flank, crossed into the middle and Jerusalem headed home a short clearance from the goalkeeper. Before Sparta's final siege, Stroh failed to capitalise on another good chance in the 83rd minute. Referee Barlassina's final whistle signalled victory for Austria, who were able to lift the second Mitropa Cup in their history, a record they shared with Bologna and Sparta. Both Meisl and Pelikan, his Czechoslovak counterpart, agreed the result was the right one.

Austria's victory was yet another confirmation of a curious trend that survives to this day: the tendency of certain teams to shine in the cups and less so in the league. Austria Vienna were the case in point: except on one occasion, in 1934, the club had always qualified for the Mitropa through victory in the Austrian Cup and at the end of fairly anonymous championships that usually ended in mid-table.

It was a classic team victory, the success of a strong and cohesive group which was a blend of leaders who had already been champions three years before, and new, young elements of undisputed value.

1937 – DR SÁROSI'S STAR SHINES

The 1937 meeting was the first one Meisl did not attend. The father of European football had died a month and a half earlier of a heart attack. Meisl had not been in the best of health for years, which is why he had taken leave of absence from Vienna and football in 1929 in order to recuperate. Over the years he had never managed to separate himself from two vices: smoking and coffee. On the fateful day, 17 February 1937, he was as busy as ever: he had summoned Richard Fischer, a young footballer from First Vienna, to question him about his age. He wanted to get to the bottom of it, as the First Vienna coach had told him three years in a row that Fischer was 17. While they were chatting, Meisl felt sick, went outside, came back in, and a second later he collapsed on the desk. Fischer ran for help but unfortunately, when Emanuel Schwarz, doctor and president of Austria Vienna, arrived a few minutes later, he could only ascertain the cause of death.

Condolences came from all quarters: Richard Eberstaller, president of the Austrian federation, underlined Meisl's sporting and diplomatic merits in shaping the world of football while Jules Rimet, with whom Meisl had collaborated in the organisation of the World Cup, travelled the same day to attend the funeral. Testimonials were printed by newspapers all over Europe: the Excelsior in Paris said goodbye to the 'Napoleon of Austrian football' and La Gazzetta dello Sport called Meisl 'the Wizard of Austrian football and a comrade who did everything possible to further the interests of Italian football'. Other European sports newspapers of the time, including Prager Presse and Nemzeti Sport, expressed themselves along the same lines. The Hungarian federation proposed renaming the competition the Meisl Cup, an idea that was later abandoned.

However, from Germany there was silence: Kicker, the main sports magazine of the Third Reich, was the only one to report the news a few days later. But it did so with a bare paragraph that only specified that the funeral had taken place and that some sports personalities had attended. Not a line about Hugo Meisl's sporting and diplomatic achievements nor about the cause of death. But the most surprising thing was the fact that the column was written by Max Leuthe, in his youth among Hugo Meisl's best friends, a journalist with whom the coach often talked about football at the Cafe Ring and other coffee houses in the capital.[109]

---

109 The two had also been colleagues at the Neues Wiener Sportblatt and then took different paths: Hugo Meisl had started to devote himself mainly to management and to his commitments with the federation, while Leuthe had expanded his contacts in journalism. One of these was Kikeriki, an openly anti-Semitic magazine later banned in 1934 by the Dollfuss government as a supporter of Adolf Hitler's movement and the Anschluss. It seems that Leuthe, at first far from certain political positions, joined the National Socialist cause a few years later. In 1938 he is said to have obtained a party card claiming to have been a member of the movement for years, even at a time when it was formally illegal.

For the 1937 edition of the Mitropa, the committee decided to admit the winners of the Romanian and Yugoslavian championships, while confirming the participation of the Swiss teams. This time, the Swiss federation could enter its two best teams without having to go through a preliminary round. To accommodate them, the four 'historic' federations, Austria, Hungary, Czechoslovakia and Italy, had to reduce their entry from four to three teams each. A week before the start of the event, the International Tournament of the Exposition Universelle was played in Paris: Bologna won the third international title in their history after eliminating Sochaux, Slavia Prague and Chelsea.

* * *

HUNGARY AND its teams had paid more of a price for the Italian football boom than Austria. The national team had not won any trophies and the Hungarian teams had not been successful in the Mitropa Cup since 1929, the year Újpest won. The only team that had managed to fly the flag was '*Fradi*', who had come close to success two years earlier, only to be defeated in the final. There was a big problem: the World Cup was just around the corner and for Alfréd Schaffer,[110] coach of the national team and once a legend of Austrian and Hungarian football, the signals were not the most comforting, despite some talents that had emerged at national and European level: Gyula Zsengellér, star of Újpest, and especially György Sárosi,

---

110 Schaffer was regarded in Vienna and Budapest as an outstanding player like no other. He had been a team-mate of a young Matthias Sindelar at Austria Vienna and was renowned for his exuberant character and constant financial demands.

now in his prime and definitely consecrated as undisputed leader of Ferencváros, were certainly the brightest stars in the Magyar football firmament. Originally a centre-half, 'Gyurka', the nickname given to him by his fans, started to play as a striker even if sometimes, according to the needs of his coach and his flexibility, he was deployed to support the forwards or went back to his original position. In other words, he was the Magyar equivalent of the Belgian Raymond Braine, although taller and stronger. Another of his outstanding qualities was his goalscoring: he was top scorer in the Hungarian championship, the International Cup and the 1935 Mitropa Cup.

In the previous years, Ferencváros's coaching line-up had changed: after the Blum era, ended in the first months of 1937, the job had been entrusted first to Sándor Bródy, but only for one match, due to an illness that had affected the former midfielder, and then to József Sándor, the coach who began the European journey of 'Fradi' that year.

* * *

Ferencváros, who were facing Slavia in the round of 16, had left for Czechoslovakia a few days earlier than usual. The group, consisting of 13 players, the coach and two staff members, had not revealed where they would be staying. No one knew, neither reporters nor their opponents. The coach and the president had decided to prepare for the match in complete peace and quiet, and for this reason the 'green-and-whites' stayed in a small village not far from Prague, Jiloviště, at the Hotel Hubertus, where they could rest and prepare for the match. There was a great desire for revenge in the 'Fradi' camp: the Hungarians had lost the national title in a last-gasp match against MTK. Their defeat against Elektromos, a now defunct club from the Hungarian capital, had been decisive.

The day of the match arrived and from the start, Slavia took the initiative and created several chances, which were foiled by the Hungarian goalkeeper Háda. However, on the half-hour he was beaten by Sobotka to give Slavia the lead. The goal didn't demotivate 'Fradi', as Sárosi, who up to that moment didn't seem to be having a great day, scored the equaliser with some great individual skill.[111]

The second half began with an attacking Ferencváros hitting two posts through Toldi and Táncos and then, in the 65th minute, Toldi himself reaped the benefits of the Hungarian dominance to put his side ahead. Only then did Slavia wake up and on one of their last attacks they scored the equaliser through Vytlačil.

The post-match comments were unanimous: the Prague newspapers acknowledged the superiority of the Magyars and the coach of the Hungarians said: 'The goals we didn't score today we saved for the return match in Budapest. Why couldn't Sárosi and Toldi score more goals? Maybe because of what Kutasi said,[112] we were too relaxed after spending wonderful sunny days in nature and resting on beautiful four-poster beds.'

Pelikan spoke of a hard-fought game, praising the Hungarian defenders and also pointing his finger at the forwards' poor scoring streak.

In preparation for the return match, which would take place exactly two weeks later, Ferencváros adopted the same strategy as the first leg: they isolated themselves in Budakeszi, a small town near Budapest, far away from everything and everyone.[113] The return leg was on 27 June.

---

111 In those years Hungarian newspapers often referred to Ferencváros as 'Sárosi and family'.

112 Kutasi was Ferencváros's backup goalkeeper.

113 Ferencváros's country retreats would become a routine throughout the competition.

Slavia, now an underdog because of the home result, had their striker Antonin Puč back from injury. Under the orders of Austrian referee Miesz, the match began and Ferencváros missed several opportunities in the opening minutes. Then they found the goal in the 32nd minute thanks to Toldi's header following Kiss's assist. That small advantage did not reassure the Hungarians: during the interval the players, the coach and the president – and founder – Springer discussed animatedly how to approach the second half. Sárosi, who had struggled in the first half, asked if he could change positions.

The 'green-and-whites' were back on the pitch with more energy than ever, doubling the score thanks to Sárosi – another header from just a few paces – and scoring the third goal in the 65th minute through Toldi, before Puč's shot deflected off Tátrai's back to make it 3-1 with a minute remaining. Toldi himself commented on the victory: 'We were stiff in the first half, then in the second half we loosened up and won deservedly.' He was echoed by Czechoslovakian defender Daučik,[114] who said '*Fradi*' deserved to win thanks to their better attack.

* * *

The quarter-finals pitted Ferencváros against First Vienna, a team that had gone downhill in recent years. They

---

114 Nicknamed 'Nandi' or 'Gandhi', Daučik was to have an intense life and career in later years. During the war years he enlisted in the anti-German resistance and in the years after the Second World War, having become a target of the Communists, he fled to Italy. Near Cinecittà he trained a team of footballers fleeing the Soviet regime, the Hungarian, among whom was László Kubala. Following a tour in Spain during which the Hungarian defeated the Iberian national team, Kubala was contracted by Barcelona but by virtue of an existing clause, the Catalans also had to put under contract the coach, who was Daučik's brother-in-law. In Spain Daučik, who also coached Athletic Bilbao and Zaragoza, won three championships and six Spanish Cups.

qualified for the quarter-finals after a hard-fought battle with Swiss side Young Boys, which lasted until the play-offs. In spite of this, the '*Döblingers*' boasted a well-tested team composed of several elements that had been playing together for years. Four players who had won the Mitropa in 1931 would be on the pitch that day: the iconic centre-forward Gschweidl, now 36 but still unmovable, Rainer, Erdl and the centre-back Hoffmann. '*Fradi*' had been forced to make some changes. Lázár had just recovered from an injury, but Kemény could not make it: in his place the young forward Gyetvai made his debut after joining the first team only two days before.

At 6pm on 4 July, the teams took the field with Italian referee Scarpi. The crowd in Budapest welcomed their favourites with chants and roars of all kinds, but then, after just a few minutes, First Vienna began to put pressure on the goalkeeper Háda who could not do anything about Pollack's goal. It was a valid goal, despite the fact that the Hungarians had protested for an offside. But only four minutes later, in the 12th minute, a misunderstanding between the defenders gave the ball to Sárosi who with an unstoppable shot, tied the score.

Ferencváros started to attack with more insistence and after some unsuccessful attempts they made it 2-1 in the 24th minute: Toldi shot from distance and the Austrian goalkeeper missed the ball, before catching it. However, it had already crossed the line and the referee awarded the goal.

The second half of the match also underlined the superiority of the Hungarians, at least for half an hour. However, Sándor's team waned as the minutes passed and First Vienna took courage and came close to equalising. In the 86th minute '*Fradi*' had a chance to add to their haul: amidst vehement protests from their opponents, the referee awarded a penalty kick, which Tatrai kicked over the crossbar. On the restart First Vienna were denied a penalty on the grounds that the foul had occurred outside the area. The first leg ended amid fierce controversy.

The first winds of war were blowing over the world. Four days before the return match, Japan had invaded China. The Japanese occupation had actually begun much earlier, in 1931, when the Japanese army took possession of Manchuria and turned it into a puppet state. The expansion continued gradually until it reached the northern city of Fengtai, a railway junction near the Lugouqiao Bridge, where the incident that provoked the advance of the Chinese army took place. It was but the prelude to a series of armed conflicts that would devastate the world.

In an increasingly uncertain political climate, although there were no signs that a conflict would break out in Europe, the return match between Ferencváros and First Vienna was played. It was 11 July 1937, and the hours leading up to the match were marked by controversy: the Viennese had complained about the appointment of the referee, Bízik, because the Czechoslovakian was born in Ruttka, a town that was part of Hungary at the time. Bízik spoke Hungarian and had also refereed some matches in the Hungarian league. In the end the protests died down and Bízik refereed the match as planned. Unbelievably, it would be the Hungarians themselves who would complain about the way the match was handled.

In the pouring rain, the match began with Ferencváros, whose team was weakened by injuries, more proactive. They created several scoring chances but in the 20th minute, due to a collision – totally accidental, according to the 'green-and-whites' – between Korányi and one of the Austrian forwards, First Vienna were awarded a penalty and Pollack scored, which brought the aggregate score back to a draw. At the end of the game, *Nemzeti Sport* did not hide their disappointment: 'You can only laugh at such a decision. Or cry,' wrote the Budapest newspaper.

'*Fradi*' were not discouraged and Sárosi masterfully launched his younger team-mates towards the goal, but they weren't calm enough to take their chances. The first half ended with Korányi disconsolate. It seems that in the changing room he said to his companions, 'Because of me we will have to play a third game,' but his team-mates encouraged him, pointing out the referee's mistake.

The hostilities resumed and the Hungarians again had a few complaints about the conduct of the referee. Sárosi was even heard to exclaim: 'Is that a referee?' Bízik did not even give a foul when the young Jakab had to leave the field injured. The diagnosis in the following hours was a fractured ankle.

The match continued with the Hungarians perhaps playing even better with ten men, although First Vienna came close to doubling the score in the end. The intense and controversial double-header was not enough to produce a winner: three days later, on 14 July, the teams would be back on the pitch in Budapest for the play-off. Numerous injuries in the Hungarians' ranks would force Sárosi back to his original position of centre-half, a not insignificant handicap, since the prolific streak of the Magyar striker would have been very useful in such a match.

In the first half Sándor's plans worked: his team created one chance after another and in the 24th minute they took the lead through Toldi. The striker's shot bounced off the foot of Austrian Machu and into the net. At the end of the first half '*Fradi*' doubled their lead: this time the goal was scored by Toldi, who beat the Hungarian goalkeeper with a shot from 15 metres after a corner kick.

In the second half, partly because of the Viennese reaction and partly because Ferencváros seemed to have qualification in their pockets, First Vienna attacked hard. Kaller made it 2-1 after a breakaway on the left and the Austrians continued to press. The game became heated: Tátrai tackled Pollack and a team-mate of the latter's attacked Tátrai. Then, towards the end, in a clash with Toldi, Kaller was injured. He left the field and returned shortly afterwards with a bandaged hand. But there was no more time: the match ended 2-1 and the Hungarians had won.

At the end of the match Polgár, a Hungarian player who had not played that day, declared: 'I lost two kilos in the second half. My nerves were completely gone.' Springer, the president, expressed his concern: 'We really gave everything, we are exhausted, I don't know how we will face Austria Vienna in the semi-final.' Ferencváros versus Austria Vienna in 1937 meant above all Sárosi versus Sindelar: the best of European football at that time.

* * *

Austria Vienna returned to the Mitropa Cup as defending champions. Between the round of 16 and the quarter-finals, they had proved their worth: they had defeated two giants, Bologna and Újpest, winning all four matches. Sindelar had scored on every occasion and looked fitter than ever, and despite suffering a slight injury in the return match against Újpest, he was able to play.

In front of a crowd of 40,000 people, Austria Vienna started off on the offensive: Jerusalem scored in the 14th minute and Sindelar doubled the score in the 38th. Sárosi, in his original position of centre-half, seemed to be groping in the dark.

But at the beginning of the second half, it was his goal that reduced the deficit: the Hungarians' star scored with a penalty kick awarded for a foul committed by Austria's Andritz. Austria took back the reins of the game and between the 57th and the 62nd minutes, Jerusalem and Sindelar made the score 4-1. A minute later 'The Paper Man' scored again but this time the referee disallowed it for offside.

At the end of the game Sárosi said that the goal was clearly invalid. He said he realised it immediately and asked the referee to consult the linesman, who after a few moments took the correct decision. Interviewed at the end of the match, Sindelar spoke of a deserved victory and said he could not wait to play in Budapest. 'The Paper Man', who besides the goal had provided all three assists for the goals of his team-mates, had been the best player on the field. *Sportagblatt* was in raptures: 'There *is only one Sindelar!*' wrote the newspaper. The opponents also showed their appreciation: *Nemzeti Sport* said that Austria Vienna were the best team in the history of the Mitropa. Looking ahead to the return leg, there was a feeling of pessimism among the Hungarians, which was not shared by Sárosi, who said he expected Ferencváros to be better than in the first leg. The striker mentioned the Easter friendly match that '*Fradi*' had won a few months earlier against Austria: the match, which had marked Sándor's debut as the Hungarian coach, had ended 7-2. The Hungarians' hopes rested mainly on that recent precedent.[115]

On 25 July the teams took to the pitch for the return match in front of 22,000 spectators who seemed to believe their team could win. The start was comforting for the

---

115 A curiosity: Sándor's brief stint at the helm of the club began and ended with two matches against Austria Vienna, the last being the semi-final return leg of the Mitropa Cup.

Hungarians: '*Fradi*' immediately took the initiative and began to besiege Zöhrer's goal. The first goal came in the seventh minute thanks to Kemény's header. The Hungarian players and public were even more galvanised when Sárosi increased the lead with a cannon shot in the 25th minute. Sindelar followed him two minutes before the end of the first half and the teams went into the dressing room with a 2-1 scoreline, a scoreline that left the Austrians feeling comfortable.

'*Fradi*' didn't give up, on the contrary, they dominated the match and thanks to another long-distance shot, this time by Kiss, they made the score 3-1. Only one goal was needed to grab the play-off place: it came shortly afterwards thanks to Kemény, who made the most of a serpentine run through the opposing defence. The 'green-and-whites' were not satisfied with the draw and kept pressing: Sárosi, who also had the ability to break away, pounced on a cross from the wing, overpowered Sesta and Nausch and beat Zöhrer to make it 5-1. The triumph was sealed a few minutes later by Toldi's sixth goal from a pass by Táncos. The match ended 6-1 and Ferencváros deservedly reached the final. The police struggled to contain the enthusiasm of the crowd that invaded the field carrying on their shoulders some of their favourites, Sárosi and Toldi above all.

'*Miracle!*' wrote a Budapest newspaper the following day. Curiously enough, at the end of the first leg, the president of the Hungarians had said: 'I am convinced that we will give our fans a nice surprise and that we will qualify for the final without going through the play-off.' A prediction at the limits of prescience.

For Austria, the European adventure had come to an end, as it had for Matthias Sindelar, who that day had played his last match in the competition. He left the Mitropa stage with his head held high: as an undisputed leader, he had led his team, a team that had never excelled in the championship, to two triumphs and that year, at the age of almost 35, he had brought them one step closer to the umpteenth final. He was certainly one of the most important players in the history of the event.

* * *

After eliminating three famous teams like Bologna, Újpest and Austria Vienna, Sárosi and his team-mates found an unexpected protagonist in their path, the classic underdog: Lazio, a team in which the star of centre-forward Silvio Piola had begun to shine. Piola, an extraordinary striker known above all for his maniacal professionalism, was in his prime and was coming off a splendid season on a personal level: he had become the league's top scorer with 21 goals that had allowed Lazio to finish just behind Árpád Weisz's Bologna. He had also scored important goals on the way to the final: seven goals out of 11 bore his signature.

Over the years the presence of Hungarian coaches in the Italian league had remained constant and Lazio were no exception as József Violak sat in their dugout. Nicknamed 'Viola' by the Italian newspapers, the coach had already worked with several Italian teams and as a player/coach had won a title with Juventus in 1924/25, but now, for the first time, he had the chance to compete in Europe. The team, until a few years earlier nicknamed 'Brasilazio' due to the large number of players of Brazilian origin, had no league titles to their name and thus risked repeating the feat of Újpest eight years earlier, which was to win their first European title before their first national title.

The 'Biancocelesti' had come to play for the cup without having to play their semi-final because of the cancellation of the second-leg match between Genova and Admira due to the riots that took place in Vienna towards the end of the first leg.[116] The tensions that were felt on the field reflected those that had been governing relations between Austria and Italy for some time: an Italy that not even too tacitly had begun to wink at Adolf Hitler's Germany. A few months earlier, the grudges had also manifested themselves in an International Cup match: towards the end of the first half, the challenge between Austria and Italy had turned into a brawl. The referee, after a series of warnings, was forced to suspend the match while the second half was in progress. It was the first match in history between two national teams to be invalidated.

* * *

Contrary to previous years, the final was supposed to be held in August but because of the controversy concerning the semi-final between Genova and Admira, the date was postponed to September. This messed up the Hungarian manager's plans since Sándor, whose contract ended before the beginning of the new championship, had left the 'Fradi' backroom staff, without being able to play the final he had earned a place in during the previous months. The team was entrusted to Emil Rauchmaul, a coach with a modest curriculum vitae and a figure about whom not much is known. He had been a footballer, had fought during the Great War – even being awarded an honour – and had then started his career as a coach. He had passed through Bocskai and that year he was presented with the best opportunity of his career: to coach 'Fradi' with

---

116 The referee had awarded a disputed penalty to the Austrians which Schall converted. A scuffle ensued which led to the expulsion of the Italian Agosteo and the departure of Morselli, who ended up with a fractured jaw. A few days later the Austrians set off for Italy for the return game and learned en route that Mussolini had decided to cancel the match. In the following days the committee would exclude both teams from the competition.

a chance of lifting the most coveted European title of the time.

Polgár, urged on by a journalist interviewing him on the eve of the match, had claimed that rather than let Piola pass he would get sent off, for which he was reprimanded by the Hungarian federation.[117] The Hungarian newspapers also dwelled on a particular event: Sárosi had graduated in law and from that moment, except for his own fans, 'Gyurka' would become 'Dr Sárosi'.

The 30,000 people who came to the stadium on 12 September sang the chorus 'Hajrá Fradi' as one man. It was the kind of crowd that many of the Lazio players were not used to. The game began with the Hungarians slightly on top but they did not create any real scoring opportunities. The first goal came in the 22nd minute thanks to Toldi's attack from the left, from which he stepped in front of Blason and beat him. But the public's enthusiasm subsided only four minutes later when Busani, in a scrum, scored the equaliser. The first half ended 1-1 and in the 15 minutes that followed, excited voices were heard from both dressing rooms. The president of 'Fradi', who had joined his team, gave his players clear advice: 'Control the ball better.'

The second half started with Ferencváros dominating. The tendency of Lazio to lose focus in some phases of the match was well known but, considering the importance of the match and the quality of the opponents, this was not the time to do it. The Hungarians took the opportunity to besiege the Lazio area: first Sárosi scored after dribbling through three defenders and then, two minutes later, Toldi had a goal disallowed for a dubious charge on Blason. But

---

117 Such a statement might seem normal nowadays. However, in an era when there were no yellow cards and expulsions were granted almost only for clearly violent and deliberate conduct, his words carried a very different meaning.

in the 60th minute 'Dr Sárosi' made it 3-1 from the penalty spot after a foul by Baldo on Kémeny.

Lazio managed to reduce the deficit four minutes later through Piola, who collected a rebound off the Magyar goalkeeper from Costa's shot. Then, at a time when confidence in the 'Fradi' camp was beginning to waver, the Hungarians benefited from a second, very dubious, penalty for a tackle by Viani on Toldi. The infallible Sárosi made it 4-2.

The following day the Italian newspapers were furious with the Czechoslovakian referee Krist even though, to tell the truth, they said that in their opinion it was not deliberate bias and admitted that some decisions had also been to the detriment of the Hungarians. The newspapers agreed that the second Ferencváros penalty should not have been given, but added that there could have been two more. It was typical of the national bias which characterised both politics and sport in those days. Toldi, who at the end of the match had bickered with Piola and had been accused by the Italians of having threatened the striker, said he was sure of the final victory: an optimism that was perhaps excessive, given that a two-goal difference did not represent such a reassuring margin.

The Hungarian team arrived in Italy two days before the return match. As always, in order to enjoy more peace and quiet and distance from the crowds, the players took refuge in the countryside, this time in the hills of Frascati. Between the two finals, Sárosi had put in an unforgettable performance in the International Cup: Hungary had beaten Czechoslovakia 8-3 and the striker had beaten Plánička seven times.[118]

---

118 The record of that match still stands today: no Hungarian footballer has scored more than seven goals in a single international match.

The match began on a soggy pitch. Light drizzle was falling in Rome, on ground which had been hit by heavy downpours a few days earlier. In addition to a large number of Hungarian fans, there were several Italian, Hungarian and international celebrities present at the stadium, unrelated to the world of football, such as the famous writer Aszlányi,[119] who wore a bizarre green hat, and the famous American actor Powell, who, to the disappointment of the Italian journalists, declared that he loved Hungarian football and therefore supported 'Fradi'.

Lazio immediately surged forward and after a few minutes Costa netted after good play from Piola and Camolese. The lead only lasted a matter of seconds as Swiss referee Wüthrich blew for a penalty in favour of the visitors. Kiss, chasing a flick by Sárosi, was brought down by Lazio's Monza,[120] although the ball seemed out of reach for the Hungarian.[121] Sárosi converted impeccably.

Lazio, demoralised, were at the mercy of their opponents for a few minutes and conceded another goal, to a header from Sárosi after a splendid team move. The Italians then woke up from their torpor and in the 19th minute, after a corner kick, Piola scored with a header to make it 2-2. The balance of the match changed completely and in the 36th minute Lazio, thanks to two more goals from Piola, levelled the aggregate score: the striker netted first by beating a defender to a cross from the right by Busani and then with a header from a free kick from Milano. But once again the enthusiasm of the Rome crowd

---

119 The following year Aszlányi, only 30 years old, is reported to have died after crashing into a tree.

120 Monza was a cousin of the left-winger Reguzzoni, a two-time champion with Bologna.

121 *La Gazzetta dello Sport* criticised that decision, claiming that in those cases, when an attack was destined to die down, Italian referees used to let things slide.

was dashed: a few moments later Toldi beat Provera – who was replacing Blason that day – with a shot. A first half full of thrills and spills ended 4-3 to the '*Biancocelesti*'. The star players, Piola and Sárosi, had put on a real show.

The second half followed a precise script: Lazio poured forward to look for the goal and the Hungarians tried to control the match. In the 61st minute there was another great opportunity for the home team. Piola was awarded a penalty but his shot, slow and central, was easily saved by Háda and then cleared by a defender. It was at that moment that Lazio's pressure eased. Ten minutes later Kiss equalised from a corner kick taken by Kemény and in the 80th minute Sárosi secured the result with a wonderful goal: he collected a back-heel cross from the right by Táncos and with a perfect bicycle kick slotted the ball in at the far post, leaving both the Lazio keeper and the Olimpico crowd stunned. '*Gyurka! Gyurka!*' the Hungarian fans shouted over and over from the stands as the 'green-and-white' players lifted their captain out of the mud and embraced him.

At the end of the match Sárosi criticised the strong tackles of the Italian defenders and jokingly commented on the goal: 'I was unlucky! I didn't manage to see one of my most beautiful goals because my back was turned.' Starace handed the cup to the Hungarian captain, won for the second time by the Budapest club. Pozzo spoke of a deserved victory due to the greater experience of the Hungarians and the referee Wüthrich called Sárosi the 'best player and strategist in the world'. Bela Nagy reports a curious statement made by Piola at the end of the match: 'I had started with the intention of kicking [the penalty] into the right corner but then, behind the goal and in front of the cup, Vittorio Pozzo signalled me to kick into the left one. In the end, in total confusion, I shot at the goalkeeper.'

1938 – JOSEF BICAN AND THE OTHER FACE OF PRAGUE

Between the evening of 11 March and 10 April 1938, Europe began its descent into the abyss. First the Austrian Chancellor Von Schuschnigg made a speech to the nation in which he resigned, concluding with the phrase 'God protect Austria.' Then, the following day, the Wehrmacht (Nazi army) marched on the Austrian capital. In Vienna, a city torn apart in the previous years by continuous protests and citizens' revolts, there were differing moods, but one was prevailing: many people looked favourably on the German invasion. Three days later, from the palace of the Hofburg, Hitler proclaimed in front of approximately 250,000 persons the union of the two nations into one great Reich. To legitimise the annexation a referendum was called for 10 April and, even if it suffered from some irregularities, it gave an almost unanimous result: 99.73 per cent of the voters crossed the box of the YES, expressing their assent to the unification between Germany and Austria.

In the preceding days Hitler's propaganda had done its utmost to boost turnout and gain the desired result. Among the celebrities the regime used to plead its cause were, of course, football stars. Exactly one week before the Austrian people went to the polls, a friendly match between Austria and Germany was organised with a double objective: on the one hand to publicise the cause of the YES vote, and on the other hand to seal the merger between the two national teams in[122] preparation for the upcoming World Cup in France. On the morning of the match, an article appeared in the *Völkischer Beobachter*, the newspaper of the National Socialist Party, which read: 'We players thank our Führer from the bottom of our hearts and we will vote YES!' Underneath it were the signatures of Austrian football icons such as Matthias Sindelar, Karl Sesta and Franz Binder.

Vienna was starting to become a fully fledged German city, and that metamorphosis would impact on every economic and social sphere. Sport was not spared: the International Cup was suspended with immediate effect and the Austrian championship, renamed Gauliga, became a sort of regional competition whose winner would challenge the winner of the other Gauligen to determine the best team of the Third Reich. In addition to the immediate expulsion of Jewish players, coaches, managers and journalists and the dismantling of the country's various Jewish-based clubs, Austrian football re-embraced the amateur model. This meant on the one hand that players would have to seek paid

---

122 The match was played in Vienna and ended 2-0 for the Austrians, with goals from Sindelar and Sesta.

employment,[123] and on the other hand that clubs in Vienna would say goodbye to the Mitropa, a competition that was the result of the transition to professionalism.[124] The Swiss teams also quit, for reasons of political expediency.

On 30 April, the committee, which in the meantime had decided to extend participation to two Yugoslav and Romanian teams, met to decide on the format and made one change: with the exception of the final, the drawing of lots (rather than a play-off) would decide the winner in the event of a draw after the first and return legs. The competition would start on 26 June.

* * *

THE WORLD Cup in France was a harbinger of confirmations and surprises: Italy had once again won the title, this time away from home and far from the suspicions and controversies of four years earlier. They had beaten Hungary in the final and Piola, who scored twice, had managed to avenge the defeat that Sárosi and his teammates had inflicted on Lazio the previous year. There were two main surprises: the premature exit of a Germany filled with Austrian players at the hands of Switzerland[125] and the even more unexpected defeat of Czechoslovakia

---

123 Matthias Sindelar, for example, who died in an accident in his partner's home on 23 January 1939, bought the Annahof, a café in his native Favoriten district.

124 At first, the possibility of including German teams in the Mitropa draw was mooted, but then the hypothesis was discarded. Without half-measures, Germany made it known that they did not want to take part in a competition invented by a Jew.

125 The first match had ended 1-1. The replay ended 4-2 to the Swiss.

against Brazil[126] at the end of a double-header. The first of these, which ended 1-1, would go down in history as one of the most violent encounters of all time, with a huge number of fouls resulting in three sendings-off and two serious injuries to the legends Nejedlý and Plánička. If Nejedlý recovered quickly enough, Plánička, who suffered a fractured arm and collarbone, said goodbye to his career that day. Doctors advised him to quit once they learned of an earlier injury the goalkeeper had suffered to the same arm in his youth.

So, another legend of Central European football left the competition, just as Matthias Sindelar had done. But what Plánička had achieved up to that day was more than enough to earn him a place in history: the 'Bohemian Swallow' (that was Plánička's nickname) had over the years stood out for his confidence, agility and ability to read the game. Rejected by Sparta, he had become a flagbearer for Slavia, a club to which he had inextricably linked his name. Plánička's move to Slavia had been a curious one: the goalkeeper, who at the time played for a smaller club called Bubeneč, insisted on joining Slavia despite his club's resistance, so he adopted the pseudonym Jakubec and went to Vienna for a friendly match with the Slavia team. Bubeneč heard about it and were not at all happy: they demanded a sanction for both the defender and Slavia. The dispute was taken to court and in the end, for a payment of 300 crowns, the goalkeeper saw his dream come true: he could finally wear the red and white colours. After a couple of years during which he competed with the more experienced Sloup-Štaplík, Plánička became an

---

126 At the time Brazil were not considered a major footballing superpower. They hadn't won as many honours as Uruguay and Argentina and their victory against Czechoslovakia was described as a 'triumph of will and commitment over technique'.

irreplaceable part of both his club and the national team. Over the years he had won eight league titles, six national cups and reached a World Cup final. Only one thing was missing: to win the Mitropa.

* * *

Plánička decided to wait before leaving the football world: in view of the upcoming edition of Mitropa, he took up the role of goalkeeper coach. To cope with the repeated physical problems suffered by some players over the years Slavia had decided to expand their technical staff by hiring three new athletic trainers. In 1936, when the first ailments started to affect the forwards Puč, Svoboda and Sobotka, the Prague club secured the services of a player who would be as much a part of the history of Slavia as Plánička: Josef Bican.

Born in Vienna of Bohemian parents,[127] Bican had been, in his youth, the undisputed favourite of Hugo Meisl, who praised his determination and hunger for success. He was a striker with extraordinary speed – he ran the 100 metres in 10.8 seconds – a strong header and an incredible nose for goal, a characteristic that would become his trademark over the years. After beginning his career at Hertha Vienna, the team for which his father František had played,[128] he moved on to Schustek und Farbenlutz, his employer's team, and then, scouted by Rapid defender Roman Schramseis, was signed by the green-and-white club. Here he became top scorer in the Austrian championship in 1934, an exploit that earned him a starting place at the World Cup. Only

---

127 He grew up on Quellengasse, the same street where Matthias Sindelar lived.

128 František Bican died in the early post-war period following an injury sustained during a match.

two years later, however, due to the player's financial demands, Bican moved to Admira although an official agreement had not been reached. Rapid had put up some initial resistance and decided to appeal in court. Meisl, who had been Bican's mentor, temporarily excluded the striker from the national team, threatening to suspend his contact for four years. The problem was solved and Bican was officially signed by Admira but only two years later the situation came up again: the striker accepted a deal from Slavia that offered him three villas and 150,000 kronen, an exorbitant sum for those times, as well as a record fee to the Austrian club. Admira, who at first had vetoed the operation and had seized the striker's passport, ended up accepting.

The first contact between Bican and Slavia had actually taken place years earlier, in 1933, when the player wore the Rapid jersey. Rapid and Slavia challenged each other in a friendly match in which Bican scored five goals and the Czechoslovaks, who initially wanted to buy Franz Binder, started to court Bican who, as legend would have it, replied: 'I'm Czechoslovakian and I've always been a Slavia fan; the day I leave, it will only be to wear your shirt.' That day would have arrived in the summer of 1936: Bican had come back to Sedlice u Blatné, his father's hometown, for his annual trip to spend his holidays, and there, during a picnic, he had been joined by Slavia's managers with a contract in tow. Those present shook hands and the deal was semi-officialised. That same day, Sparta's executives, trying to prevent Bican's transfer to their arch-rivals, had also approached the player. However, they had made a mistake: they had stopped to eat on the way and had thus arrived late. Their offer, although even more remunerative than that of their rivals, had been refused by the footballer. Bican would later recount: 'I arrived at the customs in

Břeclav on 15 April 1937. I handed my documents to the customs officers and after checking them and seeing the photo, they read my name and looked out the window. "So, you are Bican. We're good. You're finally here, we've been looking forward to this!'"

However, due to the dispute that had arisen, the inclusion of the striker was not immediate. Not only that: at first Bican was hated by his team-mates as he had agreed with Slavia to keep secret the details of his contract – which also included the match fees – something unusual at the time since the players knew how much their team-mates earned. For these reasons, the striker only started to appear permanently for the holders at the beginning of the 1937/38 season, replacing Sobotka, a player of great talent and class, but not very accustomed to team play and for some time at loggerheads with his managers. However, a series of vicissitudes meant Bican was unable to play in the 1938 World Cup: a few months after arriving in Prague, convinced that he would be able to become a citizen in a short time thanks to his origins, the striker had applied for a Czechoslovakian passport, which would have cancelled his Austrian one. But while the process was in progress the Anschluss intervened: this meant that the striker's original passport was no longer valid. Bican, who in the previous months had not answered the call of the German coach Herberger, refused to apply for the German passport and waited patiently for the bureaucratic process to obtain the Czechoslovak passport to be resolved.

Unfortunately, the hiccup lengthened the time it took and the document only arrived in August 1938 when the World Cup was already over. But there was one upside to that: Bican appeared on the Mitropa stage fresh, rested and in dazzling form.

* * *

The obstacle Slavia faced in the round of 16 was not insurmountable on paper. They were BSK Yugoslavia, an old acquaintance of Mitropa, having played in 1927 and 1928 before the Yugoslav federation was replaced by the Italian one.

The match in Belgrade began in front of 10,000 spectators with a script that lived up to expectations: Slavia on the attack and BSK in difficulty. In the eighth minute the Czechs went ahead thanks to an 'Olympic' goal from a corner kick by Vytlačil. A few minutes later Bradáč doubled the score after a serpentine run through the Yugoslav defence. In the 23rd minute Horák made it 3-0 thanks to a mistake by the goalkeeper who let the ball slip through his hands.

The second half began with Slavia giving the impression that victory was in their pocket. The Czechs' attitude gave the home side confidence and they poured forward in an attempt to reduce the deficit and towards the end of the game they succeeded, first through Podhradský and then Božović. Bokšay, Pláničkaʼs replacement, had his work cut out to prevent the final humiliation. Despite the debacle in those latter minutes, Slavia would go into the return leg with a one-goal lead.

The teams met four days later at the Letná Stadium. Despite the fact that a meeting of the Sokol, the largest Bohemian sports organisation, was scheduled for that day, the attendance was around 20,000. There was also a large contingent of Yugoslav fans who would cheer on their favourites from the first minute. After all, a one-goal difference was not an irreversible disadvantage. But the home crowd was suddenly silenced when Šimůnek gave Slavia the lead in the 12th minute. They kept the match in their grasp and continued to grind out their game without scoring any more goals before half-time.

In the 55th minute the Yugoslavs had a breakthrough when Podhradský took advantage of a mistake by Bokšay and opened up the tie that until then had been in Slavia's hands, as the corner count showed: 9-3. Slavia, who seemed to want the victory more than BSK believed in the comeback, continued to attack and in the 82nd minute they were awarded a penalty: Horák was brought down in the box and Bican scored his first international goal in a red and white shirt. The Yugoslavian defender Manola and 'Mosha' Marjanović, by now a legend of the Yugoslavian team, were sent off for insulting the referee. Despite not being particularly brilliant, the double-header went as predicted: Slavia qualified for the quarter-finals.

* * *

In the quarter-finals Slavia found Ambrosiana, a team that although not boasting an unforgettable tradition in the Mitropa Cup – they had played and lost only one final, in 1933 – were champions of Italy and had among their ranks some new world champions such as captain and talisman Giuseppe Meazza and midfielder Giovanni Ferrari. The two had played decisive roles in the previous round thanks to the goals they scored against the Hungarian team Kispest, a team that in 1938 were making their debut appearance on the international stage and that would be much more successful in the following years.

The first leg was played in Prague and began with repeated attacks by the Czechs but Šimůnek, Bradáč and Vytlačil were ineffective in the first half hour. To increase the strength of the attack, Bican and Bradáč exchanged positions and within two minutes, the 34th and 35th, Slavia made it 2-0. Bican had scored with a shot from outside the box and Horák followed up, scoring after a solo run.

The second half began exactly where the first had ended, with Slavia pressing forward and Ambrosiana entrenched at the back with all their players, including Meazza. The Czechs went on the offensive: in the 48th minute the ball reached Horák whose shot, repelled by Peruchetti, was collected by Vytlačil who made it 3-0 and only six minutes later came the fourth goal thanks to Bican, who, after making fun of the full-backs, further secured the result. Bican, unstoppable, completed his hat-trick in the 56th minute. Ambrosiana, now at the mercy of their opponents, sank further in the following minutes. Bradáč scored from a 25-metre free kick and Horák scored in the 63rd minute with a shot into the bottom corner. In the 75th minute Bican crowned a wonderful day with his fourth goal, the eighth for his side: he intercepted a pass from Buonocore and beat Peruchetti again, undisturbed. The last goal of the match came from Vytlačil after an exchange on the left wing of the Bohemian attack.

In the Prague rain, this 9-0 win was without precedent in the history of the competition[129] and the Italian newspapers could not explain it. All the 'Nerazzurri' players, with the exception of Meazza and Ferrari, ended up in the dock. Someone pointed the finger at the initial approach, which was too defensive and negative towards an adversary that, if outpaced, could be found wanting. Josef Laufer, the famous Czechoslovak radio commentator and Slavia manager, is said to have remembered the match with the following words: 'The teamwork of the forwards who were more or less the same age and were at the peak of their careers was unforgettable. Horák, Šimůnek, Bican, Bradáč and Vytlačil gave a marvellous display of football between

---

129 The highest goal difference between two teams up to that point was the 8-0 win Ferencváros had inflicted on Roma.

the 60th and 65th minutes with three signature goals. I lost my voice and my tears had started to fall as soon as the referee had whistled the end of the match. I'm only sorry that not all the Slavia fans were able to watch the match.'

Six days later Milan would host the return, a challenge that on paper was pleonastic. It was probably no coincidence that, despite the fact that an international quarter-final was being played, the stands of the Arena Civica in Milan were filled with one third of the crowd that had attended the match against Kispest. In 38°C heat, Ambrosiana took to the field with five new players compared to the first leg. The early stages of the game reflected the atmosphere of a match with a foregone conclusion: little excitement, apart from a crossbar hit by Vytlačil in the sixth minute, and almost no competition.

Vytlačil scored the first goal for the guests in the 25th minute from Bican's assist and only at that point did the match became more heated due to the nervousness of the Italians, who didn't want to lose in front of their own public. Within a few minutes Schuber fouled Bradáč, Bokšay collided with Ferrari and Černý and Šimůnek suffered minor bruises. Bradáč had to leave the field for 20 minutes to have five stitches applied to his head. It was at that stage that Ambrosiana came forward with more conviction and equalised through Ferrari.

Then, in the second half, they won the match by scoring a second and a third time thanks to Frossi, with the help of a still convalescent Bokšay, and a final goal by Ferrari. However, the fate of the contest had been decided a few days earlier in Prague. Slavia advanced to the semi-finals.

* * *

Here the Czechoslovaks found another Italian team, Genova, who at the end of the 1920s had been basically an extra at European level, before, about a decade later, making a decisive leap in quality. Although in those years they had not won the championship, the Ligurians had reached the semi-finals of the Mitropa for the second time in a row. In 1937 they had been disqualified following the Vienna scandals and in 1938 they were back with the same credibility. The double-header against Sparta in the round of 16 was their best result, and progressing to play Romanian side Rapid Bucharest, under the leadership of former Újpest legend Istvan Avar, was a further test of their maturity, especially given the heated atmosphere of the return leg.[130] In order to better prepare for facing Genova, Slavia had spent a week in Bellagio and had then arrived in the Ligurian capital on the evening of 23 July, two days before the match.

Genova, without centre-forward Bertoni, decided to implement a tactical revolution and lined up with several players occupying new positions. Despite their depleted line-up, it was the Italians who took early control of the game and they were often dangerous in the first ten minutes: Bokšay played a key role on two occasions.

The first time Slavia came close to scoring was with Kopecký's free kick in the 11th minute which finished just wide. From that point on, the game began to feature flurries on both sides but no real chances until, in the 29th minute, Italian midfielder Figliola took advantage of an Arcari corner to make it 1-0 to Genova. A few minutes later, again from an Arcari initiative, the second goal came: Morselli picked up the cross and fired a thunderbolt towards goal which smacked against the inside post before going in. But not a minute passed before Horák, forgotten

---

130 The Genoese complained about the unfair play of their opponents and the Italian newspapers harshly criticised the refereeing of the Czechoslovakian Vogl, who had not sent off anyone.

by the Italian defence, reduced the deficit with an assist from Šimůnek. A lively and intense first half ended 2-1.

Genova, knowing they deserved a bigger lead, surged forward and collected a number of corners in the opening minutes of the second half. For the third time Figliola went close to scoring with a header, but this time it was Daučík, the Slavia defender and captain, who saved on the goal line. Then Slavia found the way to the net: Bican dribbled past Genta, fired an angled torpedo that goalkeeper Agostini could not hold and Vytlačil, from just a few steps, put it into the net. That was in the 57th minute. Genova returned to the attack and claimed a foul in the box by Průha on Cattaneo, but the penalty wasn't given. However, the Italian pressure soon bore fruit: in the 68th minute an imprecise pass from Perazzolo got past Czechoslovakian midfielder Kopecký and reached Arcari, whose cross was picked up by Morselli who scored to put Genova back in front, 3-2.

Slavia seemed to be in disarray, but not Bican: the striker made himself dangerous with two solo efforts, neutralised by the Italian goalkeeper. In the 83rd minute a corner kick taken by Cattaneo generated a melee in front of Bokšay that ended with the ball in the net. The goal, in the confusion, was attributed to Cattaneo. The match thus ended 4-2 to Genova, a score that only partially satisfied the home side: according to the Italian journalists, the margin would have been greater if not for Bokšay's great day and Bertoni's absence.

The reputation that Genova had acquired over the years on a European level meant that in the days leading up to the match in Prague, tickets for the game sold out and the local authorities had worked hard to curb touting. Genova, who arrived in the Bohemian capital with their recovered centre-forward Bertoni, were received at Wilson station by the Slavia management who had prepared a similar welcome to the one they had received in Italy.

The match was played at the Stadion Letná, the stadium that Sparta had lent to their cousins. Slavia immediately went on the attack and scored the first goal in the tenth minute, through Bican. Then, four minutes later, after great play by Nožíř, Bican doubled the score, bringing the aggregate back to absolute equality. In spite of the good relations shown on the eve of the match, the game turned sour: Bertoni, on the verge of shooting towards the goal, was kicked by Černý, causing a double fracture of the tibia. The striker had to leave the pitch and was rushed to a military hospital in Prague. Slavia would play the remaining part of the match with an extra man. A scuffle began that saw Morselli, eager to avenge his comrade, hit Kopecký in the face. Nerves were frayed and Italian officials entered the field, which is why the police had to intervene and the match was suspended for a few moments. After it resumed, Bican completed his personal hat-trick, the goal marking a breakthrough for Slavia: Vytlačil shot and Bican sent the ball into the opposite corner with a wicked deflection. Nerves took over the match again and led to two expulsions, those of Morselli and Nožíř, who had come to blows. In the 78th minute, Bican completed the job with a shot from distance: 4-0, all from the same striker, and the Czechoslovaks were in the final.

La Gazzetta dello Sport dedicated a column to the match on the front page – where it summarised the elimination of Genova and Juventus at the hands of Slavia and Ferencváros – and an article on the back page. In the column, Erberto Levi argued that while the 9-0 loss suffered by Ambrosiana against the Bohemians was mainly due to the Italians' shortcomings, the 4-0 win over Genova by Bican and his team-mates was the result of superior quality. 'They play too well,' wrote Levi with reference to Slavia. The article on the back page, however, was of a completely different tone: it did not recognise the greatness of the Czechoslovaks and said that the defeat, rather than being due to technical superiority, was due to the violence of the Bohemian players.[131]

In any case, newspapers from all over the continent highlighted the performance of Josef Bican, the absolute star of the tie, but a mention was also reserved for Bokšay who, in the first quarter of an hour of the second half, made at least three saves. What better response to those who, for a long time, kept telling him 'You are not Plánička'?

* * *

In the final Slavia were faced with the reigning champions Ferencváros. The Hungarian team was largely the same as the previous year's and included three players who had come back from the World Cup disappointment, including captain Sárosi, who scored a total of three goals in the semi-final against Juventus.

This time the Masaryk Stadium hosted the event and about 50,000 spectators attended. The pitch was almost unplayable: due to the rain that had fallen heavily on the Bohemian capital in the previous days, the surface was muddy and unstable. Among the Bohemians Karol Daučík, younger brother of captain Ferdinand Daučík, replaced the suspended Nožíř. On the eve of the match *Poledni List*, a Prague newspaper, praised Ferencváros and in particular Toldi as 'an indomitable fighter and a great striker who despite being often criticised has a great heart and never gives up. A "bastard" in the best meaning of the term.'

---

131 The article that appeared on the back page did not bear any signature.

The match, restricted by the state of the ground, began quietly. Then, in the 30th minute, the first noteworthy episode occurred: the younger Daučík, visibly nervous, knocked down an opponent outside the area and from the following cross, Kemény headed the ball in. But five minutes later Bican showed up and, after receiving the ball from Horák, fired an unstoppable torpedo to make it 1-1. At the end of the first half Slavia turned the result around: Daučík Senior recovered and launched Bican's counter-attack and he served Šimůnek for 2-1. The first half ended with the Masaryk Stadium overflowing with joy.

A few minutes after the start of the second half Sárosi hit a post before his team-mate Kiss took advantage of Průcha's mistake and levelled the score. Towards the end, both sides had their chances: first Bican, once again unmarkable, supplied Horák who, alone in front of the goalkeeper, shot into the stands, and then, in the 86th minute, Hungarian Kemény's shot hit the post. The remaining minutes passed with no more score, to the disappointment of the Prague public. Much happier were the Hungarian fans and newspapers. The latter praised in particular the brilliant performance of young Béla Sárosi, brother of the more famous György. In Prague, for many people that draw looked like an elimination: to win in the 'Fradi' fortress, against such strong opponents, seemed almost impossible.

On the occasion of the final match of the competition, which took place on 11 September, the whole of Budapest was tinged with green and white: players, coaches and managers of other clubs in the capital expressed their support for 'Fradi'. Ernő Scheer, an MTK manager, was interviewed and said: 'No one will support "Fradi" as much as I do!' He was echoed by Újpest striker Gyula Zsengellér: 'As footballers we know how difficult it is to go all the way in the Mitropa and for this reason Ferencváros deserves the support of the whole country.'

Slavia had nothing to lose and went on the attack, wasting two good chances, from Šimůnek and Vytlačil. Then it was the Hungarian 'green-and-whites' who took control of the match and threatened the Czechoslovakian goal. Bokšay, on a good day, facing both Sárosi and Toldi, confirmed that although he was no Plánička, he was no slouch either.

In the second half, the balance of the game was broken after Josef Bican found Vytlačil and the striker shot from an off-centre position and put his team ahead. *'Fradi'* attacked again and again, making it difficult for their opponents, but on a counter-attack orchestrated by Vytlačil, Šimůnek doubled their lead. The next 20 minutes saw no further significant episodes and, despite a match dominated for large parts by the Hungarians – winning the corner-count 14-2 – Ferdinand Daučík was able to lift the first European trophy for Slavia.

It was a landmark moment as Slavia had taken part in the competition every year without ever winning the title. It was an incredibly exciting double final which was attended by a fantastic crowd despite the fact that ticket prices were even higher than those of the World Cup matches. Jewell, the referee of the return leg, suggested organising a challenge between the winners of the Mitropa and the reigning English champions from year to year, but the idea was never taken up.

Slavia's success was made possible above all by a group that had multiplied their efforts during that summer: as the Czechoslovak historian Vladimír Zápotocký would recount, everyone, from the managers to the players, had worked hard to reach the European summit. Zápotocký claimed that the players went into training days early, received pay rises and enjoyed bonuses with each passing round.

But one name stood out above them all: that of Josef Bican. He is known today as – official and unofficial statistics in hand – the greatest scorer of all time. *Pět Tisíc Gólu*, a book published about the player in 1971, credits him with more than 5,000 goals, although more realistic estimates stop at 830. A quick glance at the rankings of the greatest goalscorers of all time reveals the presence of forwards who were not only skilled in scoring goals but also possessed a vast technical repertoire. In this particular ranking Bican sits at the same table as Pelé, Puskás, Müller, Romario, Messi and Cristiano Ronaldo. The chronicles of the time and the striker's numbers point to an unequivocal conclusion: Bican, like the aforementioned champions, was much more than just a finisher.

The striker, who received bonuses twice as high as those of his team-mates, was one of the few players in the world capable of moving public authorities, institutions and consulates. On two occasions during the competition he had a problem: how to reach Italy to play the quarter-finals against Ambrosiana and the semi-finals against Genova? Not having received his Czechoslovakian passport and still being registered as a Viennese citizen, the player was potentially recruitable to the ranks of the Wehrmacht. Considering that at the time footballers travelled by train to away matches, both Bican and the Slavia managers feared that the Brown Shirts might raid the train, arrest the player and take him back to Vienna.

However, through its consulates Slavia was able to bribe the Yugoslav and Italian authorities so that Bican could reach Italy by ship from Split. Thus, on two occasions the striker was reunited with his team-mates once he had landed in Italy.

During the war years, at a time when Czechoslovakia had come under German influence and was renamed the Protectorate of Bohemia and Moravia, the Nazis would repeatedly try to convince Bican to join the Reich national team. Their plan was to host the World Cup in 1942 – a project that was hardly feasible as there was a war going on – and to field Bican alongside stars such as former team-mate Binder and Poland's Ernst Willimoski. Josef Pondělik, author of the book *Pět Tisíc Golů* (More than a Thousand Goals), tells his version of events, claiming that in a Prague café, the Lucerna Bar, some Nazi comrades intercepted him in order to convince him to become a German citizen and play for the national team. The footballer, however, allegedly refused. Zápotocký confirmed the player's refusal, but told the tale differently: according to him, the scene in the Lucerne Bar never took place. Sepp Herberger, the coach of the German team, is said to have been helped by Rudi Gramlich, a footballer with Eintracht Frankfurt, who often visited Prague because he was acquainted with a local athlete who was to become the mother of two of his children. Gramlich was also an admirer of Slavia and on more than one occasion he met Bican, trying to convince him to join Herberger's national team. Bican had always said no, citing the shock of losing his first wife, a girl the footballer had married who died about a year later. However, years later he would declare: 'I am Czechoslovakian, and if I had become German my father would have turned in his grave.'[132]

Bican's name has been back in the news in recent years, both globally and locally. On a global level the discussion about his number of goals is raging, being the striker –

132 Josef Bican wasn't the only player to refuse the call of Germany: Matthias Sindelar refused Sepp Herberger's call, citing as a reason his continuous knee problems.

according to official and unofficial numbers – considered the greatest scorer of all time, a record acquired mainly thanks to his achievements during the war years. At the local level, the giant picture of the striker, which had been displayed at the Sinobo Stadium, formerly called Eden Aréna, was removed in 2011, even though the player is unanimously considered a legend of the club. Ivan, his son, wanted it taken down as he did not like the change of ownership to a president who, according to him, did not exactly have a crystalline past.

1939 – BÉLA GUTTMANN: ALL ROADS LEAD TO BUDAPEST

On 30 September, shortly after the end of the 1938 tournament, Europe had taken another step toward hell. In Munich, Hitler, Mussolini – who had begun to intensify his relations with the Führer – and Chamberlain met and signed a peace treaty. The condition set by Hitler was the annexation of the Sudetenland, a region of Czechoslovakia populated by about three million citizens of Germanic origin, to the Third Reich. Back in England Chamberlain said he was enthusiastic about the agreement reached: he knew that the preservation of peace could only happen with some small concessions to the Germans. However, the English Prime Minister's hopes would soon be dashed.

More or less at the same time as the Munich Agreement, Mussolini's Italy passed the Racial Laws: announced on 18 September 1938, they came into force almost two months later. The discriminatory measures contained in the text approved by the Council of Ministers broadly followed those that had been enacted in Germany in 1933 and in Austria since the Anschluss.

Inevitably, even sport was not immune: Erberto Levi, a Jewish journalist and historic writer for *La Gazzetta dello Sport*, to whom I owe a great deal,[133] was struck off the Register of Journalists of Milan that very day along with three colleagues employed by other newspapers: Fiorenza Della Pergola, Giuliano Gerbi and Gustavo Weill-Schott.[134] One of the last columns he wrote appeared on 3 August and concerned the Mitropa semi-finals between Slavia and Genova and Ferencváros and Juventus.

The same fate befell some Jewish coaches and managers: Árpad Weisz, who had come close to winning the Mitropa in 1933 with Ambrosiana, packed his bags and headed for France, and Ernő Egri Erbstein, who had managed to stay a few months longer by moving from Lucchese to Torino, one of the cities most opposed to the regime, was also forced to flee. He had reached an agreement with Feyenoord but the train that took him to Holland was stopped at the German border and the coach was forbidden to continue his journey. So, he returned to his hometown of Budapest, where he would spend the war years.

Although it is widely believed that the theme of race in the rhetoric and propaganda of the regime in Italy had emerged since the colonial campaigns of 1936 in Ethiopia, to better analyse the phenomenon it is necessary to take a few steps back. On 10 November 1938, on the eve

---

133 Several of the chronicles which I have used in my research were written by him.
134 I thank Enrico Serventi Longhi for the information.

of the enactment of the Racial Laws, an article published on the front page of *Il Corriere della Sera* claimed with great pride that the positions taken by the Duce on the Jewish problem (as it was called) dated back as early as 1919.[135] They were not ideas that differed greatly from what Adolf Hitler had written in *Mein Kampf*: Mussolini claimed that the Jewish danger was connected to the Bolshevik danger and that the Jews, in order to 'encourage the growth of the ghetto', were cleverly able to preserve and accumulate and now to demolish and disperse assets through their bankers. And if we look closely, the early 1920s were characterised by a process of gradual fascism of the state, culminating in various kinds of harassment of the ethnic and linguistic minorities that populated northern Italy. The theme of race would reappear over and over again, for example on 1 June 1934, when the Duce gave a speech, later praised by the *Völkischer Beobachter*, in which he appealed to European nations not to follow the example of France and its colonial policy, under penalty of domination by peoples of non-European race. The escalation continued: on the one hand Mussolini would contradict himself by invading Ethiopia and on the other hand he would ally himself with Adolf Hitler.

The Steel Pact, signed on 22 May, 1939, preceded the Nazi invasion of Czechoslovakia by two months. Czechoslovakia, like Austria, would also cease to exist as an independent nation

---

135 Mussolini had written an article in *Il Popolo d'Italia* on 4 June 1919.

and be converted back into the Protectorate of Bohemia and Moravia.

The political events, of course, reverberated through to the sporting ones: at first it was suggested that the teams of the former Czechoslovakia should be excluded and replaced by two Polish or Slovakian teams, since Slovakia had remained independent. The committee finally decided to re-adopt the eight-team format and accept the Prague teams.

* * *

IN HUNGARY, the Racial Laws had appeared a full 18 years earlier, in 1920, at the end of the two-year period better known as the 'White Hungarian Terror'. The socialist regime of Béla Kun[136] had been overthrown and power had passed into the hands of former admiral Miklós Horthy, whose anti-Semitic inclinations were notorious. The first discriminatory law was named *'numerus clausus'* and restricted the presence of Jewish students in Hungarian public institutions. Although the text did not explicitly name Jews as an ethnic group, it read, 'The proportion of members of the various ethnic and national groups in institutions must represent the proportion of these groups within the population.' Many Jews, now becoming the main target of the former admiral's propaganda, decided to pack up and move elsewhere.

One of them was a 20-year-old Béla Guttmann, a midfielder with high hopes who had decided with his brother Armin to move to Újvidék, now Novi Sad, a town that had come under Yugoslav control at the end of the Great War. Here the two founded a dance school but

---

136 Born Abel Kohn.

months later, at the beginning of 1921, they returned to Budapest. The situation for the Jews seemed to have calmed down and Guttmann had decided to accept an offer from MTK, the team that dominated Magyar football in those years. Then, in 1922, mainly due to some friction with the coach Herbert Burgess, he decided to leave Budapest again, this time for Vienna. He had found a contract with Hakoah, a Jewish and Zionist club that only admitted Jewish players to its ranks and that in those years would become the favourite destination of several Hungarian Jewish[137] athletes. Hakoah had reached the first division in 1920 and in 1921 were ranked fourth. In 1922, at the end of Guttmann's first season, they finished second and then, after two seasons of finishing in mid-table, Guttmann and his team-mates won the first and only championship in the club's history.

Hakoah, who over the years had organised several tours to raise funds to finance their activities and the Zionist cause, went to the United States in April 1926 and at the end of the trip, nine players, including Guttmann, were convinced by the two main clubs of New York to settle in the new continent where they would receive unimaginable salaries compared to European standards. There is no doubt that for many, settling in New York was also a way to leave the anti-Semitic climate which pervaded in Europe.

In total, Guttmann spent six seasons in the United States and then, in 1932, decided to return to Europe. This decision, taken only a few months before Adolf Hitler came to power, depended in large part on the collapse of the Wall Street stock market in 1929. Inevitably, although the savings of many Jewish citizens had been lost, including

---

137 Hakoah was a multi-sport club that covered a variety of disciplines, not just football.

Guttmann's, the Jewish bankers, once the sole target of European propaganda, had also come under fire in New York.

Back in Vienna Guttmann made peace with the Hakoah management, played some friendly matches with the white-and-blue team[138] and in 1933 he got his first contract as a coach. He spent two uninspiring seasons at Hakoah and then, in 1935, thanks to the intercession of Hugo Meisl, he found a job at the Dutch club Enschede, which over the years would change its name to Twente. After an excellent first season, Enschede could not repeat the success and Guttmann, who was at loggerheads with the president for contractual reasons, accepted a new offer from Hakoah. However, in 1937, with the Anschluss at the gates, the problems of a few years earlier came back with even greater intensity.

Thanks to Guttmann, Hakoah, who in the meantime had returned to the second division, began to climb their way to the top flight, until German troops entered Vienna. The club was dismantled and Guttmann, who had obtained one of the few visas available to Hungarian citizens to emigrate to the United States, returned to New York. For unknown reasons, only a few months later he returned to Budapest where he was hired by Újpest. Guttmann didn't have a very good curriculum vitae, but he had important contacts: he was a friend of László Sternberg, the coach who he replaced and with whom he had shared some years in New York – Sternberg, seeing the situation deteriorate,[139] had decided to leave again for America.

Cases like Guttmann's, or rather coaches who, without enjoying great fame, were contracted by important clubs,

---

138 The Hakoah kit featured the colours of the Zionist movement.

139 Horthy had enacted another anti-Jewish law.

were not so rare: Lelovics at Bologna, Špindler at Sparta, Rauchmaul at Ferencváros and Árpád Weisz at Ambrosiana were all coaches who arrived at a big team without having to work their way up.

* * *

As a newcomer to Újpest, Guttmann won the Hungarian championship, his first title as a coach. Újpest, who had already won the 1929 edition of the Mitropa, had added four more national titles over the years and the fifth came that year. For this reason, the '*Lilák*' qualified for the Mitropa once again. The undisputed star of the club was Gyula Zsengellér, nicknamed 'Ábel',[140] who formed a dream tandem with Sárosi in the national team. Already the league's top scorer in 1937/38, the striker had improved enormously thanks to Guttmann and the coach's offensive play: he finished the championship with 56 goals – more than half of his team's goals in the league – in just 26 games.

Another curious record is that he was the first European player to wear the No.10 shirt: on 26 October 1938, on the occasion of the 75th anniversary of the Football Association, a match was played between England and the Rest of Europe. The players wore shirt numbers 1 to 11, an absolute novelty, and Zsengellér and Englishman Goulden wore number 10, a number which at the time did not have the same meaning as it has today.

The quarter-finals pitted Újpest against Ambrosiana, winners of the Coppa Italia. The teams had already faced each other in 1930, in a lengthy battle that only ended at the end of the second play-off. Meazza, who had been decisive against the Hungarians years earlier, had to

---

140 The nickname comes from the protagonist of the novels of the writer Áron Tamási, very much appreciated by the player.

withdraw this time due to an injury sustained in the final of an international friendly tournament against Hungary,[141] as did his team-mate Locatelli. The first leg took place at the same time as another sporting event: the unexpected and stunning 9-0 victory over Admira by Schalke in the German league final.[142]

The first leg of the quarter-final was played on 19 June in Milan, more precisely at the Arena Civica, in front of 10,000 spectators. The 'Nerazzurri' went on the attack and the Hungarians, who were cornered, capitulated after 17 minutes to a left-footed goal from Demaría, who entered the area after the defence had turned away a cross from Ferraris II. Six minutes later, to crown an almost total domination, Guarnieri, hunted down by the two Hungarian full-backs, resisted and scored from a low cross by Frossi. Ambrosiana continued to attack and first Frossi and then Guarnieri incredibly missed their appointments with the goal, with Sziklai, the Magyar goalkeeper, seemingly already resigned to being beaten. In the 34th minute Ambrosiana were beaten on the counter-attack by Kállai and Vincze and the latter, a few steps away from the goalkeeper Sain, scored to make it 2-1.

The second half was not quite as lively: Ambrosiana again attacked for about 30 minutes but then, in the last part of the match, it was Újpest who came close to equalising on at least two occasions. For some reason, perhaps by mistake, the English referee Worth whistled for the end of the match two minutes early.

---

141 The tournament was held in early June and featured Italy, Hungary, Switzerland, Yugoslavia, Romania and an Italian representative team (a sort of Italy B). Italy defeated Hungary in the final 3-1.

142 In Vienna all kinds of inferences were made about that result and in the course of the following months and years every time an Austrian formation faced a German one there would be enormous problems of public order.

The Italians were frustrated by the low score. The Italian newspapers, aware of the inexperience of many of the 'Nerazzurri' players, were pessimistic about the trip to Budapest. Ferenc Langfelder, president of Újpest, described the match as 'tough but fair'.

Exactly one week later the two teams met again in Budapest, this time with Ambrosiana at full strength. When they arrived in Budapest, the Ambrosiana players received an unusual gift from Langfelder: a statuette depicting a grieving shepherd. When the Italians asked about the meaning of this gift, Langfelder replied: 'This statue represents us, since you beat us in Milan, but on Sunday night it could represent you.'

In front of 8,000 people Újpest immediately threw themselves into the attack and the opening minutes increased the Italians' remorse about what had happened in the first leg: in the fifth minute Kállai, after a run by Ádám who had jumped over Campatelli and Demaría, found the target and equalised the aggregate score. Ambrosiana did not lose heart and created two clear opportunities, first through Ferraris II and then through Frossi who, after a run from the right, committed the opposition's goalkeeper. The Italians also complained about some offsides, given by referee Dale which they thought were non-existent. That, however, was one of the characteristics of Guttmann's Újpest: the ability to get forward in defence. At the last gasp of the first half, Zsengellér's close-range effort was foiled by the Italian goalkeeper.

The second half began with the Hungarians going close to 2-0 with Ádám and Zsengellér but both missed from a few metres out. From a sudden Italian attack, in the 79th minute, Ferraris II, after receiving a cross by Frossi from the right, stunned the public of Budapest with a goal to make it 1-1 and put qualification seemingly on ice. Újpest, roared on by their fans, fired their last bullets and instigated a last phase of attack: first Zsengellér scored to make it 2-1 from Vincze's pass and then, in the 89th minute, Kocsis shot a torpedo from about 15 metres that hit the crossbar and returned to the field: for the Italians it hadn't crossed the goal line, for the Hungarians it had and the referee was of the same opinion. Once the goal had been given, he was hugged and kissed by the Hungarian Ádám.

Guttmann and his team had thus succeeded in miraculously grabbing qualification at the last moment. The Hungarian coach had lost his voice and only spoke in gestures. Apart from the controversy over the last goal and the dubious offside decisions against the Italians, more or less everyone – Langfelder, Pelikan, and several Italian newspapers – agreed that the '*Lilák*' deserved their success, given the many chances they had created that day. Meazza did not look in great shape, probably due to the injury he had been suffering from the previous week. The match against Újpest, which marked the Italian star's debut in European competition with Ambrosiana, was also the end of his career: it was his last international appearance in a '*Nerazzurri*' shirt.

* * *

The main surprise of the quarter-finals was undoubtedly the exit of the defending champion, Slavia, for many the favourites for the final victory. They were eliminated by Beogradski, the team that would meet Újpest in the next round. Beogradski – or BSK – were no longer the inexperienced side that Hungária and Ferencváros had thrashed years earlier; they were a team whose experience had grown considerably and in which the now matured stars of Yugoslav nationals Marjanović and Vujadinović shone. BSK went into the double-header aware of the fact that, also because of Újpest's uninspiring performance in the quarters, the match could be decidedly open and hard-fought. Guttmann, on the other hand, showed his confidence. In the days leading up to the game he told journalists: 'If we draw or win by just one goal, I give you permission to write my name in small letters. And if you want, you can also omit the letter "u".' That's what Guttmann was, in life as well as on the pitch: a risk-taker who sought, and perhaps loved, the spotlight. Because of his relationship with journalists and his communication style, years later comparisons would be made with Herrera and Mourinho, although Guttmann's football was much more attacking. In this regard he once said: 'I don't care if my opponent scores, because I always think about scoring one more goal.'

The next day Béla Guttmann's name would appear in the Hungarian newspapers unchanged, despite the match ending 4-2 to the Yugoslavs. Božović, who scored a hat-trick, was the star of the match. Guttmann's men started the match along the same lines as the one against Ambrosiana, conceding two early goals. They fought back later and Kocsis scored to make it 2-1 before the interval, but they continued to disappoint in the second half and conceded twice more before Zsengellér managed to limit the damage with a penalty kick in the 53rd minute. BSK pulled off arguably the greatest feat in their young international history by inflicting a 4-2 defeat on a higher calibre team with a far greater tradition. According to insiders, the scoreline was narrower than the Yugoslavs deserved. Guttmann spoke of a 'bad day', claiming that his side would make up for it in the return leg, while Langfelder congratulated the opposing players, stressing that they deserved the acclaim that surrounded them. But the contest, obviously, was far from being decided.

Just five days later the two teams met for the return match. Beogradski were as fierce as in the first leg and almost immediately troubled the Hungarian goalkeeper with a shot from distance before taking the lead with a 25-metre effort from Matošić II. There was now a three-goal difference, a sizeable margin given the quality seen on the pitch so far. Újpest pushed midfielders up into the penalty area but wasted a number of good chances until, with two minutes remaining in the first half, Vincze levelled the score and reopened the qualification race.

At half-time, Guttmann berated his team and Újpest returned to the pitch with a different attitude: in the 49th minute Zsengellér made it 2-1 with a wonderful reverse kick and in the 62nd minute, again thanks to their star player, the Hungarians went 3-1 up and tied the aggregate score. Zsengellér scored his hat-trick in the 74th minute and, instead of bouncing back, Beogradski collapsed: between the 74th and 88th minutes the score became 7-1. Zsengellér's hat-trick was the only one in the history of the tournament.

Újpest reached the final and Guttmann, who was never trivial, told the microphones: 'I had said that if Beogradski had reached the final I would have stopped coaching. I am grateful to my players because thanks to this victory we will continue to work together.' He also praised the refereeing of the Italian Barlassina who, in the 83rd minute, sent off two players, Ádám from Hungary and Stojiliković from Yugoslavia, for getting into a fight after the Újpest forward had kicked the opponents' goalkeeper.

* * *

In the final the '*Lilák*' found '*Fradi*'. It was the second final in the history of the event between two teams from the same country. Ferencváros, thanks to their constant

215

presence among the finalists in the previous three years, started as favourites, also because they had eliminated giants like Sparta and Bologna along the way. Four goals scored by Toldi, one of the best Hungarian players, who had had to miss the previous matches due to injury, were decisive in the return match against the Italians. Toldi's performance was celebrated the following day by the Budapest newspapers with enthusiastic headlines such as 'Toldi! Toldi! Toldi! *Toldi!*' and 'Toldi Gésza – Bologna 4-1'.

The first leg of the match, on 23 July, was played under Bohemian referee Krist. By the stroke of half-time Guttmann's men were 2-0 up: first Zsengellér scored with a header and then Kocsis took advantage of a slip by the opposing defender Tátrai. In the 44th minute Kocsis scored again, but the referee, after consulting with the linesman, disallowed it, saying the ball had not gone into the goal. The first half ended 2-0 with Guttmann's men in control of the game.

In the 53rd minute Kocsis made it 3-0 after a short clearance by Háda. The '*Lilák*' dropped their pace and '*Fradi*' took the opportunity to get back into the game: Sárosi scored in the 73rd minute but just a minute later Zsengellér's header made it 4-1. Langfelder said: 'Our superiority was greater than the score says, I'm not very happy with 4-1 although the team played well today.' Hlavay, the '*Fradi*' coach, said he was extremely disappointed with his team's performance, except for Toldi, who had fought with all his energy. The three-goal difference was not in itself an unbridgeable margin, not for a team playing in their third consecutive final, provided the 'green-and-whites' changed gear.

The second leg of the Hungarian derby was played on 30 July, this time at Megyeri úti, the home of Újpest. The '*Lilák*' team had the same line-up as in the first leg, while their opponents changed three players, including goalkeeper Háda. The game began with a violent clash in the tenth minute that forced the Italian referee Dattilo to interrupt the match for a few minutes. Then it resumed with 'Fradi' pushing forward. Toldi's header from a corner kick landed on the hand of the opposing defender Balogh. The ball seemed to have crossed the goal line, but not to the referee, who pointed to the penalty spot. Kiszely, who replaced Sárosi as penalty-taker because of the latter's mistake against Bologna, converted to put his side ahead and put the contest back on track. After a few hard-fought minutes it was once again Kiszely who scored for 'Fradi': the forward collected a cross from the right by Kállai and, unmarked, stopped the ball and put it into the net.

In the 54th minute Újpest reduced the gap when Ádám found himself free at the far post and scored from a cross from the left. With their enthusiasm and fitness improving, Guttmann's men kept control of the game and in the 82nd minute they were rewarded with a goal to level the score at 2-2. Balogh, the defender who had conceded the penalty, picked up a deflection from the opponents' defence and from 30 yards out fired an impressive shot into the opposition goal.

The curtain came down on the competition as Futó, the Újpest captain, lifted the cup and was carried off in triumph by his team-mates. The star that shone brightest that year was undoubtedly Zsengellér. About six years later, the striker would be the protagonist of a curious handover: on 20 August 1945, in the 12th minute of a friendly match between Hungary and Austria (the second international match Hungary had played since the end of the war), he would provide the assist to newcomer Ferenc Puskás for his first goal with the national team. 'Öcsi, rúgd *be!'* – 'Shoot, Öcsi!'[143] – the older team-mate seems to have shouted at him.

Újpest, like Bologna, Austria Vienna and Ferencváros, added a second Mitropa to their roll of honour. It was a joy that would be dramatically tempered just a month later: on 1 September 1939 Germany invaded Poland and two days later war was declared.

---

143 Öcsi was one of Puskás's nicknames.

1940 – THE OLD CONTINENT UNDER IRON AND FIRE

THE GERMAN advance continued unabated. By early 1940 the Wehrmacht had invaded Denmark, Norway, Holland, Belgium and northern France. On 10 June, Italy had entered the war on Germany's side.

Despite the fact that war had been spreading across Europe, the continent's national football championships had been played without a hitch. Italy had already made its decision at the end of February: it would not take part in the 1940 edition of Mitropa. From the pages of *Il Corriere della Sera* it was said that it would be 'suspended for the current year', which shows how the perception of a multi-year war was far away at that time.

Without Italy, Austria and Czechoslovakia, the last two countries having been removed from the maps, the event was restricted to Hungary, Romania and Yugoslavia. For obvious reasons, not least the small capacities of the Romanian and Yugoslavian stadiums and the war, it was the least watched edition in the history of the Mitropa.[144] To many people, it seemed a stretch to even begin the 1940 tournament, and it did not reach its conclusion: it was

---

144 A drastic loss of interest had already been observed since the exit of the Austrian teams.

interrupted before the final that was to be played between Ferencváros – the club's fourth final in the last four years – and Rapid Bucharest. This was due to Hungary's territorial claims on Romania, which would lead to the invasion of northern Transylvania by Hungarian troops about a month later.

It was the end of an era that had lasted just 13 years and had given European crowds the chance to develop their passion for football on a more international level. The enthusiasm of the public on a large scale, the attendance at the stadiums and the resulting revenue suggested that as soon as better times arrived, Hugo Meisl's experiment would be repeated. But better times were not exactly around the corner: in the following five years the Old Continent would turn into a living hell. Those who suffered the consequences most of all were the Jewish journalists, managers, coaches and players trapped in Europe.

It is impossible to retrace the steps of every single protagonist, since no European nation was spared from the Nazi barbarism. However, I will dwell on the stories of some characters who at various levels and in various ways had made their appearance on the stage of the Mitropa.

A few months after being expelled from the Register of Journalists of Milan, Erberto Levi,[145] after a brief stay in London, took refuge in the United States, specifically in New York. When he arrived in the New Continent, he decided to change not only his life but also his identity: he took the name Erberto Landi and said goodbye to football reporting. In part, we can assume, this was a forced choice: his English would certainly not have allowed him to write for an American newspaper. But there was also a second

---

145 Levi was born with the full name of Giacobbe Erberto Minetto Levi and was originally from Savigliano, a town in the province of Cuneo.

reason, namely the unattractiveness of football in America. After the boom of the early 1920s and 1930s, an era defined as the golden age of the sport in the USA, it had ceased to arouse interest. So, Levi decided to take a new path and after a few years working for Pettinella Advertising, an advertising agency that promoted Italian products in the United States, he reinvented himself as a radio host. He had been contracted by several Italian broadcasters based in New York, including WCNW, WBNX, WHOM and WOV, and during the war years he also collaborated with the Bureau of War Information, founded by Roosevelt.

His activity did not go unnoticed especially when his past as a member of the National Fascist Party emerged. An investigation took place but it did not lead to any consequences and Levi was able to resume his duties normally. He also began to host a radio programme with his friend and former colleague Giuliano Gerbi, who had arrived in New York via Paris and Bogota. Then, starting from the 1950s, Levi recycled himself again: he became a successful entrepreneur in the field of music and cinema and imported the San Remo Festival to New York in 1960, introducing several Italian artists to the American public, including a young Domenico Modugno.

He died in New York on 10 October 1971 at the age of 63, and although he was one of the most important sports writers of the years between the wars, he is now almost completely forgotten.

The Racial Laws were also the reason why Jenő Konrád, the coach who won the Mitropa in 1936 with Austria Vienna, left Italy: in 1937 he had started working for Triestina and then, forced to pack his bags, had moved to France. He found a job with the now defunct Olympique Lillois team and, once arrived in Paris, he managed to get a residence permit for his wife Grete and daughter Evelyn.

Konrád had started his French adventure on the right foot but then, for the usual reasons, he and his family had to leave Lille. They moved to Portugal where the Hungarian, whose fame as a great coach was well known, was signed by Sporting Lisbon, but only a couple of months later the family decided to leave Europe for good in favour of a really safe harbour: New York. Here, Konrád said goodbye to the world of football. He was hired by Singer, a sewing machine company, and later became an entrepreneur in the textile industry.

Kálmán, his brother, the unintentional protagonist of the 'Konrád Case' described in the chapter on the 1927 edition, went through similar hardships: on 30 September 1938, when Germany had invaded the Sudetenland, the former player was in Brno as the coach of Židenice. Peter Brie, a Czechoslovakian journalist who had moved to Sweden and with whom Konrád was in contact, decided to help him by granting him a place in the Örebro team. Kálmán managed to save himself, and his family joined him in Scandinavia after an exhausting bureaucratic process to obtain visas. But some of their possessions – including Kálmán's priceless stamp collection – did not survive the journey: his wife Gertrud discovered this as soon as she started to unpack. The Nazis had got rid of them. At least Sweden was a lifeline and a place where the coach could continue his career for another 17 years.

Árpád Weisz and his family came to Holland via France, a favourite destination for a number of Jewish soccer players fleeing neighbouring countries. In Holland the coach signed a contract with Dordrecht, the club where Jimmy Hogan had taken his first steps in continental Europe some 30 years earlier. He made his debut in what was no more than an amateur league on 2 October 1939 and led Dordrecht to fifth place in the table, a record for the club, before the Nazi ogre began to loom over the Netherlands. Despite the fact that some of the harassment of Jews was immediately apparent, Weisz was able to continue coaching for some time and again the team finished fifth. But the political clouds began to thicken and on 29 September 1941 the coach had to leave: a missive had arrived at the headquarters of Dordrecht, ordering the top management of the club to dispose of the coach's services and not to employ him in any other task. It was the beginning of the end: bans and restrictions became more and more stringent and on 2 August 1942 the Weisz family was taken from their home in Bethlehemplein 10 to be deported to Auschwitz via Westerbork, a transit camp about 200km (125 miles) from Dordrecht. From there, exactly two months later, his wife Ilona and children Roberto and Clara were sent directly to the gas chambers. Weisz was sent to the camp of Cosel, then on to Auschwitz, where 16 months later, on 31 January 1944, he died of hunger and cold.

In the Italian football scene of those years there seems to have been a mystery, concerning a Hungarian player-coach capable of slipping through the cracks of history. He was Janós Nehadoma. The name Nehadoma caught my attention while I was analysing the reports of Fiorentina's matches during the 1935 edition. Janós Nehadoma, brother of József Nehadoma, the latter a star of Kispest and idol of a child, Öcsi, who was none other than Ferenc Puskás, had arrived in Italy in 1925, but had had to leave the country as soon as the limit on the purchase of foreign players imposed by the Viareggio Charter had been introduced. He moved to the United States and played for Brooklyn Hakoah. This suggests that Nehadoma was Jewish, since the Hakoah clubs – the main one, Vienna, we have mentioned in the course of this book – admitted only Jewish players.

However, because of the same limit on foreigners that the American federation imposed in 1930, the footballer had to emigrate once again: he decided to return to Italy, as we have noted, not as a coach, which would have been allowed by the new rules in force, but as a player, since the reports indicate his presence in the Mitropa. It would seem that Nehadoma, once back in Italy, was helped by someone, probably an employee of the Pistoia registry offices or a figure on an even higher level, someone who had the power to change or even eliminate his documents and recreate them from scratch. But even more sensational is the fact that the former striker remained in Italy to coach even after the racial laws had been promulgated, first at Triestina, where he replaced Konrad for a short period, and then at Modena. Here he continued his career, winning two Serie B championships[146] and instructing a very promising goalkeeper, the young Sentimenti IV, in saving penalties. The story, despite being discussed both in Italy and Hungary, is still unclear in parts.

Even Czechoslovakia had its Erberto Levi: Josef Laufer, a figure we have met on a couple of occasions, found himself in the same situation as Levi at the time of the German invasion of Prague. No longer able to commentate on matches on the radio – he worked mainly as a radio host – nor to appear in the management ranks of his club, Slavia, Laufer was unemployed and without an income for a few months until he was helped by Karel Herites, a former international referee he had met during the 1920s. Herites offered him a job as an insurance agent and Laufer accepted but then, due to the tightening of racial laws, he had to leave. He was also forced to separate

---

146 In the 1937/38 and 1942/43 seasons. In between Nehadoma also won a Serie C championship with Spezia.

from his wife as mixed marriages were banned. The couple managed to evade the ban with a stratagem: they pretended to have broken up. The wife continued to live in their apartment on Školská Street, while Laufer moved to the Vinohrady neighbourhood. The two of them met in the early afternoon, the best time of the day since it coincided with the time slot during which the Gestapo feared raids on Prague. During one of these visits, Laufer was discovered, but for once, luck smiled on him: an attack on the city was announced shortly thereafter, and the German police dropped the case.

During the conflict Laufer found a way to listen to the news coming from some foreign radio stations, even if now that device, his greatest passion, he could only use as a listener. He had learned of several commentators who had attacked him, wanting to take his place: one of them, Otakar Havel, whom Laufer had known for years, had written an article in the magazine *Árijský boj* (Aryan Fight) in which he harshly attacked Laufer and his work.

Laufer survived the war, returned to his profession and spent months dispelling the slanders that had been circulating about him: one of the most popular claimed that the radio presenter had committed suicide by jumping from the sixth floor of the building where he worked. According to Czech historian Zápotocký, Laufer, a person whose fame did not allow him to go unnoticed, survived thanks to the help of some prominent members of Slavia. One of them, Josef Bican, is said to have contacted Gramlich, with whom he had maintained good relations, and the latter put the Slavia leaders in touch with a group of SS who were responsible for the deportation of Jews. In order to ensure that the 'Laufer case' was treated with care, a number of coffins were filled with money and all sorts of goods for the SS. Bican, as well as contributing financially to the operation, acted as guarantor of the business, being the link between Gramlich and the Nazis. Zápotocký and Bican met several times at the end of the war, and Bican confided to the historian that he was extremely disappointed that Laufer never thanked him.

Káďa, the glorious captain of Sparta, was also in Prague when the Nazis invaded the capital. The occupying forces began to work with a local collaborationist cell, the Czechoslovak League, in order to recruit followers. They tried to convince them by presenting themselves as a check on the Bolshevik danger. Káďa received a phone call one day asking him insistently to join this group but the former player, as the Czechoslovak journalist František Steiner reports in his book *Co jsem zapomnel napsat* (*What I Forgot to Write*) never signed any documents. When Soviet tanks entered Prague a few years later, someone in *Namesti Republiky*, Republic Square, shouted, 'Look, Káďa is here! He's an enemy of Bolshevism!' The footballer was immediately identified, taken to the barracks and ill-treated for a few hours. But that same day he was released: no one had been able to find the phantom document that was supposed to prove Káďa's affiliation to the collaborationist cell. The former champion, who had just hung up his boots and entered politics, did not receive an official apology and was not even readmitted to Parliament; instead his pension was halved.

In Austria two clubs were most affected: Austria Vienna and Hakoah. Emanuel Schwarz, one of the most successful presidents of the time, with Austria Vienna having lifted the Mitropa twice under his management, left in May 1939 for Bologna with the help of the FIGC but then, due to the deteriorating situation in Italy, he had to pack his bags again. Thanks to Jules Rimet he managed to obtain a visa for France. He settled for some time in

Grenoble where he could work as a sports doctor before the Nazis arrived there. Schwarz spent the war years in hiding until, in 1944, he was captured and taken to a prison camp. Here he was subjected to all kinds of mistreatment, especially by the head of the camp, an Austrian who then inexplicably opened the gate one night and allowed him to escape.[147] Schwarz managed to find refuge in Paris thanks to Friedrich Donnenfeld, a former Hakoah footballer who had escaped to France and joined a partisan cell. At the end of the war, he returned as president of the Viennese club.

Rudolf Mütz had a similar story. The president of Austria's multi-title-winning Admira, he decided to leave the country after the company where he worked as a director, Hermann Pollack & Söhne, was Aryanised. Mütz came from a Jewish family and the fact that he had converted to Catholicism in 1900 made no difference to the Nazis. So, he fled to Yugoslavia, the destination also chosen by Josef Gerö, former president of the Austrian Football Association and Robert Lang, who had coached Austria Vienna years earlier. In order to do so, Mütz paid the huge sum of 47,000 Swiss francs. This so-called *Reichsfluchtsteuer* was an unaffordable tax that allowed German/Austrian citizens to leave the Reich. But in Yugoslavia, following the German invasion, the three were captured. Gerö, sent to Dachau, was released after a short imprisonment at the urging, it seems, of a leader of the Italian federation, while both Lang and Mütz were murdered. At the end of the war, when the International Cup was restarted, the committee decided to rename the last edition the Gerö Cup.

In Budapest, in spite of the anti-Semitic laws enacted in the years between the wars, the Hungarian Jews could

---

147 At the end of the war Schwarz made an effort to track down the guardian who had enabled him to escape, but didn't know his name.

consider themselves relatively safe: the alliance between Hitler and Horthy had ensured that Hungary remained unscathed by the German invasion. But the Second Anti-Jewish Law passed in 1939 meant that many of the Jews on the various teams in Budapest would soon have to leave their posts. The law stated that it was no longer possible to contract Jews and that the Jewish presence in the MLSZ, the Hungarian Football Federation, could not exceed 12 per cent. Some decided to stay while others, given the increasing pressure, preferred to leave.

This was what happened at MTK,[148] a club historically associated with the local Jewish community, on 8 July 1940: Alfréd Brüll,[149] the club's president, had decided to resign voluntarily. Doing so allowed the top management of his club to continue their activities. But the other managers, including Henrik Fodor, who as we have seen had also been the Hungarian federation's representative in the Mitropa committee meetings, decided not to continue and MTK was dismantled the following year. The decision was taken by Pál Gidófalvy, the newly appointed president of the MLSZ whose hatred for Jews had manifested itself on several occasions.

The situation deteriorated even more a few years later: on 19 March 1944, after Horthy had sought an armistice with the Soviet Union, the Wehrmacht entered Hungary. It had granted the former admiral's party the right to remain in government as long as it appointed a Prime Minister to Hitler's liking and willing to collaborate with the Reich. Among the Jewish footballers and coaches who were in Budapest at the time was Béla Guttmann. For many

---

148 That very year the club, which had been renamed Hungária between 1926 and 1940, had regained its original name of MTK.

149 Brüll was murdered in Auschwitz in 1944.

years it was thought that Guttmann had taken refuge in Switzerland but recent research, reported by David Bolchover in his wonderful work *The Greatest Comeback*, has revealed a totally different version. In 1944 Guttmann was in Budapest, specifically in Újpest. He had had to leave his role as coach in 1939 but, thanks to Lipót Aschner, the club's president, he had been given a behind-the-scenes role: he was to watch Újpest's matches and give his reports to the club's top brass.

On the day of the German invasion he was away at Nagyvárad and at half-time was informed of what was happening in Budapest. The coach immediately realised that the trouble had just begun and luckily he found refuge in an attic owned by the Moldoványis, the family of Marianne, his partner. The hiding place was safe and was never searched. The only time Guttmann risked being discovered was during an escapade in the city – a risk that the coach often took: he was stopped, interrogated and then, fortunately, released. That made him more cautious.

Guttmann, however, was anything but safe: hunger was looming and he needed a solution that would allow him to survive the lack of food. So, between June and July 1944[150] he accepted a call to the ranks of the army: Jewish males between the ages of 18 and 48 were called up to serve in the city. They would stay in Budapest for some time and then be transferred to Vác, a small town not far away. The reason he joined was that in the camp, Guttmann would be given board and lodging.

But on 15 October 1944 the Arrow Crosses of Ferenc Szálasi, an ultranationalist party described as even more ferocious than the SS, seized power and the situation

---

150 The army call came in June, but it's not clear exactly when Guttmann showed up.

worsened: deportations to extermination camps began. In December 1944 Guttmann and some of his fellow workers were crammed into one of the buildings where they continued to perform their duties while waiting to leave for Auschwitz. One of the companions was an old friend, another prominent face of European football in those years: Ernő Egri Erbstein. Guttmann, Erbstein and three other unfortunates gathered inside the building and planned their escape: they jumped from the first floor and then, after separating, ran like hell to escape a fate that seemed to be sealed.

It was Guttmann himself who revealed this course of events: he recounted that in the previous days, aware of what was to happen, the five had planned their escape in every detail. They had studied the times of the change of the guard and had softened up the ground on to which they would jump. The coach reportedly spent what was left of the war hidden by 'very nice people'. The most widely accepted theory is that Guttmann had once again taken refuge in the Moldoványis' attic.

Shortly after the Arrow Crosses took possession of the country, several resistance cells sprang up in Budapest, which included some of the most important faces in football. Among them were Béla Jánosi, who had led the Bocskai in one of the club's two appearances in Mitropa, István Tóth, the coach of 1928 winners Ferencváros and Géza Kertész, a former coach of several Italian teams who later joined Újpest, as well as other famous names such as Imre Schlosser and Karoly Fógl.

Tóth and Kertész joined a group called Dallam, or in some cases Mallad, consisting of about a dozen people. Dallam was primarily concerned with protecting Jews and communists from persecution by attempting to hide them or by granting them false documents. But, due to an act of stupidity, the organisation was discovered and dismantled: one evening a member of the organisation, Pál Kovács, invited Kertész to his home and the two told Mari Bényi, a prostitute whom Kovács frequently visited, about their activities in support of the Allies. The woman thought it wise to inform her pimp, Gabor Dósa, and a few days later both Kertész and Tóth were taken from their homes and sent to Fő utca prison, but then, because of the bombing, they were transferred first to the Parliament building and then to the basement of the Ministry of the Interior in Buda Castle. On 6 February 1945, five days before the liberation of Budapest and after days and days of torture, the two were murdered by SS bullets. Tóth could have escaped the tragic fate: as his son said at the end of the war, only a few months earlier the coach had been offered a job in South America but the family had decided to stay in Budapest. Tóth junior, who had been particularly against the move, would carry that burden for the rest of his life.

Ferenc Langfelder, the president of Újpest who, like Emanuel Schwarz, had won the Mitropa twice, was also a victim of the Arrow Crosses. As was often the case in 1944, at a time when the war was taking a turn for the worse for the Axis powers, Hungarian Jews and political opponents were murdered on the spot. Langfelder was killed in 1944 and the Central European football world said goodbye to another of its most iconic faces.

WHAT HAPPENED
TO THE MITROPA?

THE MITROPA Cup had formally ceased to exist in 1940. However, it was provisionally resurrected under the name of Zentropa in 1951[151] and then revived from 1955 as a tournament reserved for the top-ranked teams of some European leagues that had fallen into oblivion and the clubs who finished third and fourth in the other leagues, those who failed to qualify for the newly created Champions Cup. From 1980 onwards it was to be definitively scaled down: it became an event in which the winners of the second division championships took part, a sort of cadet Champions Cup.

What is certain is that the competition had lost its original charm and its importance had declined, along with that of the federations that had founded it. The hegemony of Central European football at continental level was coming to an end, and the football of that region does not have the same status today. The *Aranycsapat*, (the 'Golden Team'), in other words, Ferenc Puskás's Hungary, was the last great force of a sporting movement that died out with the repression of the Hungarian Revolution by Soviet

---

151 The tournament, restricted to only four participants, was won by Rapid.

tanks. It happened on 10 November 1956 and coincided with the flight of some of the leading talents of the time to the most coveted footballing shores of Western Europe. The wounds of the Second World War would take years to heal and sporting relations would suffer.

However, aware of the attraction that international football had exerted in previous years and mindful of the sporting and economic success of Mitropa, a number of federations whose relations had remained unchanged or had been repaired fairly quickly decided to set up the Latin Cup, a mini-tournament that emerged in 1949, open to the champion clubs of Italy, France, Portugal and Spain. It lasted a few days, was hosted in one of the participating nations and, like Mitropa, was held once the championships were over. The presence of the main Iberian and French teams was an absolute novelty but it also meant something else: times were changing and with them the hierarchies of football, first on the continent and then, decades later, globally.

The first edition of the Latin Cup was announced on 6 January 1949 and the newspapers all over Europe made it clear: the Grande Torino, already winners of five Italian championships in the 1940s, were the undisputed favourites. But the Superga air disaster, which occurred less than two months before the start of the event, changed the course of history. In that tragedy in May 1949, Italian football said goodbye to its best line-up, an eleven that in those years was almost exactly the same as that of the Italian national team. Ernő Egri Erbstein, the architect of the Grande Torino, Béla Guttmann's companion in his adventures and former coach of the Piedmont team before the Racial Laws came into force, died in the accident.

The Latin Cup ran for eight years and then, in 1957, was interrupted, also a victim of the growing popularity of the Champions Cup (which had begun in 1955). The latter, decidedly more inclusive and attractive, was open to all the major European federations, admitted the winners of their respective championships and was played throughout the season.

The Champions Cup was born in this way by virtue of the previous experience of the Mitropa and thanks to a curious episode: at the end of the 1953/54 season Wolverhampton Wanderers had become champions of England and had decided to invite some teams for friendly matches. The English club defeated, in chronological order, Celtic, Racing Club Avellaneda, Spartak Moscow and Maccabi Tel Aviv. The last hurdle – a kind of litmus test – was Honvéd, one of the world's strongest teams whose leader was a Puskás in his prime. Not without some cunning and a little help – the Englishmen deliberately soaked the pitch during the interval to prevent the proverbial dribbling of the Hungarians and at 2-0 to the visitors the referee awarded a penalty to Wolverhampton that appeared clearly non-existent – the home team won 3-2 and the *Daily Mail*, one of the many publications that celebrated that success, proclaimed the English 'World Champions'. In response, the French magazine *L'Equipe* replied: 'Before declaring Wolves world champions, let's play them in Moscow and Budapest.' The idea of a trophy reserved for the best clubs on the continent would take shape less than a year later.

The fact that it was held during and not at the end of the season was just one of the many differences from the Mitropa Cup. The Mitropa had always been characterised by a great balance: no team had lifted the trophy twice in a row, none more than twice in all and the four main federations involved had more or less equally shared the successes. This balance of power was due to a number of factors, not least a fledgling football market and a relatively small financial gap between the participating clubs. Several of the aforementioned stars of European football, such as Wesely, Káďa, Meazza, Sindelar and Sárosi, never played for a foreign club and all became flagships of their teams. Leaving one top club for another was not seen as particularly attractive or convenient: the difference between what one club could offer compared to another at a contractual level was slight and, with the exception of Italy, leaving one of the top Hungarian, Austrian or Czechoslovakian teams for one within the same nation, inevitably meant going to one of the bitter rivals of your own capital and risking being lynched by your former fans. In Milan a case of this type occurred with Giuseppe Meazza: Meazza, victim of a serious foot injury that occurred during the 1938/39 season, stayed put at Ambrosiana for more than a year and then moved to AC Milan. But you have to keep in mind that at the time, Milan was not one of the main clubs either in Italy or Europe: the arrival of Meazza on the opposite bank of the Naviglio was due to the desire of the man to return to action on the playing fields even if among the ranks of a lesser team. The only striking transfer that took place in this period of time and that had an impact on the event was that of Bican from Admira to Slavia,[152] but it was a case more unique than rare.

This trend changed enormously over the decades and then, starting with the Bosman ruling in 1995, any restrictions on the purchase or sale of foreign players was removed. This would allow the richest clubs to acquire the most sought-after international talent, effectively stripping the less-well-off clubs of their best resources. It was also

---

152 I have deliberately not mentioned Braine: the transfer of the striker to Sparta took place under different circumstances, since he came from an amateur league and the Belgian federation did not participate in the Mitropa.

the moment in which an important gap would be created between Old World and South American football.

Other innovations were of a tactical nature: 'the Method', the dominant system between the two wars that used only two defenders, disappeared altogether, either in favour of a more modern version of the system – a three-defender module in vogue especially in the 1950s – or of a four-man defence which, as Niccolò Mello recounts in his splendid book *Stelle di David*, was one of Guttmann's trademarks first at Sao Paulo and then at Benfica, or again of the emerging 'Catenaccio', a module that made the fortunes of both Rocco's Milan and Herrera's Inter.

The year 1955, the year of the founding of the Champions Cup, also coincided with the beginning of the first winning run of a European team, something that Mitropa had never known: Real Madrid lifted the cup for five consecutive years and, after their run of success, other clubs would win the trophy at least twice in a row. This was the case, among others, of Guttmann: the Hungarian coach won the Champions Cup twice, establishing himself as the only coach in history to lift both the Mitropa and the Champions Cup. Other series of victories would be achieved by Inter, Ajax, Bayern Munich, Liverpool, Nottingham Forest, Milan and, more recently, once again by Real Madrid.

But had the essence of Danubian football really disappeared? Not entirely. The architects of some of the continent's best teams in the years after the Second World War were either born under the Austro-Hungarian Empire or shortly after its dissolution. They had all grown up in the same sporting culture, more than a few had taken their first steps in the period between the two wars, and many of them would have re-proposed the 'passing game' philosophy of Central European football. In fact, it is widely believed that the 'Tiki Taka' of Guardiola's Barcelona is nothing more than the ultimate evolution of what had been observed in previous years in Austria, Hungary and Czechoslovakia. Some Central European coaches who had an important impact on the event were Ernst Happel, Elek Schwartz, Ferenc Puskás himself, who at the helm of Panathinaikos became the only manager to take a Greek team to a European final, Stefan Kovács, whom more than a few point to as the true architect of the 'Total Football' played by the great Ajax of the 1970s, Čestmír Vycpálek, who led Juventus to a final against Kovács in 1973 and Pál Csernai, finalist with Bayern Munich in 1982. This amounts to more than just a few, in relation to the derisory weight of the football from which they came.

MITROPA CUP FINAL STATISTICS, 1927 TO 1939

1927

Sparta Prague – Rapid Vienna 6-2

Prague, 30 October 1927; Spectators: 25,000; Referee: Van Praag (Belgium)

Teams:

SPARTA PRAGUE: Hochmann; Burgr, Perner; Kolenatý, Káďa (c), Hajný; Patek, Šima, Myclik, Silný, Horejs. Coach: Špindler

RAPID VIENNA: Feigl; Czeyka, Jellinek; Madlmayer, Smistik, Nitsch(c); Wondrak, Wesely, Kuthan, Horvath, Weselik. Coach: Bauer

Scorers: Káďa 1', Šima 14', Weselik 15', Silný 33', Wesely (R) 34', Patek 62', Silný 76', Patek 78'

Rapid Vienna – Sparta Prague 2-1

Vienna, 13 November 1927; Spectators: 40,000; Referee: Eymers (Netherlands)

Formations:

RAPID VIENNA: Feigl; Schramseis, Nitsch ©; Richter, Smistik, Madlmayer; Bauer, Horvath, Weselik, Luef, Wesely. Coach: Bauer

SPARTA PRAGUE: Hochmann; Burgr, Perner; Kolenatý, Ká©(c), Hajný; Patek, Šima, Myclik, Silný, Horejs. Coach: Špindler

Scorers: Weselik 5', Luef 55', Silný 82'.

1928

Ferencváros – Rapid Vienna 7-1

Budapest, 28 October 1928; Spectators: 20,000; Referee: Carraro (Italy)

Teams:
FERENCVÁROS: Amsel; Takács I, Hungler (c); Furmann, Bukovi, Berkessy; Koszta, Takács II, Turay, Sedláček, Kohut. Coach: Tóth
RAPID VIENNA: Hribar; Schramseis, Kral; Frühwirth, Smistik, Madlmeyer; Kirbes, Weselik, Hoffmann, Horváth, Wesely (c). Coach: Bauer
Scorers: 'Sedláček 15', Takács II 18', Sedláček 20', Kohut 56', Kohut 58', Takács II 64', Takács II 76', Horvat 85'

Rapid Vienna – Ferencváros 5-3
Vienna, 11 November 1928; Spectators: 20,000; Referee: Carraro (Italy)
Teams:
RAPID VIENNA: Hribar; Schramseis, Witschel; Frühwirth, Hoffmann, Madlmeyer; Kirbes, Weselik, Hoffmann, Horvath, Wesely (c). Coach: Bauer
FERENCVÁROS: Amsel; Takács I, Hungler (c); Furmann, Bukovi , Berkessy; Koszta, Takács II, Turay, Sedláček, Kohut, Coach: Tóth
Scorers: Kirbes 5', Kirbes 22', Kohut 33', Turay 36', Wesely 37', Weselik 50', Wesely 53', Sedláček 79'

1929
Újpest – Slavia Prague 5-1
Budapest, 3 November 1929; Spectators: 18,000; Referee: Braun (Austria)
Teams:
ÚJPEST: Aknai-Acht; Kövagö, Fogl III (c); Borsányi, Köves, Wilhelm; Ströck, Avar, Mészáros, Spitz, Szabó. Coach: Bányai
SLAVIA PRAGUE: Plánička; Ženíšek, Novak; Vodička, Pleticha (c), Čipera; Junek, Joska, Svoboda, Puč, Kratochvíl. Coach: Madden
Scorers: Spitz 42', Puc 44', Avar 60', Ströck 67', Spitz 69', Szabó 80'

Slavia Prague – Újpest 2-2
Prague, 17 November 1929; Spectators: 22,000; Referee: Braun (Austria)
SLAVIA PRAGUE: Plánička; Ženíšek, Novák; Vodička, Pleticha (c), Čipera; Junek, Joska, Svoboda, Puč, Kratochvíl. Coach: Madden
ÚJPEST: Aknai-Acht; Kövagö, Fogl III (c); Borsányi, Köves,

Wilhelm; Ströck, Avar, Mészáros, Spitz, Szabö. Coach: Bányai
Scorers: Junek 28', Kratochvíl (penalty) 57', Szabó 84', Avar 86'

1930

Sparta Prague – Rapid Vienna 0-2
Prague, 2 November 1930; Spectators: 25,000; Referee:
Hansen (Denmark)
Teams:
SPARTA PRAGUE: Bêlík; Burgr, Hojer; Madelon, Káďa (c),
Srbek; Patek, Košťálek, Braine, Silný, Hejma. Coach: Dick
RAPID VIENNA: Bugala; Schramseis, Cejka; Rappan, Smistik,
Vana; Kirbes, Weselik, Kaburek, Luef, Wesely (c). Coach: Bauer
Scorers: Luef 9', Wesely 57'.

Rapid Vienna – Sparta Prague 2-3
Vienna, 12 November 1930; Spectators; 40,000; Referee: Hansen
Teams:
RAPID VIENNA: Bugala; Schramseis, Cejka; Rappan, Smistik,
Vana; Kirbes, Weselik, Kaburek, Luef, Wesely (c). Coach: Bauer
SPARTA PRAGUE: Bêlík; Burgr, Čtyřoký; Madelon, Káďa (c),
Srbek; Podrazil, Košťálek, Braine, Silný, Hejma. Coach: Dick
Scorers: Kaburek 17', Košťálek 25', Košťálek 27', J.Smistik
67', Košťálek 87'

1931

First Vienna – Wiener AC 3-2
Zurich, 8 November 1931; Spectators: 16,000; Referee:
Mattea (Italy)
Teams:
FIRST VIENNA: Horeschovsky; Rainer, Blum (c); Schmaus,
Hoffmann, Machu; Brosenbauer, Adelbrecht, Gschweidl, Tögel,
Erdl. Coach: Frithum
WIENER AC: Hiden; Becher, Sesta; Braun, Löwinger, Kubesch;
Cisar, Müller, Hiltl, Hanke, Huber (c). Coach: Geyer
Scorers: Hanke 2', Müller 22', Tögel 30', Adelbrecht 63',
Becher (o.g.) 87'.

Wiener AC – First Vienna 1-2
Vienna, 12 November 1931; Spectators: 25,000; Referee:
Barlassina (Italy)

Teams:
WIENER AC: Hiden; Becher, Sesta; Braun, Löwinger, Kubesch; Morocutti, Müller, Hiltl, Hanke, Huber (c). Coach: Geyer
FIRST VIENNA: Horeschovsky; Rainer, Blum (c); Schmaus, Hofmann, Machu; Brosenbauer, Adelbrecht, Gschweidl, Tögel, Erdl. Coach: Frithum
Scorers: Erdl 6', Erdl 41', Hanke 65'.

1932
Bologna were declared champions on 7 November 1932 following the disqualification of Juventus and Slavia Prague, so the final was not played.

1933
Ambrosiana – Austria Vienna 2-1
Milan, 3 September 1933; Spectators: 22,000; Referee: Klug (Hungary)
Teams:
AMBROSIANA: Ceresoli; Agosteo, Allemandi; Pitto, Faccio, Castellazzi; Frione, De Manzano, Meazza (c), Demaría, Levratto. Coach: Weisz
AUSTRIA VIENNA: Billich; Graf, Nausch (c); Najemnik, Mock, Gall; Molzer, Stroh, Sindelar, Specht, Viertl. Coach: Blum
Scorers: Meazza 40', Levratto 41', Spechtl 77'.

Austria Vienna – Ambrosiana 3-1
Vienna, 8 September 1933; Spectators: 58,000; Referee: Cejnar (Czechoslovakia)
Teams:
AUSTRIA VIENNA: Billich; Graf, Nausch (c); Najemnik, Mock, Adamek; Molzer, Stroh, Sindelar, Jerusalem, Viertl. Coach: Blum
AMBROSIANA: Ceresoli; Agosteo, Allemandi; Pitto, Viani, Faccio; Frione, Serantoni, Meazza (c), Castellazzi, Demaría. Coach: Weisz
Scorers: Sindelar (penalty) 45', Sindelar 80', Meazza 85', Sindelar 88'
(NOTE: Demaría and Allemandi were sent off in the 75th and 77th minutes)

1934
Admira Vienna – Bologna 3-2
Vienna, 5 September 1934; Spectators: 45,000; Referee: Walden (England)

Teams:
ADMIRA VIENNA: Platzer; Pavlicek, Janda; Urbanek, Humenberger, Mirschitzka; Sigl (c), Hahnemann, Stoiber, Schall, Vogl. Coach: Skolaut
BOLOGNA: Gianni; Monzeglio, Gasperi; Montesanta(c), Donati, Corsi; Maini, Sansone, Spivach, Fedullo, Reguzzoni. Coach: Kovács
Scorers: Spivach 7', Reguzzoni 25', Stoiber 56', ogl 58', Schall 60'

Bologna – Admira Vienna 5-1
Bologna, 9 September 1934; Spectators: 20,000; Referee: Jewell
Teams:
BOLOGNA: Gianni; Monzeglio, Gasperi; Montesanto, Donati, Corsi; Maini, Sansone, Schiavio (c), Fedullo, Reguzzoni. Coach: Kovács
ADMIRA VIENNA: Platzer; Pavlicek, Janda; Urbanek, Humenberger, Mirschitzka; Durspekt, Hahnemann, L. Vogl, Stoiber, A. Vogl (c). Coach: Skolaut
Scorers: Maini 21', A. Vogl (penalty) 32', Reguzzoni 33', Reguzzoni 40', Fedullo 84', Reguzzoni 88'

1935
Ferencváros – Sparta Prague 2-1
Budapest, 8 September 1935; Spectators: 30,000; Referee: Walden
Teams:
FERENCVÁROS: Háda; Polgár, Korányi; Mikes, Móré, Bán; Táncos, Kiss, Sárosi I (c), Toldi, Kemény. Coach: Blum
SPARTA PRAGUE: Klenovec; Burgr (c), Čtyřoký; Košťálek, Boućek, Srbek; Faczinek, Zajíček, Braine, Nejedlý, Kalocsay. Coach: Sedláček
Scorers: Toldi 16', Kiss 27', Braine 71'.

Sparta Prague – Ferencváros 3-0
Prague, 15 September 1935; Spectators: 56,000; Referee: Fogg
Teams:
SPARTA PRAGUE: Klenovec; Burgr (c), Čtyřoký; Košťálek, Boućek, Srbek; Faczinek, Zajíček, Braine, Nejedlý, Kalocsay. Coach: Sedláček
FERENCVÁROS: Háda; Polgár, Korányi; Mikes, Móré, Bán; Táncos, Kiss, Sárosi I (c), Toldi, Kemény. Coach: Blum
Scorers: Faczinek 26', Braine 34', Braine 69'.

1936

Austria Vienna – Sparta Prague 0-0
Vienna, 6 September 1936; Spectators: 41,600; Referee: Scarpi (Italy)
Teams:
AUSTRIA VIENNA: Zöhrer; Andritz, Sesta; Adamek, Mock, Nausch (c); Riegler, Stroh, Sindelar, Jerusalem, Viertl. Coach: Konrád
SPARTA PRAGUE: Klenovec; Burgr (c), Čtyřoký; Košťálek, Bouček, Rado; Faczinek, Zajíček, Braine, Nejedlý, Kalocsay. Coach: Sedláček

Sparta Prague – Austria Vienna 0-1
Prague, 13 September 1936; Spectators: 60,000; Referee: Barlassina (Italy)
Teams:
SPARTA PRAGUE: Klenovec; Burgr (c), Čtyřoký; Košťálek, Bouček, Srbek; Faczinek, Zajíček, Braine, Nejedlý, Kalocsay. Coach: Sedláček
AUSTRIA VIENNA: Zöhrer; Andritz, Sesta; Adamek, Mock, Nausch (c); Riegler, Stroh, Sindelar, Jerusalem, Viertl. Coach: Konrád
Scorers: Jerusalem 67'

1937

Ferencváros – Lazio 4-2
Budapest, 12 September 1937; Spectators: 32,000; Referee Krist (Czechoslovakia)
Teams:
FERENCVÁROS: Háda; Tátrai, Korányi; Magda, Polgár, Székely; Táncos, Kiss, Dr Sárosi (c), Toldi, Kemény. Coach: Rauchmaul
LAZIO: Blason; Zacconi, Monza; Baldo, Viani, Milano; Busani, Marchini, Piola (c), Camolese, Costa. Coach: Violak
Scorers: Toldi 20', Busani 26', Dr Sárosi 53', Dr Sárosi (pen.) 59', Piola 63', Dr Sárosi (pen.) 72'

Lazio – Ferencváros 4-5
Rome, 24 October 1927; Spectators: 15,000; Referee: Wüthrich (Switzerland)
Teams:
LAZIO: Provera; Zacconi, Monza; Baldo, Viani, Milano; Busani, Marchini, Piola (c), Camolese, Costa. Coach: Violak

FERENCVÁROS: Háda; Tátrai, Korányi; Magda, Polgár, Lázár; Táncos, Kiss, Dr Sárosi (c), Toldi, Kemény. Coach: Rauchmaul
Scorers: Costa 4', Dr Sárosi (penalty) 5', Dr Sárosi 8', Piola 18', Piola 23', Camolese 35', Toldi 37', Lázár 71', Dr Sárosi 80'

1938

Slavia Prague – Ferencváros 2-2
Prague, 4 September 1938; Spectators: 45,000; Referee: Mee (England)
Teams:
SLAVIA PRAGUE: Bokšay; Černý, Daučík I (c); Průcha, Daučík II, Kopecký; Horák, Šimůnek, Bican, Bradáč, Vytlačil. Coach: Reichardt
FERENCVÁROS: Háda; Tátrai, Polgár; Magda, Sárosi III, Lázár; Táncos, Kiss, Dr Sárosi (c), Toldi, Kemény. Coach: Hlavay
Scorers: Kemény 30', Bican 36', Šimůnek 44', Kiss 63'.

Ferencváros – Slavia Prague 0-2
Budapest, 11 September 1938; Spectators: 35,000; Referee: Jewell (England)
Teams:
FERENCVÁROS: Háda; Tátrai, Polgár; Magda, Sárosi III, Lázár; Táncos, Kiss, Dr Sárosi (c), Toldi, Kemény. Coach: Hlavay
SLAVIA PRAGUE: Bokšay; Černý, Daučík I (c); Průcha, Nožíř, Kopecký; Vacek, Šimůnek, Bican, Bradáč, Vytlačil. Coach: Reichardt
Scorers: Vytlačil 57', Šimůnek 71'.

1939

Ferencváros – Újpest 1-4
Budapest, 23 July 1939; Spectators: 12,000; Referee: Krist (Czechoslovakia)
Teams:
FERENCVÁROS: Háda; Tátrai, Dr Szoyka; Magda, Sárosi III, Lázár; Táncos, Kiss, Dr Sárosi (c), Toldi, Gyetvai. Coach: Hlavay
ÚJPEST: Sziklay; Futó (c), Fekete; Szalay, Szűcs, Balogh; Ádám, Vincze, Zsengellér, Kállai, Kocsis. Coach: Guttmann
Scorers: Zsengellér 9', Kocsis 10', Kocsis 53', Dr Sárosi 73', Zsengellér 74'

Újpest – Ferencváros 2-2

Budapest, 30 July 1939; Spectators: 15,000; Referee: Dattilo (Italy)

Teams:
ÚJPEST: Sziklay; Futó (c), Fekete; Szalay, Szűcs, Balogh; Ádám, Vincze, Zsengellér, Kállai, Kocsis. Coach: Guttmann
FERENCVÁROS: Pálinkás; Tátrai, Dr Szoyka; Sárosi III, Polgár, Lázár; Bíró, Toldi, Dr Sárosi (c), Kiszely, Gyetvai. Coach: Hlavay
Scorers: Kiszely (penalty) 15', Kiszely 29', Ádám 54', Balogh 82'

1940

The final that was to be played between Ferencváros and Rapid Bucureşti was cancelled due to the impending war.

THANKS

MY FIRST thanks go to two people, by now two friends, who have assisted me several times, starting two years ago when I went to Germany and Austria to conduct research for my first book: Wolfgang Hafer and Georg Spitaler. I thank Wolfgang, grandson of Hugo Meisl and author of a splendid work on the life of his grandfather, for the help he gave me in better understanding the political and organisational context surrounding the event and Georg for the enormous amount of material he made available on Austrian football and its protagonists. During the writing of my book we often consulted each other and they, as always, punctually came to my aid whenever I had doubts.

I would also like to thank David Bolchover very much. David, with whom I am in frequent contact, was the author of *The Greatest Comeback*, the beautiful book about Béla Guttmann that I mentioned in the text. David gave me a great hand in tracing the vicissitudes of Hungarian football at the time.

I would also like to thank Niccolò Mello and Francesco Scabar, two authors and friends with whom I have often had the opportunity to discuss football and who have given me some interesting ideas about the schemes and forms of play adopted by the teams involved.

Another heartfelt thanks goes to Mirko Trasforini: Mirko, owner and manager of the blog *archiviotimf.blogspot. com*, has been an indispensable source for learning more about Bologna in those years.

I am equally grateful to Enrico Serventi Longhi for some information he provided me with about the situation of Jewish journalists trapped in Italy as a result of the Racial Laws. In the bibliography you can find a paper he wrote a few years ago on the subject. Similarly, I am grateful to Gianna Pontecorboli for her research on Jewish emigrants in the United States after the Racial Laws: *Americordo*, her beautiful work that you will find in the bibliography, was the first to bring to light the figure of Erberto Levi. I received further information from Alessandro Cassin, director of the Centro Primo Levi publishing house, who was also willing to support my research.

I thank my friend Fabio Brunetti, with whom I usually discuss football, who made me notice the Ferencváros Triplete in 1928, a detail that I had missed.

I would also like to thank Laurin Rosenberg, coordinator of the Rapideum, the museum of Rapid Vienna, for his enormous kindness and availability.

Thanks also go to Federico Jaselli Meazza, nephew of Giuseppe Meazza, for providing me with material from his book *Il mio nome è Giuseppe Meazza*.

Similarly, I am very grateful to Marco D'Avanzo, the owner of Soccerdata, with whom I have discussed data and statistics relating to the competition.

The last thanks goes to Béla Nagy. Nagy left us in 2006 but his writings about Ferencváros and the story of the Hungarian teams in the Mitropa Cup were indispensable.

BIBLIOGRAPHY

Allinson, Mark. Reading the Dollfuss Years. *Austrian Studies*, 14, 337-348 (2006).

Araf, J. Generazione Wunderteam. *Rise and Fall of the Wunderteam* (Pitch Publishing, 2021).

Bliss, D. *Ernő Egri Erbstein. Trionfo e tragedia dell'artefice del Grande Torino*. (Milan: Cairo, 2019). Bolchover, D. The Greatest Comeback: From Genocide To Football Glory. London (Biteback Publishing, 2017).

Brenner, G. & Reuveni, G. *Emancipation Through Muscles. Jews and Sports in Europe*. (Lincoln and London: University of Nebraska Press, 2006).

Brizzi, E. *Vincere o Morire. Gli Assi del Calcio in Camicia Nera 1926-1938*. (Bari, GLF Editori Laterza, 2016). D'Avanzo, M. European Club Competitions 1902-1940. (Soccerdata Editore, 2020).

Eppel, P., Hachleitner, B., Spitaler, G. & Schwarz, W. M. *Wo die Wuchtel fliegt. Legendäre Orte des Wiener Fußballs*. Exhibition catalogue. Vienna, (2008).

Fox, N. *Prophet or Traitor? The Jimmy Hogan Story*. (Manchester: The Parrs Wood Press, 2003).

Francka, C. *Matthias Sindelar. Una Historia de Fútbol, Nazismo y Misterios*. Buenos Aires: Librofutbol.com. (2016).

Grimaldi, M. *La Nazionale del Duce. Fatti, uomini, società e propaganda nell'epoca dell'oro del calcio italiano (1929-1938).* (Rome: Edizioni Eraclea, 2018).

Grimaldi, M. Vittorio Pozzo. *Storia di un Italiano.* (Rome: Edizioni Eraclea, 2018).

Hadas, M. *Football and Social Identity: The case of Hungary in the Twentieth Century.* The Sports Historian, 20 (2), 43-66. (2016).

Hafer, A & Hafer, W. *Hugo Meisl oder: die Erfindung des moderner Fußballs.* Göttingen: Die Werkstatt GmbH. (2007).

Horak, R., & Maderthaner, W. *A Culture of Urban Cosmopolitanism: Uridil and Sindelar as Viennese Coffee-House Heroes.* International Journal of the History of Sport, 13(1), 139-155. (1996).

Jaselli Meazza, F. & Pedrazzini, M. *Il mio nome è Giuseppe Meazza.* (Milan: ExCogita. 2010).

Jensen, N. F. *Mittel. European Football Stories.* (Hitchin: Isherwood Editorial, 2018).

Juraske, A. "Blau-Gelb ist mein Herz". (Prague: Promedia. 2017).

Marani, M. *Dallo Scudetto ad Auschwitz. Storia di Arpad Weisz, allenatore ebreo.* (Reggio Emilia: Imprimatur. 2014).

Marschik, M. Mitteleuropa: *Politische Konzepte - sportliche Praxis.* Historical Social Research/ Historische Sozialforschung, 31 (1 (115)), 88-108. (2006).

Marschik, M., *Austrian Sport and the Challenges of its Recent Historiography.* Journal of Sport History, 38 (2), 189-198.

Marschik, Matthias. *Between Manipulation and Resistance: Viennese Football in the Nazi Era.* Journal of Contemporary History, 34, No.2, 215-229. (1999).

Meisl, W. *Soccer Revolution*. London: Sportsmans Book Club. (1955).

Mello, N. *Stelle di David. Come il genio ebraico ha rivoluzionato il calcio*. (Turin: Sloth Books, 2019).

Mills, R. *The Politics of Football in Yugoslavia*. (Croydon: Taurus. 2018).

Nagy, B. *Toldi Géza. Fradi szív és szellem megtestesítője*. (Budapest: Coopinvest. 1984).

Nagy, B. *A régi, dicső KK*. (Budapest: Interpress. 1987).

Nagy, B. *Fradi futballmúzeum*, (Budapest: Ferencvárosi Torna Club 1899.) (1987).

Persson, G. *Stjärnor på flykt: Historien om Hakoah Wien*. (Stockholm: Norstedts. 2004).

Pondělik, J. *Pět tisíc gólů*. (Prague: Olympia. 1971).

Pontecorboli, G. *America Nuova Terra Promessa. Storie di ebrei italiani in fuga dal fascismo*. (Milan: Francesco Brioschi Publisher. 2013).

Rimet, J., Leblond, R., & Rimet, Y. *Le journal de Jules Rimet: Le récit rare du fondateur de la Coupe du monde de football*. (Paris: First Editions. 2014).

Rohan, L. *Rozhlasový zpravodaj Josef Laufer*. (2018).

Schidrowitz, L. *Geschichte des Fussballsportes in Österreich*. (Vienna: Rudolf Traunau. 1951).

Seddon, P. J. Steve Bloomer. *The Story of Football's First Superstar* (Derby: Breedon Books Publishing Co Ltd. 1999).

Tlustý, T. *Českoslovenští sportovci a jejich účast na Pershingově olympiádě*. (2017).

Tomlinson, A., & Young, C. *German football: History, culture, society*. (London: Routledge. 2006).

Wilson, J. *The Names Heard Long Ago. How the Golden Age of Hungarian Soccer Shaped the Modern Game*. (London: Blink Publishing. 2019).

NEWSPAPERS AND MAGAZINES
La Gazzetta dello Sport
Il Corriere della Sera
Guerin Sportivo
La Stampa
Calcio Illustrato
Il Littoriale
Nemzeti Sport
Sporthirlap
Sport-Tagblatt
Illustriertes Sportblatt
Kronen Zeitung
Prager Presse
Die Blaha

FILMS AND VIDEOS
Montevideo, Bog Te video! (2010)
Montevideo, vidimo se! (2014)
Reiscriviamo all'albo i giornalisti ebrei radiati dal
  fascismo: http://www.radioradicale.it/
Americordo. The Italian Jewish Exiles in America

SITES, ARTICLES AND BLOGS
https://anno.onb.ac.at/
https://www.history.com/
http://www.tempofradi.hu/
https://archiviotimf.blogspot.com/
http://www.ftcbaratikor.hu/
https://www.idnes.cz/
http://www.scottishsporthistory.com/
https://sparta.cz/
https://www.slavia.cz/
https://www.firstviennafc.at/

INDEX OF NAMES

Acht Aknai, János 63, 65,
  68–69, 78, 239
Ádám, Sándor 212–213,
  215, 217, 244–245
Adamek, Karl 164, 241, 243
Adelbrecht, Josef 91–92,
  96–97, 240–241
Agnelli, Edoardo 150–151
Agostini, Rodolfo 196
Allemandi, Luigi 125, 128,
  241
Amoretti, Hugh 149
Amsel, Ignác 47, 51, 239
Andreivić 50
Andritz, Karl 176, 243
Arcari, Peter 195–196
Arpinati, Leandro 59, 98,
  102, 105
Aschner, Lipót 229
Aszlányi, Károly 182
Avar, István 61, 64–65, 67,
  195, 239–240
Bacigalupo, Manlio 74–77
Baldi, Gastone 103–104, 132
Baldo, Joseph 181, 243
Balling, Karel 33, 73
Balogh, István 217, 244–245
Bán, Nandor 138, 242
Banchero, Elvio 74
Bányai, Lajos 61, 69,
  239–240
Barassi, Ottorino 57
Barátki, Iuliu, 94
Barbieri, Ottavio 76
Barlassina, Rinaldo 62, 97,
  119, 162–163, 165, 215,
  240, 243
Bauer, Eduard (Edi) 42, 63,
  238–240

Bauer, Karl 42
Beale, William 86
Becher, Johann 96, 240–241
Bednář 25, 43
Bělík, Ladislav 82–83, 240
Bensemann, Walter 43
Bényi, Mari 231
Beranek, Alois 151
Berényi, Antal 60
Berkessy, Elemér 52, 239
Bernardini, Fulvio
  (Fuffo) 90–93
Bertolini, Luigi 108, 121,
  150
Bertoni, Sergio 195–197
Bican, František 188
Bican, Ivan 203
Bican, Josef (Pepi) 133,
  135, 157, 184, 188–190,
  192–194, 196–202, 225,
  226, 235, 244
Billich, Johann 122–123,
  126, 128, 241
Binder, Franz (Child) 133,
  135–137, 158, 185, 189,
  202
Biri, János 38–39
Bíró, Mihály 245
Bízik, Ján 173–174
Blason, James 180, 183, 243
Bloomer, Stephen (Steve) 20
Blum, Josef 89, 91–92,
  105–107, 118, 127, 129,
  155, 158, 169, 240–242
Blyth, Ernest 20
Boas 154
Bokšay, Alexej 191–192,
  194–196, 198, 200, 244
Bolchover, David 229, 246

Borbás, Gáspar 15
Borel, Felice 151–153
Borsányi, Ferenc 65, 67, 239
Bouček, Jaroslav 147, 164,
  243
Božović, Vojin 191, 214
Bradáč, Vojtěch 161, 191–
  194, 244
Braine, Raymond 44, 81–
  82, 84, 103–104, 110, 144,
  146, 148–151, 153–155,
  163–164, 169, 235, 240,
  242–243
Brandstetter, Josef 24, 63
Braun, Eugen 38, 66, 109,
  138, 239
Braun, Georg 96, 97, 240–
  241
Braun, József 38
Brie, Peter 222
Bródy, Sándor 169
Brosenbauer, Anton 91–92,
  107, 240–241
Brüll, Alfréd 37, 228
Bugala, Josef 74, 80, 82, 240
Bukovi, Márton 48, 63, 239
Buonocore, Carmelo 193
Burgess, Herbert 90, 208
Burgr, Jaroslav 40, 61, 83,
  102, 146, 155, 164, 238,
  240, 242–243
Burlando, Luigi 76
Busani, Umberto 180, 182,
  243
Caligaris, Umberto 109,
  111, 123
Cameron, John 20
Camolese, Bruno 182,
  243–244

Campatelli, Aldo 212
Carcano, Carlo 109
Carraro, Albino 65, 238–239
Casanova, Ottorino 75
Castellazzi, Armando 241
Cattaneo, Angelo 196
Cejka, Friedrich 240
Cejnar, František 105, 124, 128–129, 241
Ceresoli, Carlo 126–128, 241
Černý, Karel 194, 197, 244
Cesarini, Renato 108–111, 123, 151–153
Chamberlain, Neville 204
Chapman, Herbert 94
Chini Ludueña, Arturo 90
Chrenka, Gustav 87
Cisar, Franz 240
Čipera, Karel 239
Combi, Gianpiero 110–111, 121–122, 151
Comini, Cherubino 148
Corsi, Giordano 160, 242
Costa, Giovanni 181–182, 243–244
Cottenet, Maurice 48
Cscrnai, Pál 237
Čtyřoký, Josef 150, 240, 242–243
Czejka, Leopold 82
Dale, Leslie 212
D'Aquino, Raffaele 91–92
Dattilo, Generoso 217, 245
Daučik, Ferdinand (Daučík I) 171
Daučík, Karol (Daučík II) 196, 198–200, 244
De Manzano, Renato 241
De Vecchi, Renzo 22, 73, 75
Della Pergola, Fiorenza 205
Di Stéfano, Alfredo 155
Dick, John (Johnny) 30, 32–33, 80, 83, 146, 240
Dóczé, István 134
Dollfuss, Engelbert 131, 141, 167
Donati, Aldo 104, 141, 242
Donnenfeld, Friedrich (Fritz) 227
Dósa, Gábor 231
Durspekt, Karl 242
Dvořáček, Jan 35
Eberstaller, Richard 166
Egri Erbstein, Ernő 205, 230, 233

Eisenhoffer, József 22
Erdl, Franz 97, 172, 240–241
Evaristo, Juan 11
Eymers, Willem 41–42, 238
Faccio, Ricardo 127, 241
Faczinek, Ferdinand 145, 149–150, 154, 163, 242–243
Fasanelli, Cesare 91, 93
Fedullo, Fraancisco 100, 132, 136, 142, 242
Feigl, Walter 40, 42, 238
Fekete, Jenő 244–245
Feldmann, Gyula 48–49
Felsner, Hermann (Umazz) 101, 143
Ferrari, Giovanni 123, 150, 152, 192–194
Ferraris, Pietro (Ferraris II) 211–212
Ferretti, Mario 57
Fiala, Adolf 109
Figliola, Emanuele 195–196
Fiorini, Dino 136, 138, 160
Fischer, Mór 55, 69
Fischer, Richard 148, 154, 166
Fodor, Henrik 24–25, 33, 38–39, 58, 94, 145, 228
Fogg, Albert Edward 153–154, 242
Fogl, József (Fogl III) 60, 62, 65, 77, 239
Fogl, Károly (Fogl II) 60
Földessy, János 48
Foni, Alfredo 153
Fraiponts, Jean-Norbert 155
Franzl, Friedrich 35, 53
Frione, Francisco 125–126, 128, 241
Frithum, Ferdinand 91, 240–241
Fritz, Alajos 15–16, 87–88, 105, 121
Frossi, Hannibal 194, 211–212
Frühwirth, Josef 239
Furmann, Károly 239
Futó, Gyula 217, 244–245
Gabrovitz, Kornél 47
Gall, Karl 123, 127, 241
Gasperi, Felice 103, 107, 138, 242
Genta, Mario 196
Gerbi, Giuliano 205, 221
Gero, Ferenc 35

Gerö, Josef 113, 143, 227
Geyer, Karl 117, 240–241
Gianni, Mario 103, 106, 134–136, 138–139, 141, 242
Gidófalvy, Pál 228
Goll, János 60
Göring, Hermann 144
Goulden, Leonard Arthur (Len) 210
Graf, Karl 126, 241
Gramlich, Rudolf 'Rudi' 202, 225–226
Gramlick, John 14
Gringa, Carlos 149
Gschweidl, Friedrich (Fritz) 87–88, 91–92, 96, 106–107, 172, 240–241
Guardiola, Josep (Pep) 237
Guarnieri, Umberto 211
Guttmann, Armin 207
Guttmann, Béla 199
Gyetvai, László 172, 244–245
Háda, József 138, 170, 172, 183, 216–217, 242–244
Haftl, Otto 62
Hahnemann, Wilhelm 142, 158, 242
Hajný, Ferdinand 35, 61, 238
Hanke, Walter 95, 97, 240–241
Hansen, Sophus 82–83, 240
Happel, Ernst 237
Havel, Otakar 225
Hejma, Karel 82–83, 240
Herberger, Sepp 190, 202
Herites, Karel 224
Herrera, Helenio 214, 236
Herzog, Edwin 24
Hevesi, Sándor 134
Hiden, Rudolf (Rudi) 81, 94, 96, 141, 240–241
Hiltl, Heinrich 94, 240–241
Hirzer, Ferenc 37
Hitler, Adolf 144, 167, 179, 184, 204, 206, 208, 228
Hlavay, György 216, 244–245
Hochmann, František 42, 61, 238
Hoffmann, Leopold 88, 91, 105, 172, 239–240
Hogan, James (Jimmy) 18–20, 37, 90, 157, 222
Hojer, Antonín 82, 240

Holec, Wilhelm 147
Holub, Johann 55
Horák, Václav 191–193, 195, 199, 244
Horejs, Josef 38, 41–42, 238
Horeschovsky, Karl 91, 240–241
Hóri, György 162
Horthy, Miklós 207, 209, 228
Horvath, Hans (Hansi) 40, 42, 63–64, 131, 238–239
Howcroft, James 19
Hribar, Franz 239
Humenberger, Karl 141, 242
Hungler, János 52, 239
Hussak, Ludwig 16
Iszer, Károly 66
Ivanicsics, Mihály 126, 148, 151
Jakab, László 174
Janda, Antonín 32
Janda, Anton 33, 242
Jánosi, Béla 230
Jellinek, Otto 40, 238
Jeny, Rudolf 38
Jeřábek, Luboš 45
Jerusalem, Camilo 128, 158, 160–161, 163, 165, 175–176, 241, 243
Jestrab, Karl 136
Jewell, Arthur James 140, 200, 242, 244
Jiran, Antonín 61
Joska, Bohumil 68, 118–119, 239
Junek, František 66, 68, 82, 111, 239–240
Kaburek, Matthias 65, 74, 76, 79, 83, 133, 158, 240
Kállai, Lipót 162, 211–212, 217, 244–245
Kaller, Otto 106, 175
Kalocsay, Géza 149, 152–153, 242–243
Kaszala, Károly 54
Katscher, Robert 73
Kemény, Tibor 172, 177, 183, 199, 242–244
Kenyeres, Árpád 84, 98
Kertész, Géza 230–231
Kirbes, Willibald 54, 64–65, 76, 79, 239–240
Kiss, Gyula (coach) 48, 60
Kiss, Gyula (footballer) 153, 171, 177, 182–183, 199, 242–244

Kiss, Tivadar 48
Kiszely, István 217, 245
Klein, Árpád 122–123
Klemens 140
Klenovec, Bohumil 153, 164, 242–243
Klug, Ferenc 126, 241
Kocsis, Géza 162, 213–214, 216, 244–245
Köhler, Franz 34
Kohut, Vilmos 48, 54, 79, 239
Kolenatý, František 36, 41, 43, 61–62, 238
Konrád, Evelyn 221
Konrád, Gertrud 222
Konrád, Grete 221
Konrád, Jenő 22–24, 39, 158
Konrád, Kálmán 22–23, 39, 222
Kopecký, Vlastimil 118, 161, 195–197, 244
Korányi, Lajos 155, 173–174, 242–244
Košťálek, Josef 82–84, 150, 240, 242–243
Koszta, Imre 239
Kovács, Lajos 132, 148
Kovács, Pál 231, 237, 242
Kovács, Stefan 132, 134, 136, 148, 231, 237, 242
Kövagö, Károly 239
Köves, János 64, 77, 239
Kral, Franz 239
Kratochvíl, Karel 68, 239–240
Kreisler, Friedrich-Max (Fritz) 121
Krist, Augustin 88, 133, 163, 181, 216, 243–244
Kun, Béla (born Abel Kohn) 207
Kubesch, Rudolf 240–241
Kurz, Karl 87
Kutasi, Károly 170
Kuthan, Richard (Rigo) 65, 72, 238
Lang, Robert 227
Langfelder, Ferenc 62–63, 69, 162, 212–214, 216, 231
Laufer, Josef 111, 193, 224–226
Lázár, Gyula 172, 244–245
Lelovics, Gyula 100–101, 105, 108, 114, 132, 210
Leuthe, Max Johann (John Mac) 167

Levi Landi, Erberto 220
Levratto, Virgil 74–76, 125–127, 241
Locatelli, Ugo 211
Lombardo, Nicolás 90–91
Löwinger, Ernst 240–241
Löwy, Izsák 60
Luef, Johann 42, 74, 76, 82–83, 238, 240
Lyka, Antal 80
Machu, Leonhard 147, 174, 240–241
Madden, John William 30–31, 67, 109, 239
Magda, Béla 243–244
Maini, Bruno 103–104, 106, 134–135, 137–139, 141–142, 159, 242
Madlmayer, Josef 238
Majorszky, Ferenc 64, 102
Maloun, Josef 35
Mann 68
Manola, Petar 192
Marat, Leopold 91–93
Marchini, Libero 243
Marjanović, Blagoje (Mosha) 50, 192, 213
Markos, Imre 134
Martelli, Gastone 103
Masetti, Guido 91–93
Mátéffy, Attila 89
Matošić, Frane (Matošić II) 215
Mattea, Francesco 95, 240
Mauro, John 57, 97
Mazal, Otakar 32
Meazza, Giuseppe (Peppin) 12, 77–78, 124–129, 132, 159, 192–193, 210, 213, 235, 241, 247
Meisl, Hugo 17–22, 24–27, 30, 36, 39, 43, 55, 57, 59, 70, 79, 86–88, 94, 105, 110, 115, 119–120, 122, 126, 130–131, 142–144, 149, 154, 157, 165–167, 188–189, 209, 220, 246
Meisl, Willy 18
Messi, Lionel 201
Mészáros, István 239–240
Miesz, Adolf 102, 110, 112–113, 171
Mikes, Károly 242
Mirschitzka, Josef 242
Mock, Johann (Hans) 119, 158, 164, 241, 243
Modugno, Domenico 221

INDEX OF NAMES

Moldoványi, Marianne 229
Molzer, Josef 122, 124, 128–129, 241
Montesanto, Mario 106, 137–138, 142, 242
Monti, Luis (Doble Ancho) 122–123, 127, 150–152
Monza, Alfredo 182, 243
Monzeglio, Eraldo 100, 107, 132, 134–135, 137–138, 242
Móré, János 242
Morocutti, Wilhelm (Cutti) 241
Morselli, Arrigo 179, 195–197
Mourinho, Jose 214
Müller, Gerd 201, 240–241
Müller, Heinrich 96
Mussolini, Benito 99, 131
Mussolini, Bruno 100, 135, 142
Mussolini, Vito 142
Mussolini, Vittorio 100, 135, 142
Mütz, Rudolf 53, 227
Myclik, Josef 41, 238
Nagy, Béla 101, 183, 247
Nagy, József 114,
Najemnik, Matthias 241
Nathan 38
Nausch, Walter 121, 126, 128–129, 153, 158, 162, 164, 177, 241, 243
Negro, Alfonso 150
Nehadoma, Janós 223–224
Nehadoma, József 223–224
Nejedlý, Oldrich (Olda) 103–104, 146–150, 152, 163, 187, 242–243
Nitsch, Leopold 41, 238
Novák, Antonín 239
Nožíř, Otakar 197–198, 244
Onzari, Caesar 104
Opata, Zoltán 38, 89
Orsi, Raimundo 109, 111, 122, 143
Orth, György 33, 37–38
Pálinkás, József 245
Pasolini, Carlo Alberto 100
Pasolini, Pier Paolo 100
Pataki, Mihály 52
Patek, Adolf 35, 38, 40–41, 62, 82–83, 238, 240
Pavlicek, Robert 242
Pekarna, Karl 18

Pelé, Edson Arantes do Nascimento 201
Pelikan, Rudolf 113, 165, 170, 213
Pentland, John 20
Perazzolo, Mario 135, 139, 196
Perner, Antonín 41–42, 61, 104, 238
Pershing, John Joseph 31
Peruchetti, Joseph 193
Pešek, Karel (Káďa), 33
Peškova 146
Pesser, Hans 137
Petrone, Pedro 100
Pilát, Václav 32
Piola, Silvio 178, 180–183, 186, 243–244
Pitto, Alfredo 241
Plánička, Františsck 40, 44, 51, 67–68, 110–112, 119, 160, 181, 187–188, 191, 198, 200, 239
Platzer, Peter 141–142, 242
Pleticha, Josef 239
Podhradský, Jan 191–192
Podrazil, Karel 83, 103–104, 240
Poláček, Jaroslav 33
Polgar, Alfred 125
Polgár, Gyula 138, 175, 180, 242–245
Pollack, Gustav 148, 172–173, 175, 227
Pondělik, Josef 202
Pozzo, Vittorio 12, 19–20, 102, 132, 140, 143, 157, 159, 183
Pressler, Alfred 50
Provera, Vincenzo 183, 243
Průha, Karel 196
Puč, Antonín 66, 108, 111, 118–119, 160, 171, 188, 239
Puskás, Ferenc (Öcsi) 201, 217–218, 223, 232, 234, 237
Pusztai, Ferenc 162
Raftl, Rudolf 135
Rainer, Karl 91, 172, 240–241
Rappan, Karl 79, 158, 240
Rauchmaul, Emil 179, 210, 243–244
Rázsó, Izidor (Mor) 52–53
Reguzzoni, Carlo 100, 102–103, 106, 132–139, 142, 159, 182, 242

Reichardt, Jan 244
Richter, Johann 238
Riegler, Franz 161, 165, 243
Rimet, Jules 100, 166, 226
Robinson, John William 17
Romario de Souza Faria 201
Ronaldo, Cristiano 201
Roosevelt, Franklin Delano 221
Rosetta, Virginio 122, 151
Rothschild, Nathaniel Meyer von 86
Rumbold, Gyula 16
Runge, Franz 35–36
Ruoff, Paul 76
Sain, Orlando 211
Sallustro, Attila 140
Sándor, József 169, 172, 174, 176, 179
Sárosi, Béla 199
Sárosi, György 109, 132, 137, 168, 199
Sassi, Othello 147
Scarpi, Joseph 164, 172, 243
Schaffer, Alfréd 22, 37, 117, 168
Schall, Anton (Toni) 34, 36, 51, 141, 179, 242
Scheer, Ernő 199
Schiavio Angelo (Anzlèn) 100, 102, 104, 106–107, 132–136, 138–139, 142–143, 159, 242
Schidrowitz, Leo 117
Schlosser, Imre 15, 37, 101, 230
Schmaus, Willibald 240–241
Schmieger, Wilhelm (Willy) 16
Schönecker, Dyonis 54, 73, 117, 145
Schönwetter, Franz 106–107
Schramseis, Roman 63, 74–75, 80, 83–84, 188, 238–240
Schuschnigg, Kurt Alois von 184
Schwartz, Alexandru (Elek) 237
Schwarz, Emanuel Michael (Michl) 120, 126, 162, 166, 226–227, 231
Schwarz, Ernő 22
Scorzoni, Raffaele 161
Sedláček, Ferenc 53–54, 146, 153, 155, 239, 242–243

Seidl, Rudolf 87
Seipel, Ignaz 26
Seitler, Károly 16
Sentimenti Lucidio
(Sentiments IV) 224
Serantoni, Pietro 241
Sernagiotto, Pedro 109, 111
Sesta, Karl 94, 158, 161–
162, 177, 185, 240–241,
243
Sigl, Ignaz 36, 51–52, 141,
242
Silný, Josef 35–36, 38, 40–
45, 62, 81, 104, 238, 240
Šima, Josef 40–41, 238
Šimůnek, Ladislav 191–194,
196, 199–200, 244
Sindelar, Matthias 12,
87, 115, 117–129, 153,
157–165, 168, 175–177,
185–188, 202, 235, 241,
243
Skolaut, Hans 242
Skoumal, Stefan 79
Sloup-Štaplík, Josef 108,
187
Smistik, Josef 63, 84,
238–240
Sobotka, Jiři 160, 170, 188,
190
Spechtl, Viktor 122, 127,
241
Špindler, Václav 32, 35,
210, 238
Spitz, Illés 65–67, 239–240
Spivach, Aldo 141, 242
Springer, Ferenc 171, 175
Srbek, Erich 82, 240,
242–243
Stable, Guillermo 31
Starace, Achille 183
Stefanovsky, Ladislav 73
Steiner, František 226
Steiner, Karel 38, 226
Sternberg, László 60, 209
Stoiber, Karl 36, 51, 141,
242
Stojiliković, Đorđe 215
Ströck, Albert 60–61,
64–65, 67, 239–240
Stroh, Josef 119, 128, 158,
160–163, 165, 241, 243
Studnicka, Jan 16
Svoboda, František 118,
160, 188, 239

Szabó, Gábor Péter 61,
65–68, 239–240
Szálasi, Ferenc 229
Szekany-Cicagne,
Etienne 75
Székely, Béla 243
Székely-Sonnenfeld,
Ábris 60
Szigeti, Imre 55
Sziklai, Ferenc 211
Szoyka, Kornél 244–245
Szűcs, György 244–245
Takács, Géza (Takács I) 48–
55, 80, 239
Takács, József (Takács
II) 48–55, 80, 239
Tamási, Áron 210
Táncos, Mihály 138, 170,
177, 183, 242–244
Tátrai, Sándor 171, 175,
216, 243–245
Taurer, Josef 15
Teleki, Pál 88–89, 133
Tögel, Gustav 89, 96,
240–241
Toldi, Géza 138, 140, 153–
154, 170–172, 174–175,
177, 180–181, 183, 198,
200, 216–217, 242–245
Torberg, Friedrich 125
Tóth, István 48–49, 101,
230–231, 239
Turay, József 48–51, 54, 239
Tusch 67
Ugró, Gyula 60
Urbanek, Johann 242
Uridil, Josef (Pepi) 72–73
Vacek, Bedřich 161, 244
Valinasso, Cesare 151–153
Van Praag, Raphaël 40, 238
Vana, Johann 82, 240
Varglien, John (Varglien
II) 123–124
Varglien, Mario (Varglien
I) 109
Vecchina, John 109
Veselý, Evžen 35–36, 38
Viani, Giuseppe (Gipo) 150,
181, 241, 243
Viertl, Rudolf 119, 122,
126, 128, 158–159, 162,
241, 243
Vincze, Jenő 88, 134, 211,
213, 215, 244–245
Violak, József 178, 243

Vodička, Antonín 239
Vogl, Adolf (Adi) 141–142,
195, 242
Vogl, Leon 141–142, 195,
242
Volk, Rodolfo
(Sciabbolone) 90, 93
Vycpálek, Čestmír 237
Vytlačil, Rudolf 161, 170,
191–194, 196–197, 200,
244
Walden, William
Walter 140–141, 153–
154, 241–242
Weill-Schott, Gustavus 205
Weisz, Árpad 205
Weisz, Clara 223
Weisz, Ilona 223
Weisz, Roberto 59, 78,
125–126, 159, 178, 205,
210, 222–223, 241
Weselik, Franz 74, 76, 84,
238–240
Wesely, Ferdinand 40–42,
54, 63–65, 74–77, 79, 82,
84, 235, 238–240
Wetzer, Rudolf 61
Wilhelm, János 65, 239–240
Wilson, Jonathan 37, 67, 196
Witschel, Anton 239
Wondrak, Karl 238
Worth, Friedrich 81, 175,
211
Wüthrich, Hans 182–183,
243
Zacconi, Benedicto 243
Zajíček, Oldrich (Olda) 148,
151, 163, 242–243
Zamboni, Anteo 99
Zanetti, Giuseppe 57, 98,
113
Zápotocký, Vladimir 200,
202, 225–226
Ženišek, Ladislav 68
Zischek, Karl 158
Zöhrer, Rudolf 158, 160–
163, 177, 243
Zsák, Károly 69
Zsengellér, Gyula
(Abel) 163, 168, 199, 210,
212–217, 244–245